Publications of the Graduate School of
Business Administration of the University of Virginia

Bank Expansion in Virginia, 1962–1966: The Holding Company and the
Direct Merger. By Paul Foster.

Business Ethics Bibliography, 1971–1975. By Donald D. Jones.

A Financial Planning Model for Private Colleges: A Research Report.
By William J. Arthur.

A Selected Bibliography of Applied Ethics in the Professions, 1950–1970:
A Working Sourcebook with Annotations and Indexes.
By Daniel L. Gothie.

Stettinius, Sr.: Portrait of a Morgan Partner.
By John Douglas Forbes.

J. P. MORGAN, JR.
1867–1943

J. P. Morgan, Jr.
1867–1943

by

JOHN DOUGLAS FORBES

University Press of Virginia

Charlottesville

The Publication of this book has been
assisted by the Graduate School of
Business Administration, University of Virginia.

THE UNIVERSITY PRESS OF VIRGINIA
Copyright © 1981 by the Rector and Visitors
of the University of Virginia

First published 1981

Library of Congress Cataloging in Publication Data

Forbes, John Douglas, 1910–
  J. P. Morgan, Jr., 1867–1943.
  Bibliography: p.
  Includes index.
  1. Morgan, J. P. (John Pierpont), 1867–1943.
2. Bankers—United States—Biography. 3. Capitalists
and financiers—United States—Biography. I. Title.
HG2463.M62F67 332.1'092'4 [B] 81–1787
ISBN 0–8139–0889–2   AACR2

Printed in the United States of America

For Alex, Anne, and Sophie

CONTENTS

Preface

THE YOUNGER J. P. MORGAN WAS THE THIRD GENERATION OF THE Morgan banking dynasty. Morgans have long been leading figures—and still are—in the important business of making available large sums of money for productive purposes. Each Morgan has been a distinct personality very different from the others. Each has lived in a different time from the others, each era marked by an entirely different set of conditions and problems from those characterizing the other periods. A common point of view, however, has linked the successive generations of Morgans. All have, in the words of J. P. Morgan, Jr., at the 1933 Pecora congressional hearings, been concerned with "doing only first-class business, and that in a first-class way."[1] Except for a brief excursion into holding-company shares in the late 1920s, they have maintained this standard with extraordinary consistency.

Founder of the family and the least well-known was Junius Spencer Morgan (1813–80), partner in London of the financier and philanthropist George Peabody. Most colorful was his son, John Pierpont Morgan, Sr. (1837–1913), about whom a great deal has been written.

We are concerned with *his* son, John Pierpont Morgan, Jr. (1867–1943). Our Morgan has been referred to incidentally in biographies of his father and in histories of J. P. Morgan & Co. (labeled grandly the House of Morgan) and has been the subject of a *New Yorker* profile and an extremely perceptive *Fortune* biographical sketch. But no full-length life has appeared before now.

This lack is remarkable, because he was without question the most important figure in world financial history of the first third of the twentieth century. If he had done nothing else, his part in financing and supplying the Western Allies in World War I and in financing the postwar reconstruction would entitle him to that distinction, although these activities were actually peripheral to his principal business of providing funds for the expansion of American businesses and helping companies in trouble.

The reasons for the neglect are understandable, however. Morgan thought of himself as a private person. He lived quietly. He was very much involved with his immediate family. He abhorred flamboyance whether of action or in public utterance. It has proved virtually impossible to bring him to life on the printed page. That he had a quiet charm for his friends is undeniable. They adored him, yet almost the only expressions of his warmth and whimsy that survive are found in his lifelong series of letters to his mother. We know that he was subject to rages when angered—explosions that came suddenly and vanished as quickly—but we don't know what triggered these outbursts. We also know that they were not really spectacular, because he had no gift for invective and lacked a colorful profane vocabulary.

Morgan was a team player and submerged his own personality in the firm, where he managed with consummate skill to hold together a group of highly skilled and individualistic partners and make maximum use of their separate gifts to achieve very substantial results. Possibly it helped in directing the energies of prima donnas not to compete with them.

But it should be stated at the outset that while J. Pierpont Morgan, Sr., captured more headlines, inspired more books, and was altogether a more picturesque figure, the son—our subject—accomplished every bit as much during his own lifetime as his father had during his.

The life of John Pierpont Morgan, Jr., falls conveniently into three successively shorter periods, which are reflected in the pattern of this study.

1867–1913

This is the period from this birth in 1867 until the death of his father, John Pierpont Morgan, Sr., in 1913. It includes his childhood and youth, marriage and early manhood, and prolonged apprenticeship for greater responsibility.

1913–33

In 1913, J. P. Morgan, Jr., became the senior partner of J. P. Morgan & Co., bankers, at the age of forty-five. He immediately came to the forefront of the international banking community and remained a very important figure for more than twenty years. These were the active years of the first world war and its aftermath, the booming 1920s, the crash, the start of the depression, and the coming of the New Deal.

1933–43

In 1933, the Roosevelt Administration came into office, and the government moved to investigate and to alter the American financial system. New Deal legislation forced J. P. Morgan & Co. to change its character drastically by separating the banking and securities-underwriting functions. J. P. Morgan & Co. elected to remain a bank, while an entirely new and separate concern, Morgan, Stanley & Co., was formed to take over the underwriting business of the old partnerships. The final dozen years was a period in which J. P. Morgan, Jr., gradually withdrew from the affairs of the firm, which was changed from a partnership to a corporation in 1940, and during which he left more and more decision making and policymaking to his younger associates.

In writing Morgan's biography, we encounter a most baffling situation: For Morgan's youth and early manhood as a schoolboy at St. Paul's and an undergraduate at Harvard, we have a detailed and voluminous record in the carefully preserved letters written to his mother. This record is resumed for the years of his London apprenticeship (1898 to 1906) and for various other times when he did not live next door to his parents on Madison Avenue in New York. From this wealth of material, we are able to present a remarkable social and human portrayal of a man in his time.

Our sources for Morgan's career as an international banker are quite different in nature. There is an enormous body of surviving correspondence relating to good works and public or quasi-public concerns throughout his life—charitable, educational, and other matters. The greatest gap is in the area of business; most business transactions at 23 Wall Street were carried on orally.

For the more important later years, the material is generally more impersonal, more fragmented, and narrower in approach. Gaps must be filled, where possible, from published sources. The result of this extraordinary disparity in the quantity, the quality, and even the nature of the material available is that we have two separate books within one set of covers. This presents problems of adjustment for the reader—problems particularly difficult for any who may assume that the biographer invariably had the full story readily available and that his failure to tell everything that happened is the result of negligence or of intentional suppression of facts! To clarify the unavoidable textual inconsistency, the two books are separated and labeled parts I and II, but the chronological subdivision is retained.

Morgan spent part of almost every day he was in New York at the Pierpont Morgan Library, next door to his house on Madison Avenue. He followed this routine from his inheriting the library in 1913 until his death in 1943. We have therefore deviated from a strict chronology to devote a chapter to the financier's consuming interest in the library and its collections.

In attempting to present an accurate, impartial account of the life and career of J. P. Morgan, Jr., we shall encounter difficulties of another kind. Too few readers will come to a consideration of Morgan with an open mind. Morgan was a public figure for so many years that many people believe that they know a great deal about him and will resent any presentation that differs from what they had always heard or wanted to believe. It is human nature for a reader to judge a book by the degree to which it conforms to his own preconceptions. If the serious writer has presented facts that make the subject out to be less attractive or honorable than the reader hoped, the cry is "Smear!" If the reverse is true, the charge is "Whitewash!"

In the case of J. P. Morgan, Jr., this is an unusually grave problem, because he was seized upon by writers of the political Left and was made a symbol of all the evils those writers could attribute to the capitalist system. Following his succession to the senior partnership of the family firm in 1913, he remained an object of intermittent attack, derision, and abuse throughout his entire career. An extension of this situation is the fact that Morgan was involved in specific cases of controversy. To question the assertions or the reasoning of one side or the other of such differences is to invite charges from the opposition.

Acknowledgments

THIS STUDY OF THE LIFE OF THE YOUNGER J. P. MORGAN, LIKE ALmost all historical work, owes its existence to the help of a large number of individuals. I wish to thank them all and to mention those to whom I am particularly indebted.

Henry Sturgis Morgan, son of the subject, is the person most responsible for the book's coming to be written. Not that it was his idea or that he was ever happy about the prospect of a life of his father being written—he shares his father's feelings about privacy. But once he accepted the fact that such a study would be attempted, he very generously made available at the Pierpont Morgan Library a great body of letters and other materials and even released from a twenty-five year seal the collection of letters from J. P. Morgan, Jr., to his mother. The only string attached was that there were no strings attached; he would help but would in no way try to influence what he believed should be a dispassionate, warts-and-all portrait of his father.

The staff of the Pierpont Morgan Library were more than helpful with their time and effort. Herbert T. F. Cahoon was in immediate charge of my activities at the library and was a very thoughtful guide to the collections. I am also under deep obligation to Francis S. Mason, Jr., assistant director of the library, and to Mrs. Evelyn W. Semler, Miss Christine Stenstrom, John H. Plummer, J. Rigbie Turner, William M. Voelkle, Thomas V. Lange, David W. Wright, and Miss Priscilla C. Barker. In a very special category are Mrs. Gale D'Luhy and Reginald Allen. Perhaps the greatest day-to-day help came from William G. Reichert, superintendent of the library, and his staff.

At the Darden School, University of Virginia, Dean C. Stewart Sheppard and Research Committee Chairmen William Rotch, R. Jack Weber, and Charles O. Meiburg have been encouraging throughout the entire project. Particularly patient and long-suffering in this enterprise were Miss Barbara S. Smyth and Mrs. Beth S. McDermott.

At other institutions, I am indebted to Robert W. Lovett, formerly head of the Manuscript Division, Baker Library, Harvard Business School, for giving me access to the Lamont Papers; to John Lancaster, Archivist, Amherst College, for allowing the British scholar Miss Priscilla M. Roberts to examine the Dwight Morrow Papers on my behalf; to Harley P. Holden, Curator, and Mrs. Bonnie B. Salt of the Harvard Archives; to John H. Beust, Vice Rector of St. Paul's School; and to the staffs of the National Archives, the Library of Congress, the New York Public Library, the New-York Historical Society, and the Huntington Library at San Marino, California.

My debt to the late Margaret Forbes—who lived for years with Mr. Morgan as an unseen presence in our house—is very great.

PART I
1867–1905

Introductory Note:
Morgan on Morgan

JOHN PIERPONT MORGAN, JR., WROTE AN AUTOBIOGRAPHICAL NOTE
not unlike a *Who's Who* entry at the request of his associate
Thomas W. Lamont sometime during Morgan's second term as
Overseer of Harvard College (1916–22). A covering note, which
omits the year, handwritten on Matinicock Point, Glencove [*sic*],
L.I., notepaper reads:

> Dear Tom:
>
> I wrote this out last Sunday and forgot to give it to you.
> It seems to me it is fairly apposite.
>
> Yrs
> J.P.M.
>
> May 15[1]

This summary is a useful introduction to a more detailed treatment of his life and is particularly illuminating as an expression of
the aspects of his career he himself considered important.

> MORGAN, JOHN PIERPONT (1867–   ), American Banker, son of
> the late John Pierpont Morgan, grandson of Junius Spencer
> Morgan, and head of the international banking house of J. P.
> Morgan & Co. Born at Irvington-on-Hudson, he prepared for
> college at St. Paul's, Concord, New Hampshire, and received
> his A.B. from Harvard in 1889. He secured his preliminary

training in banking at Boston and in January 1892 he became a partner in the New York firm of Drexel, Morgan & Co., of which his father was the head. Four years later the partnership name was changed to its present form, J. P. Morgan & Co. In 1898 Mr. Morgan became a member of J. S. Morgan & Co., of London, now Morgan, Grenfell & Co., and of Morgan, Harjes & Co., of Paris. Soon after admittance to the British house Mr. Morgan went to London and for several years was active in the business of the house. Upon his return to the United States he at once became active in the work of the New York firm, and upon the death of his father at Rome on March 31, 1913, he became senior member of the several houses allied in the firm. His experience as member and head of this leading firm of private bankers, has covered a wide range of constructive finance, domestic and international, and of active civic service as well. Perhaps his most conspicuous service in recent years was in connection with the financing by his firm of a considerable part of the enormous purchases made by Great Britain and her Allies in the United States between the outbreak of the World War and the entry to it of the United States, which then took over the task previously borne by Mr. Morgan and his partners. After the signing of peace he was active in the post war financing required in the United States by Great Britain and France. Mr. Morgan was married December 11, 1890, to Jane Norton Grew, of Boston, and they have four children, Junius Spencer Morgan, Jr., Mrs. George Nichols, Mrs. Paul G. Pennoyer and Henry Sturgis Morgan. The honorary degree of LL.D. was conferred upon Mr. Morgan by Trinity College, Hartford, in 1918 and by Cambridge University in 1919. He received the freedom of the Goldsmith's Company of London in 1919, and the same year the Government of France made him an officier de la Legion d'Honneur, in recognition of service to the republic, subsequently advancing him to Commander of the Order. Mr. Morgan is keenly and successfully interested in small boat racing. He has also more than once been a leading member of the group formed to finance and manage the American cup defender in the international cup races. He is an ex-Commodore of the New York Yacht Club and flies his flag on the steam yacht Corsair. His other recreative interest lies largely in his library which contains a notable collection of books, manuscripts, letters, and other objects of art. He has long been a Trustee of the Metropolitan Museum of Art in New York and for two terms has been an Overseer of Harvard College.

CHAPTER I

Boyhood
1867–85

The First Thirteen Years, 1867–80

JOHN PIERPONT MORGAN, JR., WAS BORN ON SEPTEMBER 7, 1867, at Irvington-on-Hudson, New York. His parents, the elder J. P. Morgan and Frances Tracy Morgan, and their year-and-a-half-old daughter Louisa were spending the summer as houseguests of his aunt Sarah Morgan and her husband George H. Morgan at Woodcliff, their country house in the Hudson Valley, away from the heat of New York.[1]

J. P. Morgan, Sr., commuted to the city, where he was a partner in Dabney, Morgan & Co., bankers and brokers and representatives of his father's firm, J. S. Morgan & Co. of London, successors to George Peabody & Co.

With the coming of fall, the Morgans moved back to New York and their rented town house at 227 Madison Avenue on Murray Hill. For the next three years they followed the same pattern of living in the city, but during the summer renting Stonihurst at Highland Falls, near West Point on the Hudson.

In 1871, J. P. Morgan and his partner and cousin James Goodwin dissolved Dabney, Morgan & Co., and Morgan accepted the invitation of Anthony J. Drexel of Philadelphia to join the Philadelphia firm Drexel & Co. and form the partnership Drexel, Morgan & Co. in New York—the partners in the one firm to be partners in the other as well. Morgan was in poor health, however,

largely from overwork, so in the summer of 1871, before becoming immersed in the new venture, he took the whole family to
Europe for a year and a half. This was young Jack's first trip
abroad. He was four years old. The Morgans visited J. P.'s parents, the Junius Spencer Morgans, at 13 Princes Gate in London.
They traveled through France from Paris to Pau, in the Pyrenees
foothills. They then went to Austria and visited Karlsbad, the
Tyrol, and Vienna. In the winter, the family went south to Rome
and on to Egypt. They cruised up the Nile to the First Cataract.
On returning to Italy they stopped at Rome, the Italian Lakes,
and Venice. They visited Austria again in the spring of 1872, then
went back to London, and returned to New York in the fall. While
abroad, Morgan learned that the country property called Cragston at Highland Falls near Stonihurst had come on the market, so
at the urging of his father, J. S. Morgan, he bought it by cable.

Morgan came back fully restored from more than a year abroad
and returned to his active business and civic affairs. For the next
few years the usual family routine was to spend the cold months
at 6 East Fortieth Street in New York and to move up the Hudson
to the rural pleasures of Cragston in the spring.

By the spring of 1876, Morgan had worn himself out again, so,
after the four children (now including Juliet, born in 1870, and
Anne, born in 1873) had recovered from the measles, the whole
family again went to Europe—accompanied this time by two
nurses for the children—and spent almost a year there. They visited the Junius Morgans at Dover House, Roehampton, in the
London suburbs, and traveled through the Lake Country to Scotland. In the fall, they crossed over to Paris and in December went
to Italy—Milan, Venice, and down the Adriatic coast—and on to
Egypt for Christmas. They returned north in February by way of
Brindisi and Rome at carnival time. They revisited Paris and
London and were back in New York in May 1877. Jack was now
nine and better able this time to appreciate the sights he was ex-
posed to on the family travels abroad.

The alternating seasons in New York and Cragston continued.
Life at Cragston became more active as J. P. Morgan's business
became more prosperous and the children grew older. Morgan
raised prize-winning Guernsey dairy cattle, drove fast trotting
horses, and with his wife did a lot of entertaining.

The first letter from Jack to his mother that has survived is from
Cragston, written in July of 1878. The house party had been to

watch the parade at West Point. Father had just bought a new steam launch and named it after his daughter Louisa. Rehearsals were in progress for amateur theatricals.[2] These included, Morgan recalled almost fifty years later, ". . . one French one that we performed under the auspices of Miss Eustis who was governess to us children. I think the play was done in 1878, and if I remember rightly the name of it was *La Niaise de St. Fleur*, and I know that Louisa took the part of the heroine. Father promised us each a dollar if we brought it off, and we each received a silver dollar of the at that time new coinage, which impressed itself on my mind very much."[3]

The Morgans' social life in New York became more active in the late 1870s. Throughout this entire period, J. P. Morgan played with his children a great deal. He took them on outings in the city, brought them back to Cragston for sleigh rides in the winter, made Christmas a great event, and organized summer picnics around Cragston to places reached on the launch *Louisa* or by horse-drawn buggy. But he remained an aloof and reserved figure to his son. In the spring of 1879, Morgan took his daughter Louisa and a cousin of hers to England with him. A year later it was Juliet's turn to go abroad with her father.

On November 2, 1879, he took Jack, age twelve, down New York Harbor on a chartered tug to greet grandfather Junius S. Morgan on his arrival from England. That Christmas, Morgan dressed up as Santa Claus and drove around in a carriage distributing presents to friends and relatives. Christmas was always a day of giving and receiving presents under the decorated Christmas tree, but it was also a day when the family attended Christmas services at St. George's, Stuyvesant Square. Young Morgan was reared in a church-going tradition, and throughout his life he was an active layman in the Episcopal Church.

Meanwhile, J. P. Morgan was becoming more and more prominent in the business world. In 1869, he out-maneuvered James Fisk, and thus his boss, Jay Gould, in keeping the Albany & Susquehanna Railroad Company out of the control of the Erie Railroad, which enabled it to lease its properties to the Delaware & Hudson Canal Company. In 1877, an acrimonious political battle in Congress caused that body to adjourn without appropriating any money for the army payroll. Morgan grasped the situation and volunteered to lend the money to the War Department at not to exceed the legal rate of interest so the soldiers could be paid.

The offer was accepted. Morgan was reimbursed when Congress reconvened in the fall.

In November 1879, Drexel, Morgan & Co. entered the railroad-financing field by organizing a syndicate to buy 350,000 shares of New York Central stock from William H. Vanderbilt, which it sold to British investors through J. S. Morgan & Co. J. P. Morgan became a director of the road, representing the British stockholders. Railroads became the Morgan specialty.

St. Paul's School, 1880–84

In mid-September 1880, Mr. and Mrs. J. Pierpont Morgan took their only son, J. P. Morgan, Jr., thirteen, to Concord, New Hampshire, to enter St. Paul's School.[4] Jack wrote to his mother regularly. He emerges from the correspondence as a very attractive, candid, fair-minded, and natural school boy. He had an inquiring mind and a pleasant sense of humor with a whimsical gift of expression. He enjoyed reading; was a conscientious, if not brilliant, student; and liked outdoor activities, though he was not good enough at organized athletics to be invited to play on school teams.

Family life at the Morgans' continued in its usual course while Jack was off at school, except for the decision to move from 6 East Fortieth Street to a brownstone at 219 Madison Avenue, northeast corner of Thirty-sixth Street.

Christmas of 1880 followed the previous year's pattern, with Morgan dressing up in costume and setting forth to distribute presents to friends in New York on Christmas Eve. This year he took Jack—home after his first term at boarding school—along with him. Returning to school after the holiday festivities was an anticlimax, but Jack wrote to his mother that he had had "great fun in the train and did not have time to be blue." A month later he wrote enthusiastically of the Washington's Birthday celebration at the school, the excitement of sleighing, and the fairyland beauty of the New Hampshire winter with the evergreens weighted down by snow. These raptures were modified by the school's mumps epidemic.[5] In his first year at St. Paul's, Jack stood fourth in a class of thirty-two.[6]

The summer of 1881 found the family at Cragston on the Hudson, but this time the rural peace of the place was shattered by the blasting and excavating for the West Shore Railroad tracks. In

July, Grandfather Tracy and his two daughters, Frances (Mrs. Morgan) and Daisy, took Louisa and Jack for a trip to the West.

Jack returned to St. Paul's in the fall of 1881 to enter the third form.

In December 1881, the elder Morgan was invited to join his father on a yachting cruise of the Mediterranean. He took the train up to Concord, New Hampshire, to say good-bye to Jack at St. Paul's. A tangible result of the cruise was that it confirmed Morgan in his decision to buy the steam yacht already christened *Corsair* by C. J. Osborn, her original owner, on which he had taken an option before sailing to England in December. Jack, meanwhile, completed his second year away at school. At the end of 1881–82, he stood tenth in a class of forty-two students.

The summer of 1882 found Highland Falls even more congested and torn up by the West Shore Railroad construction than it had been the year before. The newly renovated house at 219 Madison Avenue was finally ready for the family when they returned from the country in the fall of 1882, but Jack had little time to arrange his new room before it was time to go back to Concord for the opening of school. That fall, St. Paul's School beat Harvard in cricket, and Jack wrote, "I don't think there is any pleasure so great in a cricket match as having one's side win." He read books that were not on class-assigned reading lists and found *Cupid M.D.* "very nice . . . although the love parts are a little sick perhaps." The following week he reported, "Football began on Monday and today I tried alas in vain to get on the team of the form." Indian summer came to New Hampshire and Jack went horseback riding. He continued, "Riding is much nicer than football. Still football is a most delightful game and I am very sorry I am not on a regular team."[7]

Jack wrote that he looked forward with great pleasure to a visit from his mother in November. In the next letter he told of substituting in a football game. He reread Thackeray's *Henry Esmond* and found that it was a "thrilling story and ends so deliciously that I could begin again and read it right through tomorrow." He hoped the family wouldn't be shocked by his low grades. He was doing "horribly" in Greek and falling behind. His headaches had returned for periods of four to five days.[8]

Christmas was celebrated in the usual way in 1882. This was the first Christmas at 219 Madison Avenue. Nearly a half century later Morgan wrote:

I still remember the . . . excitement and interest that I felt
on the occasion of my return from school for the Christmas
holidays in 1882, when, at the coming of dusk, the [electric]
lights began to glow. That was the second time I had seen that
form of light; the first was when my father was considering
the question of putting it into the house in the spring of 1881,
and took me down to Mr. Edison's place, then at Menlo Park,
New Jersey, to see how it looked. At the same time, Mr. Edison had just invented the phonograph, and he showed me (I
was aged 14) a cylinder phonograph into which he spoke and
which at once returned his exact words and tone, to my intense surprise and delight. What he said was "Hello, hello,
Mr. Phonograph, this is Mr. Edison talking to you and you
will please say it back again."[9]

He wrote back from school after the holiday, "Don't imagine I
feel happy for I don't but I am not uncomfortable." He added,
"We had our first Greek lesson this morning and I knew it!" He
decided (temporarily) to keep books out of his desk to avoid the
temptation to read when he ought to be studying. He refused
Egisto Labbri's offer to lend him *The Count of Monte Cristo*. School
remained a dull business.[10]

Studies looked up early in February. He was "ahead of a testimonial" (honors) in Greek and Latin, "Hoo Roar!!!!" Lent soon
began. The services were "not too bad." He had given up "four
square inch pie" for Lent, "which I cannot bear and never eat
anyhow. Don't you think that this is an opportunity for great self-
denial?" He read *Little Dorrit*, but didn't see why his sister Louisa
liked it as well as the rest of Dickens.[11]

Jack reassured his mother that he was taking care of his health
and wearing a flannel nightshirt. He wanted to join the "Racket
Club," but didn't have the money and didn't want to have to sell
his bicycle. He wrote, "Of course if Papa thinks it is too expensive
a luxury there is nothing more to say." The younger Morgan was
not spoiled by his austere father. The cheque did come, and he
joined the club. But life at school continued dull with "no new
girls to get mashed on."[12] With March came the doldrums. He
was tired of winter. Could his mother arrange to have flowers sent
to him, as she had the year before, one or two blooms a week to
brighten his alcove. A week later he "almost screamed with delight" when he opened a box of roses.[13]

He enjoyed the Easter visit with his parents and hoped that his mother was cheerful now that Papa had gone off to Europe, taking Louisa along.[14] J. Pierpont Morgan was away a great deal, and one wonders if Jack's solicitude about his mother and his faithful writing to her might not have been an attempt to compensate for her husband's long absences.

Spring finally reached New England in April, with flowers and birds. A number of boys' eyes were giving out from the winter's study. Jack wrote that he planned to have sore eyes and go outdoors and skip Greek. The arbutus bloomed, he received a "good" on a paper on the literature of Queen Anne's reign, and he read the *De Coverly Papers*.[15]

Toward the end of the 1882–83 school year, Homer was turning out to be more fun to read than Xenophon had been.[16] Jack played a good deal of tennis. He had hoped to get on the cricket team, but had no luck. But he was in good shape from playing racquets all winter. He spent seven dollars for new tennis shoes and hoped his mother didn't think that was too extravagant. He was reading Sir Walter Scott's novels and wished the author had condensed them somewhat. And the leaves were coming out on the trees! It was good to learn that Papa and Louisa were on their way home from Europe. Cousin Joe Kirkland introduced him to Frank Stockton's *The Lady or the Tiger* in *Scribner's*. The approaching Harvard examinations were a source of dread, but the new foliage was lovely. By the first week in June 1883, it was hot in New Hampshire. Could his mother send two quarts of strawberries from Cragston?[17]

At the end of his third year at St. Paul's, Jack stood eighth in a class of forty-four.

The summer vacation of 1883 saw a great deal of activity on board the new steam yacht and frequent cruises.

There is a gap in the mother-and-son correspondence for the fall term of 1883. We find Jack back at school in January 1884 after the Christmas vacation. Work was not going well: "Lessons were NASTY today. You don't know how hard it is to fix your attention on the reason for a Greek verb being in the subjunctive instead of the indicative after you have not been working for a long time." Rector Coit took Jack aside and lectured him "for his own good." He reported, "He told me I did not hold a high enough place in the school and among the boys, that I did not exert myself for the

general benefit enough; and that he knew I knew (which was true)
that if I should go away now the hole I made would be felt but
very little except by a small knot of fellows 'very nice fellows, my
dear, but very few of them.'"[18] Greek had its ups and downs. One
week he could report, "we are at Herodotus' account of the Battle
of Thermopylae and I never thought ancient history could be so
interesting. It is really as if H. had been there and seen everything." A week later all was gloom. "I studied on it for two hours
today and couldn't make any sense out of it and then when it is
translated in class it seems so easy."[19]

Meanwhile, the founding of a rival boarding school at Groton,
Massachusetts, was disturbing to the headmaster of St. Paul's.
"Mr. Coit spoke of the new school of which Mr. Peabody is the
head in a most contemptuous sort of way and wishes to know why
the Lawrences did not give their money to some existing school
rather than founding a new one, for instance St. Mark's at South-
borough. You may suppose I was rather annoyed with the reference to Mr. Peabody because he is Papa's friend."[20] J. P. Morgan,
Jr., was later to send both of his own sons to Mr. Peabody's
Groton School.

That spring he became editor of the student paper. About his
editorship, Jack wrote, "It is not a sinecure to be head editor. But
it will do me an immense lot of good in the way of teaching me to
act for myself on my own responsibility. You see, I am very defi-
cient in self-reliance." Nor was his self-confidence buoyed up
much by Rector Coit: "We took a 20 minute walk. It was chiefly a
small sermon. . . . The only thing it has done is to make me think
that perhaps I had better have died a very small boy."[21] In moments of stress, Rector Coit let the mask of polite concern fall.
Morgan recalled forty-five years later an incident when the boys
returned from a horseback ride later than expected: "Dr. Coit
called for me, and laying all the blame on me, and dropping all the
usual suavity of manner (he stopped calling me 'my dear,' which
he always did even when most vexed), he said to me, 'you must
know that this school is an absolute monarchy, of which I am the
head, and you must obey my rules or get out.' It was quite a shock
to me, but I recognized the justice of his position in that particular, although I could not agree with him that I was largely to
blame."[22]

Jack graduated from St. Paul's School in 1884, eleventh in a
class of thirty-five.

Wanderjahr I, 1884–85

The West

Mrs. Junius Spencer Morgan died in London on February 23, 1884, at 13 Princes Gate at the age of sixty-seven. In an age when mourning was a drawn-out matter, this even had a sobering effect on the family's 1884 summer at Cragston.[23] Jack was at loose ends. Finally, it was agreed that he could accept the invitation of the Reverend William Rainsford to visit the clergyman's rustic lodge, Sunlight, in the Rocky Mountains. This experience of roughing it in the wilderness was something totally new to young Morgan and a drastic change from boarding school and a world otherwise bounded by summers in the Hudson Valley and winters in the city.

Rainsford, the new rector of the Morgans' church, St. George's, Stuyvesant Square, was an outdoorsman of the type coming to the fore with Theodore Roosevelt and John Muir. While the minister was about twice Jack Morgan's age—the one in his thirties, the other not seventeen until September—they became very close as the result of shared hardships and dangers in August of 1884. High point of that western holiday was a blizzard that overtook the party on the trail and forced them to take shelter in an improvised camp for three days.[24]

Europe and Boston

Following his return from the west in the fall of 1884, young Morgan took a year off between preparatory school and college. Part of this year Jack traveled abroad.[25] Upon his return, he settled down in Boston and was tutored by Dr. Franklin Dexter of the Harvard Medical School faculty. Since he had already been accepted by Harvard, this study seems to have been for its own sake.[26] He wrote home to have some pictures and a few of his books sent up: Pepys's diary, Evelyn's diary, the Waverley novels, the *Life of Sydney Smith, The Arabian Nights*.[27] His sister Louisa came up for a visit early in January, and he met her at Back Bay Station. He went to some shows: Karl Millöcker's Viennese operetta *The Beggar Student* and, better, he thought, *The Queen's Lace Handkerchief*. He became assistant treasurer of the Trinity Church Sunday School.[28]

The correspondence lists events, diary fashion, as they occurred. Pierpont Morgan came up to Boston in mid-January, and

Jack was glad to see him. Jack went to the theatre with George Fiske to see Thomas Kean as Richard III. He observed, "He rants tremendously." He attended Trinity Church. A seasoned church-goer, he commented, "Mr. [Phillips] Brooks' sermon . . . was on foreign missions and was not very different from any one else's sermon on that subject."[29]

He became increasingly social, but was essentially shy. He declined an invitation to a sleigh ride and dance in February 1885, saying, "I didn't want to go as I didn't know one of the girls and cannot make myself useful in the gay and lightsome dance." He continued to read and noted that he agreed with his mother's criticism of Kingsley's *Westward Ho!*[30] He was glad that his mother was becoming more interested in society. Her secret, he wrote, was her genuine interest in listening to young people on their own level.[31] A fortnight later, he saw Ellen Terry in *Much Ado About Nothing*. He was enraptured: "As soon as Beatrice came on the steps I collapsed and remained so till she went off, when I temporarily recovered."[32]

A short financial rein is a recurring theme. He wrote in March 1885, "I need a new hat for purposes of swellness and as Papa don't want me to get things without permission may I get one, also some small things as collars, etc.?[33]

In the spring of 1885, there was the prospect of spending another summer in the Rocky Mountains in company with the young and earnest clergyman William Rainsford. Jack hoped that Papa would approve. He wrote to his father in Europe and begged him to cable back "Jack Rainsford yes." Meanwhile, he needed fifty dollars for pew rent at Trinity Church, and his social life was looking up. He dined with the Bangs family and wrote, "I am much in demand for I had two other invitations, one from Mrs. Endicott Peabody and one from Mrs. Lothrop."[34]

Harvard became more of a reality for the coming fall when Jack secured a room in Beck Hall in May. The other important event of the week was going to see Joseph Jefferson in *Rip Van Winkle*.[35]

The West Again

The elder Morgan approved the proposal to join Rainsford for another western summer; we have a letter from Jack to his father—few such letters have survived—dated "Pacific Express, June 25, 1885," filled with details of the trip and the stop at Miles City, Montana Territory, for camping supplies.[36]

The party of six left Mammoth Springs National Park on about June 29. The mosquitoes were bad, as they always are at snow line in early summer. Jack spoke of killing ten at a slap. They hunted mountain sheep, and Jack bagged the only one. They saw three bears and bear tracks. The weather was uneven. Sometimes there was rain mixed with hail. The wildflowers in the Alpine meadows were luxuriant—forget-me-nots and wild roses and wild onion plants in bloom.[37]

CHAPTER II

Harvard
1885–89

J. P. MORGAN, JR., ENTERED HARVARD COLLEGE IN THE FALL OF
1885 as a member of the Class of 1889. The school year began in
early October. Jack planned to have his breakfast and lunch at the
Memorial Hall dining room, where the food was "not so vile" as
reported. He resolved on a course of "absolute tea-totaling during these four years." His earliest friends were a boy named
Painter, the Sears twins, and Will Osborn. Another early friend
was J. C. R. "Jake" Peabody.[1] There was another Morgan in his
class, a "gentlemanly" youth from St. Mark's School. Hazing of
freshmen was practiced, but he told his mother not to worry, he
had been successful in avoiding it.[2]

Later in the fall, he went to see *The Mikado* with Jake Peabody at
the Hollis Street Theatre. He thought he really ought to receive a
pass to the theatre because it was formerly the Hollis Street
Church, where Great-grandfather Pierpont had preached.[3]

Jack's candor with his mother and ease in confiding in her indicates a very pleasant, relaxed friendship between mother and son.
He was able to write with complete unselfconsciousness—no
touch of bravado—"I had a smoke today and it has made me feel
gay as a lark."[4]

Jack expressed a sense of social responsibility beyond his years
on learning of the death of the financier William Henry Vanderbilt on December 8, 1885, at the age of sixty-four—the man perhaps best known outside the business world for bringing the

obelisk *Cleopatra's Needle* to New York. "How terribly sudden Mr. Vanderbilt's death was. . . . But what a fearful thing it seems for one man to have had so much money as that. It seems too much even to understand the responsibility of it." In the same letter, he spoke of seeing Salvini in *King Lear*, which he found less fine than *Othello*, "But I cried of course, like a fool, at his mad scenes and his waking scene . . . I wish my tears were less near the top."[5]

When he came back to Cambridge after the holidays in mid-January 1886, Jack reported, "Last night I treated myself to the opera: *Rigoletto*. Nordica sang Gilda and De Anna Rigoletto. His voice is not so fine as it might be but she is so handsome it made up for it."[6]

On St. Valentine's Day, 1886, he wrote about the floods in Cambridge, "It gives one a sick feeling . . . the people who must bear [the loss] are those who cannot well afford it." He went on to tell of having a cup of tea in his rooms in Beck Hall, the second time he had used his kettle, "and it does feel fine to have it under one's own vine and fig tree." In the same letter, he wrote, "I have received an undeserved and unwelcome honor . . . an invitation to President Eliot's for lunch tomorrow. I think I had rather die than go. (Burn this letter). . . ."[7]

He read R. L. Stevenson's new novel, *Dr. Jekyll and Mr. Hyde*, and "was much struck with it, but the horror of it was almost painful."[8] His social life continued active. He spoke of "a delicious time at the Cushings," where his friend was Grafton Cushing.[9] He liked Mrs. Cushing but would "not say she was particularly intellectual."[10] March 10, 1886, was a very special day. He called on the Gurneys and observed of his host: "He is rather a pompous gentleman and shows the bad effect of having been Dean of the College. It causes him to utter forth moral reflections which might be called commonplace were it not a Professor of Harvard who invented them." That night he went to the Franklin Dexters' for dinner and to the play afterwards to see Modjeska in *Camille*. He preferred happy endings; his criticism was that, of course, it had "to end badly in a perfectly unnecessary manner. . . ."[11]

Young Morgan discovered the Russian writers in the spring of his freshman year. He wrote: "I finished Anna [Karenina] last night and was much entertained with Levin's feelings and thoughts about faith and the effect it has on him. One feels as if Tolstoi had been through it." Later in the season, he told his mother, "I get a little time for *War & Peace* which is enchanting."[12]

In the long vacation between his first and second years at Harvard, Jack Morgan went on his third trip to the Rocky Mountains with the Reverend William Rainsford. Back again in Miles City, Montana Territory, in July 1886, Jack noted that the party, which included his cousin Junius Morgan, would soon be in camp and, "when one gets on his flannel shirt and ancient duds one feels the savage instinct very strong and hankers for no one to see him."[13] Upon his return in September, he wrote from New York to his mother at Cragston and described his cousin Junius as "a first class camper, shot, and companion all around." He was reading *Wanda*, "incomparably the finest of Ouida's books and is clean besides, except in spots." He went on a yacht-race house party that included Jake Peabody and his parents. He reported to his mother, about his father, "Papa is looking better than I have seen him in a long time."[14]

The elder Morgan promised to get his son a horse to ride in Cambridge when Harvard opened. This last puzzled Jack who told his mother, "I cannot exactly understand his kindness about the horse. He must have been much better satisfied with my report than I was."[15] Father and son also came to an agreement about smoking. It was permissible but "to be done within limits." Morgan, Sr., had just put through his plan for reorganizing the Philadelphia & Reading Railroad Co. in such a way that he controlled the road. Jack noted, "Papa is simply triumphant about the Reading business. . . ." He even went to a ball after signing the papers.[16]

It was the fall of 1886, almost time for Jack to return to Harvard for his sophomore year. But he wasn't happy at the prospect. "As the time approaches I feel more and more how entirely I hate Cambridge and everything connected with it." Perhaps James Gore King, a classmate at St. Paul's and now a classmate at Harvard, helped to reconcile Jack to returning. They arranged to return to Boston on the train together, and Jack planned to sit next to young King if he decided to board at Memorial Hall. Later in the fall, he wrote, "I see more and more of Jim King,"[17] and we know that this friendship lasted the rest of their lives, until King's death in 1932.

Another thing that made the second year more pleasurable was the horse his father gave him. But the single most important factor was his joining DKE, the "Dickey" Club, despite the initiation ordeal. He wrote, "I am more than glad I did go through with the disagreeable part of it for the sake of the change it has made in my feelings towards and position in college life." Apparently the feeling of belonging was very important. Moments of gloom thereafter tended to be only temporary—as when Princeton beat Harvard twelve to nothing in football in November 1886.[18]

The elder Morgan was a stickler for the businesslike handling of money by his son. Mrs. Morgan thought it would be simplest if Jack submitted a written statement of accounts, but her son pointed out that it would be better to do it orally, with supporting bills and cheques, so that misunderstandings could be cleared up immediately. In a subsequent letter, however, he said he had decided to write after all, because Papa would be so busy upon his return.[19]

Social life continued brisk in the spring of 1887. On April 24, Jack had lunch at the Osborns' and dinner at the Jacob Rogerses'.

Jack was brought up in a religious household and was convinced of the validity of the Christian tenets. In writing of a discussion of "purity" with the skeptic Eliot Norton, son of history of art professor Charles Eliot Norton and a student in the Harvard Law School, he said: "A man who starts by believing in the law of Christ and the Gospel starts with an immeasurable advantage over one who has not such a belief to start with. The latter must first work his way . . . into the position of the former and makes many mistakes before he does. For any man who is very earnest is bound to reach the conclusions which the Gospels lay down as principles and which were seen by the divine power before man ever began to think of them."[20]

In the spring of 1887, Jack, now a member of Delta Phi, the Delphic Club, was appointed a committee of one to figure out a way for the club to evade the Massachusetts liquor law that forbade clubs to keep bars. He observed of this assignment: "It seems rather queer to me because I don't drink; however, I am in favor of allowing a man a glass of beer if he wants it, or in other words, I believe in the inalienable right of every man to make a beast of his self whenever he wishes to. But really I don't believe in compulsory *total abstinence* and Prohibition for I think it makes a man want to get drunk more than ever. . . ."[21]

Spring brought boat races, and Jack won the club pool of forty-five dollars by winning at auction the ticket with the winning order of Harvard class shells on the river. The spring of 1887 was a particularly pleasant one, and spring in Cambridge—even today's built-up Cambridge—can be very lovely. "The country nowadays is simply glorious with the orchards in full bloom and all the shrubs beginning to blossom." Jack's spirits were high. He wished that his mother could come up and visit him as she had the previous year, but he could say that her "presence here is not as necessary to keep me in good spirits as it was last spring."²² Jack's letters were usually on notepaper imprinted "6, Beck Hall, Cambridge." The one sent on Monday, May 16, 1887, was on paper marked "Delta Phi Club, 7 Brattle Street." He wished his mother well on her birthday the day before and told of his horseback riding, both alone and with Jake Peabody.

The visit of a friend sad at leaving college caused Jack to reflect upon "the fact, sad but true, that I shall feel the same way in two years. Can you fancy my feeling that way when last year I felt so pleased at the idea of a whole year being past?" He reported that work was about to begin on the new Delta Phi house, a fact that brought him satisfaction, "for I am one of the two fellows who have done all the work."²³

He had an attack of jaundice followed by a severe headache in the middle of final examination week. A companion in discomfort was James Gore King, who suffered from rheumatism. It was the end of term, so he felt obliged to make a number of duty calls. He found Canon Wilberforce's Trinity Sunday sermon at Trinity Church a mistake: "The doctrine of the Trinity cannot be explained and why try to do so for three quarters of an hour?"²⁴

In the summer of 1887, J. P. Morgan, Jr., went to Europe with his cousins Will Goodwin of Hartford and Junius Morgan. They sailed on the *Germanic* in company with a contingent of doctors including Franklin Dexter. As they approached Queenstown on the Irish coast, Jack wrote, "The passage has been wonderful, never in the least rough and sails up more than half the time," an observation that gives us a picture of the steamships in 1887. He noted: "There is only one girl on board who can be called a belle and I have kept very clear of her because she struck me as being *common*. I can fancy Louisa turning up her nose at that and saying I am stuck up but I do like girls to be ladylike." He found Will Goodwin a bit difficult to make conversation with, but was himself: "the most contented of the crowd apparently for I am fond of loafing and here there is no duty which conscience makes one feel uncomfortable about if not performed. So I take my ease with a pipe and a book while others more actively disposed fret at the confinement."[25]

The *Germanic* docked at Liverpool on Friday, July 8, 1887, and Jack and Junius set out at once for London and their grandfather's place, Dover House, in the suburb of Roehampton. A house party was in progress, which included other cousins, the Walter Burns family of Copt House. It was the weekend of the Eton-Harrow cricket match, and the two American college boys went into Lord's cricket ground with the others and enjoyed it greatly. Jack wrote, "It was gay and bright and the match itself was entertaining. But it was rather fatiguing for we got to Lord's at 11 and stayed until four with a swell lunch there." The Walter Burnses were difficult to talk with at first but soon proved most congenial. Walter Burns was amusing, "but continually making remarks which are rather worse than doubtful."[26]

At Roehampton, the English servants treated Jack with more deference than they did Junius, because Jack had precedence as the son of old Junius's son while Junius was only the son of his daughter[27] (who had married a man with the same last name as her own).

On Thursday, July 14, Jack and young Junius went into town to see an exhibition of contemporary British painters, where old Junius Morgan's recent portrait was on display. The following evening they dined at the Criterion and went to the theatre to see Henry Irving as Mephistopheles and Ellen Terry as Marguerite in *Faust* (the play, not the opera). As usual, Jack was disturbed by the tragic ending and wrote, "The absolute certainty of the triumph of evil over good is so fiendishly worked out, it is worse than an old Greek drama." A diversion was the presence in the theatre of the Crown Prince of Germany, who the following year was to ascend the throne as William II (and lose it with considerable help from J. P. Morgan). Jack found the future Kaiser "such a wonderfully handsome man!"[28]

In the same letter, Jack mentions a friend of the family or a relative, referred to only as "Luie," whose husband, Ernest, had been "ordered off to a German *Bad* with an unspellable name on account of supposed gout," leaving Luie "an interesting grass widow." When Jack and Luie went to the theatre to see Windham in *David Garrick*, Jack was apprehensive all through the performance because Luie's dress was "of the 'shoulder strap and waist band' order" and he "feared a catastrophe. However, none occurred."

The climax of Jack's English summer was going down to Spithead on July 23 as the guest of Sir John Rose to see the great naval review.[29]

Jack returned to his junior year at Harvard in the fall of 1887. He usually addressed his letters "Dearest Mama"; it is interesting to find him experimenting with the "dear-less" letter affected by some businessmen today. The December 4, 1887, letter begins: "I can't begin to tell you, dearest Mother, how good it seemed to get your letter." He went on to say, "I am becoming quite a society swell now and am having invitations from all directions." Throughout the correspondence there is always this note of modesty and light poking of fun at himself, never bombast or smugness. He had become interested in science in his last year at St. Paul's and had tutored in science between school and college. He had a small laboratory area in his dormitory at Beck Hall and wrote home for more equipment for his Zeiss microscope. He and Sam Dexter planned "to put in some rather effective work there during the winter if all goes well." One December evening, he and Jim King went to see the Stock Museum Company's performance of *The Barrister*. He found it hilariously funny. He kept social fences mended—called on Mrs. Louis Agassiz and went to the Rogerses' for tea.[30]

In December 1887, Jack reported on a call on a Mr. Hopkinson, "who was as kind as could be, but much disgusted at the idea of my going into business after leaving college." He went on, "I don't know why so many people, chiefly those who are engaged in tuition or some literary pursuit, seem to look upon business as if it were the general sewer in which all ambition and intelligence disappear or, worse, get turned into 'money getting' arrangements. I must confess I don't see any harm myself in making a little money, provided it can be done honestly and reasonably."[31]

Jack found the Christmas holidays in 1887 somewhat disappointing, since the Morgan family was not all together. Late in January, after the spring term had started, Mrs. John Cushing gave a ball in Boston. Jack and Jim King were invited, so they dressed right after dinner and went into town to spend the first part of the evening before the party listening to *Tannhäuser* presented by the American Opera Company. Jack said he felt as sad as Elizabeth did when Tannhäuser threw away his second chance! A few days later, the room at Beck Hall was entered and a number of his favorite possessions were stolen, including his razor and strop, ivory-backed military brushes, and clothes brush. He called in the police, but was so relieved at the thief's modest haul that he was not too downhearted.

In the winter of 1888, Jack wrote, "I have been steeping myself in Browning lately and, do you know, I have at last found poetry I liked. . . . As for its being hard to understand, there don't seem to me to be a very great foundation for that except in one or two poems. . . ." He partly explained his new interest: "But you see, living in Boston or near it, I was bound to catch the Browning craze."[32]

Almost exactly a year later, he spoke of Browning's *Rabbi Ben Ezra*. He liked it, "not that the words were so fine, but because the poet did not try to separate the physical part of the human being from the soul." He deplored the kind of poetry "which means to appeal to the soul as apart from the body, that sinks the body in a sleep of sweet melody (a la Shelley) and then goes on to tell the soul how it ought to feel."[33]

The class of 1889, then in its junior year, held a dinner at the Parker House in Boston on the evening of March 7, 1888. The main events of the occasion were the delivering of a poem, an oration, and an address. The poem by Carleton Hunneman was a lighthearted piece of doggerel that poked fun at members of his class. The reference to Jack Morgan tells us how he appeared to his contemporaries and the influence on his outlook of the trips to the West with William Rainsford:

> Jack Morgan, the wonderful talking-machine, and human-type-writer combined
> Will spout three straight hours on "Life on the Plains" and eventually talk himself blind.[34]

There is a break in the correspondence for the rest of the spring term until the letter of June 11. He had been social, with calls on old friends, the Bangses, the Osborns, and Mrs. Agassiz. Final examinations were in progress. He was hopeful about natural science, and optimistic about German, in which he came into the examination "simply loaded to the muzzle with facts and constructions." The big event of the semester was being invited to join "O.K.," which he characterized as "a society literary in its aims."[35]

Jack returned to Cambridge in October 1888 for his senior year at Harvard. He was working eighteen hours a week in the science laboratory. One October day he had a pleasant walk in the woods looking for fungi with Professor Farlow, the botanist. He wanted his mother to ask his father how he should register to vote. His twenty-first birthday had been on September 7. He had a long discussion of religion with Jim King and Newton Stokes, son of Canon Phelps Stokes. He read *Sartor Resartis* again, which he did every year at this time. In Boston, he went to see *Little Lord Fauntleroy* as a play.[36]

The study of natural science narrowed into a specializing in seaweed, a field that Jack said "is going to make the chief pleasure of my year here, I am sure, and probably teach me how to work for myself after I leave here."[37] Peering through a microscope in science laboratory caused Jack to strain his eyes seriously, however, and his oculist ordered him to rest his eyes.[38]

A short-lived rift between mother and son developed in the fall of 1888. Apparently he failed to write as regularly as she wished and she administered—verbally—what he called a slap in the face, which continued to smart until his letter of October 21. He enjoyed hearing Phillips Brooks preach at Trinity Church, and he had a pleasant horseback ride in the fall coloring. He and Jim King read poetry aloud.[39]

Christmas at 219 Madison Avenue found Mrs. Morgan and the girls away. Jack and his father went to hear William Rainsford preach at St. George's and then took the train to Hartford for a visit. Jack wrote of the elder Morgan, "He is very well and jolly by fits but sometimes I see he feels as lonely as I do and he looks as glum as if he hadn't a friend in the world."[40]

January 1889 found Jack Morgan back in Cambridge for his final semester of college. Two new items appear in the correspondence: his activity as business manager of the Hasty Pudding dramatic production and his increased interest in the Grew family of Boston—Ned Grew had been a classmate at St. Paul's and was now a classmate at Harvard. Jack sent a sketchy Grew genealogy to his father: Mr. Grew was connected with the Sturgis clan, and Mrs. Grew was born a Wigglesworth.[41] He went to lunch and then ice skating with the Grews one day in the first week of February. That week he also read *Fraternity* and liked the story, but thought its socialistic ideas unrealistic: "humans are too selfish to pull together for the common good, won't change overnight to make a new system work."[42] But Jack's thoughts were not on socialism. They were on Jessie Grew. Normally very restrained and controlled, he seems to have let himself go. He wrote his mother: "The more I see Miss Grew and the more I talk with her the surer I am that I am not only wise in my choice, but also that it could not have happened any other way; that wherever or whenever I met her the result as far as I was concerned would have been the same." His concern and apprehension about telling his father of his feelings are sad to read. There are few sorrier states than that of being so financially dependent as to be subject to parental opinion in the matter of falling in love or considering marriage. Happily, the elder Morgan was most sympathetic.[43] Jack was greatly encouraged to learn that the Grews were making inquiries about him and especially about his moral character, through a family friend connected with the ownership of his dormitory, Beck Hall.

He was kept very busy raising money for the Hasty Pudding Show—lining up society women to be patronesses. At the same time, the O.K. Society had the idea of having the members write successive chapters of a collaborative novel. Jack was assigned to do the penultimate chapter, by which time the heroine, newly recovering from brain fever, and a married man have fallen in love. Jack's dilemma: to solve the problem by killing off the inconvenient wife would be immoral, to kill off the heroine would cause the reader to lose interest, to kill off the man would be to kill off the heroine too, with a relapse of the fever. He observed with some understatement, "It seems an awkward situation."[44]

The great news the following week was Jack's making a laboratory discovery that proved a theory about seaweed held by his mentor Farlow—as opposed to one advanced by a Professor Barnet—thus practically insuring him a grade of *A* in the course.[45]

While he did not consider himself a lover of music, young Morgan was certainly interested in it. He attended Walter Damrosch's course of lectures on Wagner's *Ring* cycle and observed, "I don't think I ever enjoyed anything of the kind as much—the music and the lecturer's enthusiasm made a charming mixture." Characteristically, he was put off by the sad ending. "But the end of the Cycle is so utterly painful. . . . Certainly, the whole scheme is grand and magnificent as much as you like but it is painfully low in its moral tone. The love which should have been the one part of Siegfried which could stand against all treachery is lost so instantly and utterly. Certainly the heroic age was a brutish time."[46]

By May, Jack had begun to think about final examinations and whom to invite for Class Day exercises. He saw a Lyceum School performance of Sophocles's *Electra* given in English. He found it "effective," but noted that Charles Eliot Norton walked out in the middle. Perhaps the professor was put off by Clytemnestra's Arkansas twang.[47]

It is entertaining to find Jack speaking of the delays in the arrival of his mother's letters from Europe with a reference to the governor of North Carolina's celebrated remark to the governor of South Carolina! He was surprised to find how sad he was at the prospect of leaving Harvard, even with the summer's European trip before him. He found his association with the O.K. the pleasantest experience of his four years—even if they did resuscitate the heroine of their joint-effort novel after he had killed her off![48]

J. P. Morgan, Jr., received his bachelor's degree from Harvard College in June 1889. His academic record at Harvard was slightly above a *C* average for the four years. He did well in French, indifferently in mathematics, unevenly in natural science and English—sometimes well, sometimes not. He did receive the hoped-for *A* in the final science course after the seaweed triumph![49]

Wanderjahr II, *1889*

Following graduation, Jack went abroad for a change of scene between college and the start of his business career. During this interval, he planned to learn French and German. There was a tradition within the family of interest in German. The elder Morgan had been a student at the University of Göttingen from April 12, 1856, until the early summer of 1857.[50] That year at Göttingen later led to an ingenious attempt to extort money from the Morgan family. In 1936, a German citizen wrote claiming to be the illegitimate son of J. P. Morgan, Sr., and a German girl who was living in Göttingen when Morgan was a student. He said that his birthdate was November 30, 1864, which led the younger Morgan to inquire of his father's biographer whether Pierpont had been in Göttingen at the appropriate time. He had not.[51]

In company with Ned Grew, Jack sailed for England early in July. He went first to London, then stayed for a week at Dover House, Roehampton, with his grandfather, Junius Spencer Morgan. From London he crossed over to Paris.[52] The Exposition was in progress, and the Eiffel Tower had just been completed.

Since the first objective of the European visit was to learn French, Jack made arrangements to go to Beauvais and live and study at the house of the Protestant clergyman Pasteur Diény. He was very homesick but resolved to show his determination and learn the French language. He *lived* French. He found Beauvais a dull provincial town, which probably helped him concentrate. A diversion was the arrival of a carnival in the public square with a merry-go-round and a shooting gallery. Tennis helped. But delays in the arrival of letters from Jessie Grew caused him anxiety.[53]

A recurring note in Jack's letters to his mother is his concern about his father: pleasure at his interesting business moves, but worry about his health and possible overwork. This is summed up in the remark in his letter of August 18, 1889. "It is good to think of papa as having a good long holiday. I hate to have him so over-worked in the hot weather. Ah for the time when I can help him!"[54]

Jack had moments of poetic expression. He wrote of being caught in a driving rain while out walking with the Diény family and looking down from the top of a hill. "Beauvais behind us and in front a beautiful valley with a forest and a château with the wonderful sea-clouds driving in from the ocean. It looked like a Gainsborough landscape, and I did not really much mind the wetting I got for having gone there." He expressed pleasure that his mother was finding Jessie Grew a pleasant young woman.[55] Perhaps the most enjoyable single episode of the Beauvais stay occurred a week before his departure—an afternoon spent crawling all over the cathedral among gargoyles and flying buttresses, enjoying the view from various high places on the church.[56]

On September 2, 1889, Jack said goodbye to the Diény family and set out for Germany by way of Paris and another look at the Exposition. He went from Paris to Berlin by way of Cologne.[57]

Life in Germany turned out to be much less grim than Jack had feared—actually very enjoyable. He went to parties, to dinner with new friends, to hear *Götterdämmerung*.[58] In retrospect, it seemed less pleasant. Looking back at the Berlin experience after fifty years, Morgan wrote Addie Prince: "I, too, well remember the time at Frau von Schack's, although my three or four months there are really a very painful recollection because I wanted very much to come home and did not like the Germans or their ways—of which trouble I have never been cured."[59]

He made good progress with the language but felt he only

wanted it for utilitarian ends, not for the pleasure of German it-self.[60] He wrote, "The needful awkwardness of phrasing, the crabbed letters and harsh sounds are all unpleasant to me." He preferred French, although he wrote his mother in the last surviv-ing letter of the German visit that, "well done as the writing is" he did not like the writings of de Maupassant because of the view of life which he opens up, "so hopeless and so inhuman" that it de-pressed him.[61]

CHAPTER III

Apprenticeship for Business
1890 – 1905

Boston, 1890

UPON HIS RETURN TO THE UNITED STATES, YOUNG MORGAN WENT to work early in 1890 for the Boston banking house of Jacob C. Rogers & Co. to learn the business.[1] Mr. Rogers was a former partner of J. S. Morgan & Co., London, and since 1879 had been an agent of the firm in Boston.[2] Mrs. Rogers was a member of the Peabody clan of Massachusetts.[3]

After all the anguish and waiting on parental opinion that marked the early stages of their courtship, Jack and Jane Norton ("Jessie") Grew became engaged during 1890. They were married on December 11, 1890. The festivities were reported on the front page of the *New York Times* the following day under the heading "Society Wedding at Boston." It was a gala affair at the Arlington Street church, with a reception afterwards at the Grew house on Beacon Street. The best man was Jack's kinsman Junius; the bridesmaids were his sisters Louisa and Juliet and the bride's sisters Elsie and Rita Grew. The ushers were his lifelong friend James G. King, and Stewart Brown, Arthur Sturges,[4] T. S. Bradlee, G. W. Wheelwright, Edward W. Grew, J. S. Codman, and Samuel Dexter. The Reverend Brook Hereford performed the ceremony. The mother of the groom is described as "superb in gray and silver brocade and wearing a magnificent necklace of pearls." The mother of the bride wore "a gown of olive satin, and diamond ornaments."[5]

Following their marriage, the junior Morgans moved permanently from Boston to New York. Mrs. Grew gave Jessie's jewelry to Mrs. Morgan to carry back with her to New York, so that Jessie would have it there when she arrived from the wedding trip.[6]

New York, 1891–98

In January 1891, J. P. Morgan, Jr.—Jack—went to work in New York for his father's firm, Drexel, Morgan & Co. This tour of duty would last until January of 1898, when he was transferred to London.[7] Jack was back in the United States in the fall of 1891, when he was called upon by his father to christen the new *Corsair*, on its launching.[8] On January 1, 1892, he became a partner of Drexel, Morgan & Co. His first child, Junius Spencer Morgan, Jr., named for his great-grandfather, was born on March 15.[9]

During 1892, the younger Morgans lived at 8 East Fortieth Street in New York,[10] but that year the Boston architect R. C. "Chip" Sturgis of Sturgis & Cabot designed a new house for them at 8 East Thirty-sixth Street, completed in the summer. Morgan instructed the architect to spare no expense on the structure, but to go slowly on the decoration—no $1800 frieze and not too much stained glass![11] The young family got out of the city during the hot summer months and rented a series of houses in Westchester County by the shore.[12]

Morgan's longtime interest in small-boat sailing on Long Island Sound may date from his purchase in the spring of 1895 of the knockabout sloop *Marianne*, nineteen feet at the waterline, twenty-nine feet overall length.[13]

Anthony J. Drexel, senior partner of Drexel, Morgan & Co., died in Karlsbad on June 30, 1893.[14] A year and a half later, on January 1, 1895, the firm name was changed to the subsequently renowned name of J. P. Morgan & Co. The younger Morgan automatically became a partner in the new firm.[15] The Paris house became Morgan, Harjes & Co.[16]

On November 14, 1893, a second child, Jane Norton Morgan, was born.[17]

The period of the younger Morgan's New York apprenticeship (1892–98) was the time that began with the firm's undertaking a series of railroad reorganizations related to the business troubles leading up to the panic of 1893. These included the Richmond (Virginia) Terminal reorganization of 1892, the Erie Railroad reorganization of 1894, the creation that same year of the Southern Railway System by a consolidation of some thirty companies, and the Northern Pacific reorganization of 1896.[18]

The most dramatic financial episode of this period was the 1895–96 rescue of the United States Treasury from the potentially disastrous decline in gold reserves by the syndicate organized by the elder Morgan and August Belmont. It was also a period of security issues and the financing of the emerging electric industry.[19]

Meanwhile, young Morgan had become active in the financing and managing of two philanthropic organizations, St. Luke's Hospital and the New York Trade School at Sixty-seventh Street and First Avenue.[20]

During these seven years in New York, J. P. Morgan, Jr., was learning banking and the related securities-underwriting business, but as a young man in his twenties with a forceful father as head of the firm, he could hardly have exerted great influence on the course of the firm's affairs, even assuming that he had wished to.

London, 1898–1905

1898

J. P. Morgan, Jr., became a partner in the London house of J. S. Morgan & Co. on January 1, 1898, and a fortnight later, with his wife Jessie and their three children (a second daughter, Frances Tracy Morgan, had been born on January 17, 1897), he left New York and took up residence in England for the next eight years.

Morgan was sent to London to do two specific things. The first was to learn at first hand how the British carried on a banking business under a central banking system dominated by the Bank of England. Morgan, Sr., anticipated the establishment of the Federal Reserve System in the United States and wanted someone who would eventually have authority in the Morgan firms to know how such a system worked. The second was quietly to look about the City and select British partners to convert the elder Morgan's privately owned J. S. Morgan & Co. into a British concern. The old George Peabody firm was still basically an American company; among the leading members of the firm, the Walter Burnses, father and son, were Americans and so was Clinton

Dawkins, however Anglicized they had become. It was Jack Morgan who found the partners of what became Morgan, Grenfell & Co.—E. C. Grenfell, Vivian Smith, and others.[21]

Jack looked forward eagerly to the London assignment. He wrote, "There begins the new work for me!"[22] But it turned out to be largely routine.

One is tempted to draw a rough parallel between the careers of Morgan's older British contemporary the Prince of Wales (the future Edward VII) and the heir to the senior partnership of J. P. Morgan & Co. Victoria denied her eldest son any participation in matters of state, and J. Pierpont Morgan sent his son to the London office from 1898 to 1905. Despite the nominal dignity of a partnership, Jack's London duties were not very exciting during a time when more spectacular concerns, like the formation of the United States Steel Corporation, were in progress in New York.

The reaction of the Prince of Wales to his enforced inactivity was to engage in a lighthearted succession of sporting and amorous adventures. He felt frustrated and frequently sought through his mother's ministers to be given some work to do. Such a comparison would not be entirely appropriate, however, as the purposes of Morgan's mission shows. Morgan accepted his role in a resigned spirit. He saw the logic of the move, and he had great affection and almost awe for his father. But he chafed at his virtual exile. He turned to the pleasures of an almost hyperactive social life with a titled group to which the firm's prestige and his own family connections gave him entrée. It was a breathless round of dinner parties, dances, theatre parties, country-house parties, shooting parties. On arrival in London, the Morgans were immediately caught up in a social whirl, with calls and dinner parties. One of the first topics of conversation was the matter of Jessie's presentation at court.[23] Jack wrote, "Father has arranged that Jessie is to be presented on February 25 or 26, I forget which. It now appears that Louisa's friend Victoria R I won't receive any young married women whose husbands haven't been to a Levee so I am booked for February 21 with court dress and all; sword and cocked hat, too, I believe, to go and see *my* friend Albert Edward, Prince of Wales. It will make me feel like seven kinds of jackass, but Jessie wants to go to court at all hazards and at any cost. Sad isn't it?"[24]

The elder Morgan was in London at this time, and he was also at some of the dinner parties, including those at the Burnses. The younger Morgans saw a lot of the Burns family. Walter Spencer Morgan Burns was a relative and a partner in J. S. Morgan & Co. He was the son of Walter Hayes Burns, also a partner in the firm, who had died the previous year.[25]

Pierpont Morgan seems to have stepped easily into the role of grandfather and took the Jack Morgan children to the pantomime—that strange, stylized English holiday-time theatrical entertainment.[26] He also took his son and daughter-in-law to the theatre to see *Bachelor's Romance*. The round of dinner parties continued. One wonders how a young banker could stay awake to work in the countinghouse the next morning after so many late nights. They dined with a Mrs. Clifford, whose husband had been lost in a Swiss glacier. At this party the butler announced the guests portentously. They were particularly impressed by his calling out, "The Lord Chief Justice of England and Lady Russell!" Another night it was to the Maurice Glyns' and on to the play *Julius Caesar*, with sets by Alma-Tadema. Then to the Burnses' again.[27]

Pierpont Morgan crossed over to Paris, but the parties continued for the young Morgans: to the Bulteels' (Mrs. Bulteel had been a Grenfell), where they found Lord and Lady Grey, Lord Revelstoke (head of the Baring family), and what Jack referred to as other "swells"; to Lady Tweeddale's for a party of eighteen at dinner; to the Charles Eric Hambros'.[28]

The Morgans met Henry James and also went to two private art showings, a watercolor exhibition at Agnew's and one at the National Portrait Gallery, the latter courtesy of Mr. Christ, the director. Jack also took up riding in the park.[29]

They dined with Henry White, American Ambassador John Hay's secretary of embassy. Jack sat next to Arthur Balfour's sister. Also there were Lord Landaff and Lady Harcourt (née Motley of Boston). One Sunday, Miss Gregory, daughter of the Dean of St. Paul's, took them to that cathedral for services.

Jack Morgan was presented to the Prince of Wales at the levee at St. James's Palace on February 21, 1898. Secretary of Embassy White led him through the ambassadors' door into the presentation chamber. He enjoyed every minute of it. The dinner parties continued. At Lady Lyttleton's, Jessie sat next to the bishop of London, which led Jack to observe, "England can never come to any good until they relearn how to talk to the Almighty without intoning through their noses at Him." Lady Lyttleton was a funny little old lady who had "stepped out of Trollope or Charles Reade, full of charities and the Church of England."[30]

At length the great day of Jane Norton Morgan's presentation at court arrived. It was a Queen's Drawing Room—an afternoon affair at Buckingham Palace—on February 25, 1898. The *Daily Mail* described the Queen's Drawing Room the following day:

> Her Majesty looked wonderfully well in her black robes, glittering with jewels and many-colored orders, and, as usual, she stayed for some time after the entree people had passed by, and did not leave the throne room until after four o'clock. . . .
>
> Next to her Majesty stood the Princess of Wales, sweet and lovely as ever, and loaded with diamonds; with her was the Prince of Wales, while the Prince and Princess Christian and the Duke and Duchess of Connaught were also in the circle, and the Duchess of Devonshire was noticeable, among those who stood by. . . .
>
> Far and away the loveliest woman in any of the rooms was Lady Helen Vincent, tall and graceful in white, with something of soft blue and a deep, unbroken band of diamonds across her hair, while round her neck were entwined beautiful pearls. . . .
>
> Quite the most beautiful dress in the whole room was the one worn by Mrs. Pierpont Morgan, whose husband is one of the big American financiers, and who is herself a pretty woman—tall, slender, with fair hair and blue eyes, and a very charming smile. The dress itself was of soft muslin applique with lace, and with a soft waist-band of the same, and the train (which marked a new era in the world of fashion, and which was slung loosely from her shoulders almost like a coat) was made of white satin, lined with turquoise-blue miroir velvet and ruffled with pink roses.[31]

During the week of the Drawing Room, the Morgans went to see Henry Irving and Ellen Terry in *Madame Sans Gêne.* They found that age was telling on Terry. They also dined at Walter Heinemann's and there found "the men, on average . . . more attractive than the women." But not every minute was devoted to the social life. Both husband and wife read English history. Morgan found that he was rusty on the period before the Restoration and his "friend Mr. Pepys." They missed the elder Morgan, off in France, and Morgan wrote that his father "has been dear to us."[32]

There was a brief respite from social activity late in February, so the Morgans went out to suburban Roehampton to look at Morgan, Sr.'s, Dover House and found fruit ripening in the greenhouses.[33] With the Grenfells, they visited the Tower of London with a special pass. A day or so later, Jack went to lunch with Hugh Smith at the Bank of England and was given the tour of the bank and its vaults. He was particularly taken with the machines that took worn coins out of circulation, "charming little intelligent machines which drop the light sovereigns to one side and the full weight ones to the other. (It looks like the day of Judgement and is I believe almost as infallible, the error being on the side of severity, however, which we hope will not be the case then.)" He dined with a Mrs. Colgate, whom he described as "not quite our kind" and given to "hinting at improper stories."[34]

The subject came up of how long he was to remain in England. Jack said that the family planned to come home to the United States in the summer of 1898, but he would have to stay in England until the partnership of J. S. Morgan & Co. was due to expire at the end of 1899. The firm actually continued for ten more years and was dissolved on December 31, 1909.[35]

Rumors of a war between the United States and Spain were disturbing the business community in March of 1898. In the same week, the Morgans dined with Chief Justice Russell and his wife; other guests were Mrs. Gully, wife of the Speaker of the House of Commons, Sir Andrew McCormack, President of the College of Surgeons, and a couple named Maguire, of whom it was reported, "She couldn't stand the dullness of her honeymoon and sent for her sister to join them!" They also went to services again at St. Paul's, where the "sermon by the Archdeacon of London was too awful for words." At Julian Sturgis's they encountered the literary lions of the day. Jack spoke of "Henry James, who has been most polite ever since we came," and "the Barries (such a disappointment after his book he is. I don't know why his mother should have loved him!)"[36]

The sluggishness of the stock exchange from the uncertainty over the prospect of war with Cuba led to a semipanic. Jack felt utterly useless at his job. Nor was his mood helped by his reading. He felt "much disgusted . . . by a book . . . recommended by various dinner companions as being an excellent type of American life, written by a person called Gertrude Atherton and called *Patience Spark* . . . trash."[37]

In mid-March, the Morgans gave a dinner party to repay some of their social obligations. March 15 was Junius's birthday, and he received a boat from his grandfather, so Jack came home from the office early and took Junius to sail his new boat on the Serpentine in Kensington Gardens.[38]

Late in March, the Morgans' social activity became even more strenuous, with a dinner party almost every night as people wound up the season before Lent. Among the names that recur are those of the Harcourts, Lady Tweeddale, the McIlvaines.[39]

Morgan expressed himself bitterly about the approaching Spanish-American War. "I do not like to see a civilized nation taking up the cause of the Cuban insurgents who are of so low a kind as to shoot a man under a flag of truce, as they did the other day." He asked why there should be war when Spain was ready to yield.[40] Such a needless waste of life and property. "I am depressed by the conduct of my countrymen!" The motive of this senseless conflict was, he was sure, that a great many Americans "want to see our new navy used and any excuse will do for a row."[41] He was distressed to hear that his brother-in-law Ned Grew had volunteered to serve in Jake Peabody's battery. He was irritated because American newspaper reporters in their zeal for a story reported to the world, and so to the enemy, United States fleet movements, while the enemy kept his moves secret.[42]

At length the round of dinner parties came to a stop with Lent, and J. P. Morgan, Sr., returned to America in late March.[43] The Morgans turned to other interests. They attended a performance of Bach's *St. Matthew Passion* at St. Paul's. Then they went over to Paris for an Easter holiday, stopping at the Hotel Bristol. They saw the actress Réjane in performance and then "went to see Coquelin play the new play about which everyone is raving called *Cyrano de Bergerac*. It is really quite wonderful, with splendid lines and acted as no one else could do it." In Paris they also went shopping: "In order to keep up the tradition of the family I went with Jessie to Worth where we found some things which are going to be most satisfactory." He added with incredible naiveté, "I find our name a passport in most of the places where we buy things!"[44]

Upon their return to London, the Morgans planned two dinner parties, and Jack noted that in preparing for them, "questions of precedence have occupied us a good deal. . . ." Who goes into dinner before whom? The first was a party of twelve, the second for sixteen.[45] They dined with Sir Charles Tennant, but Jack did not like Tennant and felt very much out of it at that dinner for twenty-two in the first week of May. On the evening of May 3, Jack and Launcelot Smith went to the Albert Hall to hear Lord Salisbury address the Primrose League. That was a busy week. The Morgans heard *Lohengrin* sung by Edouard de Reszke. They had a box for the season for Monday and Thursday nights, and the Bulteels joined them for *Lohengrin*. The Prince of Wales also attended the performance. That week Jack saw Queen Victoria for the first time. Jessie, of course, had already been presented to her at court.[46]

On the evening of May 12, they dined with James Bryce, later Lord Bryce, and author of *The American Commonwealth*, and a Miss Rathbone, a kinswoman of Mrs. Bryce and of Jessie Morgan, and then went to a ball at the Seymours'.[47]

In a letter to his father, Jack thanked him for letting them live in his London town house, 13 Princes Gate, and noted that guests at the two dinner parties with which they paid their social debts liked the paintings on the walls.[48]

This was another active week. The Queen's birthday was celebrated with the ceremony of trooping of the color at the Horse Guards, and only a day or two before, W. E. Gladstone had died.[49] Jack planned to go to the lying in state at Westminster Hall, he explained, "because I want to have seen it." On top of everything else, Jack joined a stag party of nine to drive out in a "brake" to Epsom Downs to watch the running of the Derby. He found the crowd rowdy but good-natured.[50] By now the season was really under way, and activities crowded upon each other. The Morgans went to the Wagner *Ring* cycle over a period of several weeks in June and early July. In contemplating that massive dose of music, Jack observed, "I expect to die before Saturday night but it will be a pleasant death."[51]

The court ball, postponed because of Mr. Gladstone's death, was given on June 6. Henry White provided the tickets. It was a splendid affair with superb gowns and diamonds in a room decorated with paintings and with silver brought from Windsor Castle for the evening.[52] The recent visit to Paris contributed to the occasion. Jack wrote, "Very swell was Jessie in her finest new Worth gown!" Some of the other guests were less decorative: "The duchesses have a row of seats and such a collection of queer looking people you never saw." The Morgans got back to Dover House at two o'clock in the morning.[53]

Meanwhile, the Wagner *Ring* was in progress. On June 9, *Siegfried* was presented—as Jack described it—"à la Bayreuth," i.e., broken by a dinner interval.[54]

A little more than two weeks later, on June 28, came *Die Walküre*, described as "a delicious opera . . . except for the fact that they would not cut a note of the long scene between Wotan and Brünhilde which is very dull as to action and not particularly interesting from a music point of view."[55] The climax came with *Götterdämmerung* on the fourth of July, a glittering cast with Jean and Edouard de Reszke, Lillian Nordica, and, in two lesser roles, young Ernestine Schumann-Heink. Earlier in the day, the annual Fourth of July reception at the American Embassy was the scene of considerable jubilation over the recent naval victory over Spain at Santiago.[56]

Morgan found that the Church of England service compared unfavorably with the American Episcopal service to which he was accustomed. "Even the service which at home makes up for the sermon is spoilt here by elaboration and whining."[57]

Mrs. Morgan particularly enjoyed the springtime move from the center of London to the suburbs. "Jessie is simply mad about Dover House and the gardens and lawns and spends all her off time sketching. . . ."[58]

Morgan was appointed a trustee of the Peabody Hospital Fund set up by the banker and philanthropist, George Peabody, his grandfather's partner. This was in accordance with Junius Morgan's interest that a member of the family be on the board.[59]

Following a visit to Windsor for tea with Lady Antrim (mother of Lady Sybil Smith, wife of J. S. Morgan & Co. associate and later Morgan, Grenfell partner Vivian Hugh Smith, and lady-in-waiting to Queen Victoria), Morgan wrote, "I find more and more that we (Jessie and I) feel much more at home with the swells who are *real* swells, not wildly gay ones but the very best, than with almost anyone." While at Windsor they looked at the Holbein portraits and the da Vinci drawings in the royal collection.[60]

A play by John Oliver Hobbs, *The Ambassador*, was dismissed as "almost too clever." On Saturday, July 8, the Morgans went to the final afternoon of the Eton-Harrow cricket match at Lord's. Eton made a poor showing. On Monday they attended the performance of Luigi Mancinelli's new opera *Ero e Leandro* conducted by the composer and found it "disappointing."[61]

In late July there were two social events of particular interest.

On Wednesday, July 20, Jack was a guest at a dinner of the Cloth-workers' Company in Clothworkers' Hall. He enjoyed the cere-mony and took particular interest in the fur-lined gowns of the Master and Wardens of this ancient society. The toastmaster was a great pleasure to observe, and Jack enjoyed such details as the rosewater bowl into which one dipped the napkin instead of a finger bowl and the loving cup passed around from left to right, a cup presented by Samuel Pepys in 1677 when he was the Wor-shipful Master.[62] On Saturday, July 23, the Morgans went down to Hatfield House with Sir William Harcourt and the Japanese minister and his wife to Lord Salisbury's garden party. They met Lady Gwendoline Cecil, who was acting as hostess, and "wan-dered about those enchanting gardens." Secretary White, an inti-mate of the Cecils, took the Morgans inside to see the family portraits.[63]

At the office, Robert Gordon, a partner in J. S. Morgan & Co. since 1885, planned to go on vacation and leave young Morgan and Walter Burns in charge.[64]

Early in August, the Morgans went on a house party at Ross, Herefordshire, with their friends the Lyttletons. Fellow guests were the Biddulphs. Lady Elizabeth Biddulph was "fierce on the temperance question." World news included the prospects of an early peace in the Spanish-American War and increased tension between Russia and Britain.[65]

August was the traditional month for the opening of the Scot-tish shooting season, and Walter Burns planned to go to Scotland for the event. In view of Morgan's many subsequent seasons as host to shooting parties at Gannochy, it is revealing to read his views on the subject in 1898. "I could find other amusements which would appeal to me much more than killing birds for mar-ket, which is the way most of the results of the big kills is disposed of. But you see we are not trained in our youth to enjoy killing for the sake of the fun it gives without anything to show for it after-wards. However, it takes them all out of doors for many hours a day and gives the unoccupied something to think about and to discuss, which is a good thing in itself."[66] The fact is that Morgan never really did enjoy killing birds, but he did enjoy the comrade-ship and the exercise in the open air.

There was speculation in the American colony in London as to whom President McKinley would appoint to succeed John Hay as ambassador to the Court of St. James's. Many hoped that it would be Whitelaw Reid. Morgan observed, "Personally, I don't think much of him, but he has many qualifications for the place and would be popular over here which is a most important job just now. But would New York State Republican boss Platt oppose confirmation unless he received some political favor?" Morgan, like others before and since, thought it regrettable that the United States position before foreign nations should be influenced by ward politics.[67] The new ambassador was Joseph H. Choate. Reid followed him in 1905.

Morgan wrote during August Bank Holiday that he was reading Nansen's Arctic adventures and enjoying particularly reading about Greenland during the English summer hot spell.[68]

The young Morgan family came back to the United States in the fall of 1898 and returned to England at the end of October on the *Teutonic*. It was a rough passage. It was pleasant to be so warmly welcomed back to England by the domestic staff at Princes Gate and by many friends. And it was good to be back at the office, though business was quiet, and Robert Gordon was out ill.[69]

The fast pace of London living started immediately. The Morgans took the children to the Lord Mayor's Show. That excitement was followed by the festivities, including fireworks, to celebrate the Prince of Wales's birthday. There was a dinner party at the Savoy Hotel, given by John Hays Hammond of South African mining fame, one of the participants in the Jameson Raid. Morgan sat opposite Rudyard Kipling, who talked of "Empire administration as applied to Asiatics and the handling of bodies of men, armies or other." He was not favorably impressed, noting, "He is a dreadfully common specimen and I shouldn't care to be very intimately associated with him."[70]

Morgan had a weight problem, so he and Eric Hambro went regularly to Sandow's gymnasium, which specialized in reducing exercises.[71] The Hambros and the Morgans became close friends. One November evening both couples and the Vivian Smiths went to that peculiarly English place of light entertainment, the music hall. The party were all of an age, and Jack Morgan noted how pleasant it was to spend an evening with young people. "Our position here has pushed us so far ahead of our years socially speaking. That is a great advantage in the quality of people one meets but a change is pleasant sometimes."[72]

November brought a series of London fogs, that wretched

mixture of water vapor and coal smoke. Social life quieted down slightly—to not more than four dinner parties a week! At one such party, Sir Stanley Clarke's, the Morgans met a number of intimates of the Prince of Wales. And the exercises at Sandow's continued.[73]

Meanwhile, the children occupied much of Jessie Morgan's time. She read aloud to them Thackeray's *The Rose and the Ring*. By coincidence, the original manuscript of that book was the younger Morgan's first gift to the Morgan Library.[74]

Young Junius became ill with severe abdominal pains late in November. Appendicitis was feared, and he was a very sick little boy for almost three weeks.[75] Surgery followed a recurrence of the trouble in late February.

During this time, there was a steady stream of visitors from America, most of them from Boston: a Mrs. Bowdoin, the Endicott Peabody's from Groton, Jon Sturgis—of whom Jack wrote, "the fascination which he undoubtedly has for many people don't extend to me"—the Osborns (though not Fairfield, "the most attractive of the lot"), and the Murray Forbeses.[76]

Jack always found time to read, even with the demands of business, an active social life, and the family. He read Savage Landor on Tibet and Eastern tortures: "The man blows a good deal, but I believe he is fairly truthful." This was followed by Sven Hedin, *Across Asia*, more attractive than Landor, more like Nansen. After Hedin came Stevens, *With Kitchener to Khartoum*, then there came an account of whaling, *The Cruise of the Cachalot*.[77]

The engagement of May Burns (sister of Morgan kinsman and business associate Walter Burns) to Lewis "Loulou" Harcourt led to frequent social encounters. The Morgans became acquainted with Sir William Harcourt, the great Liberal statesman, and spent Christmas with the Harcourts and the Burnses at the Burns country place North Mymms Park.[78]

The elder Morgan came over for a visit and sailed for home on December 28.[79] Jack said of his father, "There never was a man who had such uniform luck as he has about all sorts of things, little as well as big."[80]

Jack contrasted the "jumping about" at 23 Wall Street with the quieter pace of the firm's London office, where "profoundest peace reigns."[81]

1899

J. Pierpont Morgan's return to London right after the new year 1899 was an event in the younger Morgans' lives.[82] His arrival had been preceded by his Christmas presents: "Father's cheques . . . arrived to our great delight so we are feeling very rich indeed."[83] The elder Morgan and his daughter Louisa promptly got caught up in the festivities of May Burns's engagement to Lewis Harcourt.[84]

The father's aloofness and unwillingness to share his thoughts with his son is a recurring theme. "Father went over to Paris on Monday and is coming back Friday, I believe. As to what his future plans may be, I can't say." May Burns wanted him to go to Egypt, which became one of his favorite places until a few days before his death. "He has not decided at all as yet however nor has he unfolded anything which may be in his mind as to future arrangements as to this office." The son accepted this state of affairs with resignation. "In the fullness of time we shall probably hear something and in the meantime we are getting on very well as we are."[85] "I suppose [he] will go away somewhere before long if he can get the future of this office arranged to his satisfaction. It looks now as if it were taking some sort of shape, but it's not yet definite enough to talk about."[86]

Social life continued. The Morgans dined at Lady Westbury's on the Cromwell Road with the Speaker of the House of Commons, the Japanese ambassador, their wives, and Francis Bret Harte—"the original Heathen Chinee, and very amusing he was, too." They were scheduled to dine with the elder Morgan and Sir Thomas Lipton "and a lot of old admirals" to discuss the yachting prospects for the following summer. Young Morgan quoted Gordon of the Morgan office on Lipton, who was described as "one of nature's noblemen, I love him—of course I do, he brings me business."[87]

The future of the London office continued to be a matter for speculation. A difficulty was the senior Morgan's unpredictability. "You never can tell what he will do till he starts to do it."[88] At length the elder Morgan seems to have made a decision on the eve of his departure with his daughter Louisa for Monte Carlo, and its effects on Jack Morgan's plans were far-reaching. On February 21, 1889, he wrote, "Matters have now taken such shape over here that it's certain I shall be here for a few years more; it seems to be the place where I can be most useful just now so we must make up our minds to it, I suppose. There are many delightfully pleasant things about it too, but when I think of home the time does seem a bit long."

In view of the prospect of a long stay in London, Jack leased the town house at no. 2 South Street, off Park Lane, a pleasant property with sunshine assured from the south, which was protected by the gardens of Dorchester House and from the west by Hyde Park. Neighbors on South Street were Miss Florence Nightingale, now eighty, at no. 10, and Earl Grey at no. 22.[89] For summers they would have the choice of Dover House or the adjoining Roehampton House, recently purchased by Morgan, Sr., to provide space as the city built up around him.[90] The length of the family's stay abroad was still not entirely accepted. "It won't be forever . . . for us over here . . . and yet I hope we shall always have more or less to do with this side and more or less of a home over here."[91]

Pierpont Morgan reluctantly sailed for the United States late in February. Jack wrote, "I had a note from father before he sailed! He ends by saying he 'hates to go more and more every moment.' I am more than sorry he felt he had to do it. But I suppose when a man finally reaches the point when he thinks nothing can move along without him a holiday becomes an impossible thing." He ends on a wistful note that suggests feelings of inadequacy in comparing himself to his more famous father. "I only hope it will never come to that with me. Probably it won't owing to the fact that things always will move on without me."[92]

He was struck by the similarity between the New York and London offices: "On the whole, I find the work here as interesting as in New York, though there is not so much of it." He reflected on the differences between the British and the American point of view about work. He mentioned a British acquaintance, an eldest son without "a single idea . . . beyond his hunting and a little shooting . . . I hope in America that a young man would rebel and try to do something to make him independent."[93]

He remarked that the family's social life was quiet even though the London season had begun, then listed a full schedule of events: a visit to Parliament to hear the Liberal Sir William Harcourt attack the government's budget from the Opposition benches, a royal levee with Lewis Harcourt (while one might attend a levee every other year, it was considered more polite to go to one annually), a dinner party at the Morgans' for James Bryce to meet the Jack Chapmans,[94] and the gift to May Burns of a munificent wedding present, a Victoria carriage ("She has jewels").[95]

In September 1899, the younger Morgans were houseguests of Lord and Lady Antrim—already noted as the parents-in-law of Vivian Smith of the Morgan London office—at their Irish country house. The property had been enormous at one time, "but was raced away" with legendary Irish irresponsibility by the great-grandfather of the current lord. It was race week, and there were gala parties and balls. There was shooting in the Antrim forests, and Jack bagged a buck, the first animal he had shot since 1888 in the Rocky Mountains with William Rainsford.[96]

The chief thing on people's minds and the main topic of conversation in Britain in the fall of 1899 was the Boer War. Young Morgan noted, "War checks business at every turn." But more important to Jack was the number of their friends whose sons had gone off to South Africa. A nephew of Eric Hambro was killed, age twenty-one.[97] He observed, "War . . . pulls [people] together and emphasizes the point all are agreed on."[98] But that was not universally true of the Boer War. Many British families were divided on the issue of the war. The losses were severe,[99] and Morgan remarked on the "anxious faces and loneliness" of war and the effect on the British public of a war after so many years of peace: the tendency to overreact, as in the United States in 1898.[100] There was no gaiety that Christmas of 1899.

On November 24, 1899, the Morgans moved into their newly renovated house on South Street off Park Lane. The family liked having their own house, but they did miss the works of art at the grander establishment at Princes Gate.[101]

Social life continued active despite the war. On the evening of December 8, the Morgans dined at the Macmillans', where they found Mr. and Mrs. Samuel Clemens (Mark Twain) and Sir Donald Wallace, the writer on Russia. A few days later at the Burnses' they met Mr. Choate and Sir Colin Scott, engineer of the Nile River. That same week they took the Lionel Bulteels to the play *Lord Quex*, a "horrid, dirty piece."[102]

Christmas at the Morgans' was a busy time. The children's letters to Santa Claus asked for impossible things like real steam engines and sailboats. Morgan wrote, "It shows the older ones are getting beyond the age when their imaginations can supply all the deficiencies in their equipment." But he found them more interesting as people. They were beginning to read to themselves.

They planned a Christmas party for their parents, with Junius playing the piano and the others reciting French poetry. The Walter Burnses gave a family house party at North Mymms Park. There was a children's party with a conjurer and a ventriloquist. On Boxing Day, December 26, the men went shooting in the park.[103]

At the end of 1899, Morgan's brother-in-law, William "Billy" Hamilton, Juliet's husband, was admitted to J. P. Morgan & Co., and Morgan commented to his mother on the advantages of belonging to that concern: "After all, there is no place in the world of the kind which begins to compare with it for position and dignity; besides which it has the added charm of being profitable, which is more desirable too."[104]

1900

On New Year's Day, 1900, the young Morgans returned to London from their holiday with the Burnses, and Jack plunged into the year-end business at the office, "which, while . . . nothing to N.Y. is enough, done as it is here, to keep us rather busy." He was saddened by the news of the death of his former Boston employer, Jacob Rogers. On New Year's night they heard the *Messiah* at Albert Hall and "enjoyed it to the full." The following weekend, Jack and Jessie went to the Hambro country house, Hayes Place in Kent, for a day's shooting. Before going down, they took Junius and Janie to the pantomime. "The children were splendid, and the ripple of high pitched laughter around the place was bewitching."[105]

In his letter of February 1, 1900, Morgan described the ceremony of the opening of Parliament, which he found "rather amusing to see, for once," with the summoning of the Commons and the reading by the lord chancellor of the Queen's message. It had been a very active week socially, including an evening at the Hippodrome (twenty-one lions) with the Eric Hambros as the high point. He was unenthusiastic about going to the Blakes' to dinner, preferring to stay home and read *The Transvaal from Within*.[106]

He read Robert Louis Stevenson's letters and found them "quite delightful," but he questioned the writer's sincerity at times, feeling that "he seemed to consider his feelings and thoughts as more or less literary material and used them as such."

He saw no chance of a vacation in the States "with the changes in partnership here." He could expect to get off only for "a Saturday now and then." "Until [C. E.] Dawkins gets himself used to the job."[107]

Early in March he took the family for a brief holiday at Brighton, where they were "established in rather a dreary hotel" during the early days of Jessie's pregnancy, which was to continue until October 24. He visited them on weekends. They had left London after experiencing one of the great moments in modern British history, the relief of beleaguered Ladysmith in South Africa. On March 1, cheering, flag-waving crowds packed the streets all day and far into the night. Morgan wrote, "I never saw that sort of crowd before; it was very thrilling. Now there is only Mafeking to be relieved."[108]

Mrs. Morgan, Sr., was at Newport, Rhode Island, in March. Her son observed that this was the agreeable time to be in Newport, rather than during the summer, "when the people who really live there are swamped by the horrid vulgar lot who make or rather ruin the reputation of it." So much for the "cottage" dwellers and high-society types of Bailey's Beach. Mention of Newport brought up the subject of wealth, and we get another expression of Morgan's conviction on the matter: "the power to help is really in the person and not in the money," and "the desire to help without the power to do so . . . is really the worst part of lack of means." Meanwhile, his golf game was very poor.[109]

The coming of the queen to town caused him to write, "And that wonderful little old woman in black and sables with the big spectacles means so much to so many—she represents in a concrete form so much of the past that it is very stirring to see her driving through the crowd."[110]

News of the death of Charles Henry Coster of the Morgan firm in New York reached London on March 13. Jack's great concern was the added burden that the loss of such a strong figure in the company would cause, and he worried that his father, "who already has so much more than enough on his shoulders will have to do even more." He hoped the older man would not be forced to miss his Aix cure.[111]

Jessie was feeling well enough to attend a royal Drawing Room with Mrs. Bulteel. "The stuff of her train is really lovely, a sort of creamy satin with a big pattern of velvet, painted poppies in very faint colors on it, and a little lace at the edge." Morgan wrote the next day, "the dress was a great success, graceful and becoming and *I* was much pleased as I hope the Royalties were!" The other news was the birthday treat planned for young Junius, who was to go to Erith to visit the Vickers Maxim works.[112]

On Saturday morning, May 12, the Morgans went to a dinner party for the king of Sweden at the Levenses'. The distinguished company included the lord chancellor, Lord Halsbury, and his wife, the elderly Duchess of Cleveland (who was Lord Rosebery's mother and the last of Victoria's bridesmaids—a spry octogenarian who had gone to India by herself and ridden on elephants), Lady Susan Melville, and Mr. Goldschmidt—Jenny Lind's husband. Jenny Lind's daughter, Mrs. Moore, came with her daughter after dinner and sang. Then the king of Sweden sang and played his own accompaniment, explaining that he was a bit out of practice because he was kept busy ruling both Norway and Sweden.

In a family reference, Morgan expressed amusement that he should live to see the day that his independent sister Louisa would want to get back from her travels with her father to see a man (Herbert Satterlee)![113]

The business outlook in the spring of 1900 was gloomy. "Even Father can't rake any up which is unusual," Jack wrote. But the great news was the relief of Mafeking in the Boer War. London crowds went mad and swarmed about until all hours, as they had for Ladysmith. He saw "a ladylike looking girl" kiss a large and stolid policeman in the general carnival atmosphere.[114]

Our next letter from Jack to his mother was written on October 24 to announce the arrival that morning of his fourth child, second son, Henry Sturgis Morgan, weighing 9¼ pounds and described as "really a buster." Jack noted "an extraordinary likeness in this one to Father. The shape of head (which was not squeezed at all) and the ears and the setting of the eyes are exactly like—let us hope he may help as many people during his life."[115]

1901

Jack returned to New York briefly at the end of 1900, so the preserved correspondence resumes in late January 1901, with comments on the greatest news event of the day, the death of Queen Victoria. "Her death is I suppose a real sorrow to more people in the world than any other death could have been, and London this morning is extraordinary with the crowds of quiet people walking about."[116]

By great good luck, Morgan was in front of St. James's Palace in time to witness the proclaiming of Edward VII as the new monarch. "It was exactly like a scene in one of Shakespeare's historical plays even to the cheers of the populace and the delightful sound of the silver trumpets and the quaintness of the wording of the proclamation. . . . Moreover, the Heralds and pursuivants with their gorgeous clothes and old world look and names were most beautiful to behold." He was glad the new king had not been named Albert. "Albert makes me think of biscuits and the style of art popular in the 50's and 60's. But Edward VII seems to give some sort of historical character to him at once." But the old queen was not forgotten in the enthusiasm over her successor, "*Everyone* has gone into mourning, you never saw anything so black as the streets."[117] From their house at 2 South Street, the Morgans could look into Hyde Park and up and down Park Lane. They invited thirty guests—taking advantage of the opportunity to invite people they had wanted to have to the house—to watch the funeral cortege go by. "The procession was long and uncertain in its progress, stopping at times to re-establish the distance between the units. The coffin looked so small to carry such a weight of symbolic sovereignty in the crown and orb and sceptre and to be the central figure of such a pageant! . . . The Queen never had a more superb expression of affection and loyalty than the dead silence of that enormous crowd as her coffin went by." Morgan noted that the new king seemed to be off to a good start in public goodwill. He then changed the subject entirely and mentioned that he had spent part of the Christmas cheque from his father on a small portrait of a man by Joshua Reynolds.[118]

February of 1901 found the family down with the influenza— upper respiratory illness was a frequent condition at the Morgan household during the damp London winters. Jack was dismayed to find that hard work and riding a horse in the park were not enough to keep his spirits up and his disposition even. He was pessimistic about the state of the theatre. Plays nowadays were so unpleasant and were concerned with the lives of such unattractive people. "The Woman with a past was ceasing to interest"; everyone seemed "to be following the history of the Man with a past (and present) equally unsavory." He preferred old-fashioned melodrama with "lots of adventures and plot and very little character study."[119]

Modern improvements were extended to Dover House with the installation of electric lighting. The excitement of the change of sovereign continued with Edward's opening of Parliament on February 14, with impressive "flummery."[120]

Morgan's lurking Protestant Episcopal prejudice against the Church of England came to the fore with young Harry's christening, which was held in the drawing room at South Street because the young mother was not well enough to go out, even though technically a child could only be "received into Christ's flock" in a church. Morgan expressed himself with vigor to the Reverend Mr. Poynder, telling him that his own "idea of Christ's flock was that it was larger even than the Church of England." The cleric replied "with evident pride that he was broad church enough to think so too!" and they parted friends.[121]

Morgan was amused to read in the papers that private individuals were taking out life insurance policies on J. Pierpont Morgan to a total of two million pounds. He felt that this put his father "in the same category with Queen Victoria and other rulers on this side of the Atlantic!"[122]

The New York Chamber of Commerce sent a delegation to England to felicitate the new monarch. The group included the Morgans, father and son. On June 2, 1901, the whole group put on frock coats and went out to Windsor by train to pay their respects and attend a reception.[123] The senior Morgan was in England that June and was active socially, although Jack did not always inquire who his friends were.

In the spring of 1901, young Morgan rented a country place, Aldenham Abbey, near Watford in Hertfordshire. He wrote enthusiastically about the house and 300 acres under cultivation around it and the parish church about a mile away, "a sort of patchwork of all sorts built during the last six hundred years and full of quaint brasses and monuments." He added, "the farm is most entertaining and I expect soon to appear in the office with leather gaiters and a straw in my mouth instead of a cigar." He anticipated considerable shooting in the fall since the place came stocked with pheasants, and wild game birds abounded.[124] In December 1910, he bought the property outright in Mrs. Morgan's name, and they promptly changed the name of the place from Aldenham Abbey to the more prosaic Wall Hall.[125] Some people wondered why Morgan had made that change, and he later replied to an inquiry: "'Aldenham Abbey' was never an abbey and had no historical interest whatsoever."[126] He was correcting a misnomer.

The two Morgan country places in England, the Senior's Dover House and the Junior's Wall Hall, each had a cricket team. Jack was gratified that his team beat his father's in the summer of 1908.[127] At his new place in the country, Jack reported that he was "in clover." He had a place where he could set up his microscope and resume his study of natural history and had already "got a lot of lovely beasts out of the various ponds in the vicinity" and found "several hours interesting enjoyment in watching their little ways and tricks." He also had a photographic darkroom built, in which he made early experiments with color photography, which was to become one of his activities in retirement.[128] The Morgans took long automobile drives in the surrounding countryside, where motors were almost unknown, "to train people's horses into indifference."[129]

One of Morgan's pleasures—though interrupted by two world wars—was shooting game birds, whether partridges, pheasants, doves, grouse, or quail. For some years, in addition to doing some shooting at Wall Hall, he had held a shooting tenancy at Six Mile Bottom just east of Cambridge. This arrangement ended when Sir Ernest Cassel, financier and great companion of the late Edward VII, acquired the property, and Morgan last used the place in 1916.[130]

One day in late June 1901, Jack and Clinton Edward Dawkins of the London office went with Pierpont Morgan down to Gravesend at the mouth of the Thames to dine with Leopold, king of the Belgians, since Morgan, Sr., could not go over to Brussels. They spent the night on board the royal yacht. In a totally unrelated burst of generosity, the following day the senior Morgan dispatched a cable to the Harvard Medical School offering to give them a building in memory of his father, Junius Spencer Morgan.[131] Shortly afterwards, Pierpont Morgan sailed for home. Jack was sad to have his father return to New York. Morgan, Sr., took Dawkins with him, leaving Jack and Walter Burns to mind the store. Jessie sent word to her mother-in-law, her love, and an inquiry: had she read Winston Churchill's "(the American Winston Churchill)" latest, *The Crisis*, about the American Civil War?[132]

President William McKinley was shot by an anarchist on September 6 and died on the fourteenth. Morgan was astonished at the public display of sentiment for the American president. "London was really not more in mourning last winter at the time of the Queen's death." He found himself committed to attend memorial services at both Westminster Abbey and St. Paul's and had his "fill of funeral marches and gloomy music." He was hopeful that Theodore Roosevelt would establish a "reasonably permanent" civil service and not talk too much.[133]

The Morgans spent the Christmas holidays of 1901 in New York and returned to England on the *Majestic* in early January 1902. It was an uneventful crossing except for the sight of an abandoned schooner, which had been set on fire.[134]

1902

Once back in London, the Morgans were again mildly social. There was a shooting party that included Dawkins of the Morgan firm and his brother-in-law Lord Chichester, Frederick Duleep Singh, Vivian Smith of Morgan's, and G. Watson. Following dinner at the Maurice Glyns' they went to see Marie Tempest as Becky Sharp in a dramatized version of *Vanity Fair*.[135]

In June he wrote of Ascot. "The racing is quite a secondary feature, it's a garden party with lots of pleasant people. . . ." The following week, Jack "came to town and made all the official calls on all the regular embassies and legations, getting through 29 calls and leaving hundreds of cards, a horrid farce but it had to be done." Later in the week, they "Ascoted again" and were all ready to attend the ball at Windsor Castle "when the inconvenient old King of Saxony had to go and die 24 hours earlier than was necessary." Great was the disappointment because there had not been a ball at Windsor for about seventy years.[136] Jack had been appointed by Theodore Roosevelt to the United States delegation to the coronation of Edward VII so he was busy with Ambassador Joseph H. Choate in the preparations. The cynical expressed the view that this appointment was a gesture of conciliation toward J. P. Morgan, who had not been in agreement with Roosevelt about government regulation of business affairs.[137]

The new king subsequently presented the Coronation Medal to each member of the American special embassy to the coronation. By an absurd and awkward bureaucratic mistake, the medals—which were received by the U.S. State Department on October 12, 1902—were mislaid and did not come to light until February 1912! Taft's Secretary of State Philander C. Knox wrote to Morgan on February 7, 1912, apologizing for the ten-year delay and enclosing the medal.[138]

J. Pierpont Morgan was expected from Paris for the coronation with his youngest child, Anne, but Jack was not sure that his father would actually come. ("He is not easy to keep track of and I have almost given up"). Jack hoped that his father would take them on the *Corsair* to watch the naval review at Spithead, "but," he added wistfully, "he will probably not think of asking us."[139]

On the very eve of the coronation, the country was shocked by the news of the king's sudden emergency surgery for an internal abscess. London was caught with flags and decorations everywhere, but sadness and concern replaced the noisy anticipation of a few hours before. There was some exasperation too, as so many plans had to be changed. The American Special Embassy was now to go to the Whitelaw Reids' on the evening of June 24 instead of dining in state at Buckingham Palace, as planned.[140]

The disappointment over the canceled coronation was so great that the prospect of the king's recovering was almost an anticlimax. Jack's final duty as a member of the Special Embassy was to attend the special service of intercession at St. Paul's for the king's recovery. Morgan, Senior, entertained at Dover House and then planned to "run off to Kiel."[141]

A number of old friends from the States came to England in the summer of 1902, and the Morgans did a lot of shepherding about and a great deal of entertaining at Aldenham. Among the houseguests was Jessie's cousin Joe Grew, just graduated from Harvard College.

The Morgans took a new town house in the summer of 1902 at 12 Grosvenor Square. Their last night at South Street was July 10, when they came in from Aldenham for dinner with Julia, Lady Tweeddale, and some Schleswig-Holstein royalty. Later in the week, they were to go to Moor Park overnight to visit the Eburys, where they would meet the king's sister Princess Christian and see the Maurice Glyns again (Mrs. Glyn was a daughter of the Eburys).[142]

Princess Christian had been described as "very good, very dull and very dowdy," but she turned out to be not dowdy at all but with "a great deal of distinction and dignity" and "really very grande dame indeed, though very friendly and pleasant." One of her daughters was there too "a very nice simple person—very homely." The princess told them that the king wanted so much to have a coronation ceremony, despite his close call, "that the queen and all of them were afraid of the effect on him if it was not allowed."[143]

The movements of Morgan, Sr., remained unpredictable, but he was clearly not getting as much rest as he should. His son noted, "He is always imprudent in his eating and his liver has been somewhat upset which naturally makes him rather blue. Moreover, he thinks he has lost weight which alarms him."[144]

The social season ended with a gala dinner at Lord and Lady Landsdowne's. Among the guests were some very pleasant Indians and Siamese and "the old Duchess of Manchester . . . a rum old thing very fat and painted and twitchey." Jack found himself "very sympathetic . . . with her husband who had every excuse for seeking rest and refreshment elsewhere!" This last reminded him that Uncle George Morgan was in town with his wife. Jack feared he had not been very cordial to his distant relative, Cousin Junius's father.[145]

It seemed clear that the coronation would take place on August 9, but it would be a very modest affair with no special embassies. Even Ambassador Choate was planning to be away so as to not complicate matters. Jack had enjoyed the association with him.

The house in Grosvenor Square would not be ready until September 29, but they already liked it enormously. The children all came down with whooping cough, "four small barkers."[146]

The coronation, while less spectacular than originally planned, was most impressive. Jack wrote, "Nothing ever gave me so strong a feeling of the historical continuity of things here."

Mrs. Morgan, Sr., was at Bar Harbor, Maine, at this time. Her spirits were very low, as indeed they might be with her husband virtually ignoring her for several months of every year.[147]

1903

It is not until the summer of 1903 that we pick up the mother-and-son correspondence again. The elder Morgan owned a painting by Sir Thomas Lawrence, *Portrait of Miss Croker*. On June 25, 1903, the younger Morgans drove out in their motor to a small cottage near Hampton Court and called upon Lady Barrow, the Miss Croker of the portrait, now ninety-three, with grown great-grandchildren. With her was her daughter, a Mrs. Woodridge, a sprightly seventy-three, "who might have stepped out of *Cranford*." Jack was charmed and wrote, "You who know my sentiments in regard to old ladies will understand how much pleasure it meant."[148]

Junius was now away at boarding school, and his mother and

father were preparing to see him on parents' weekend.[149]

The next letter is dated Brandon Park, Suffolk, October 16, 1903. The Morgans were visiting the Almeric Pagets for a couple of days' shooting. The current literary sensation was John Morley's *Life of William Gladstone*, which Morgan found "stodgy and heavy."[150] The book got better as one got into it, but he didn't care for the man, thought he had a "curious attitude of mind about the Church and all the questions which centre about the Church as distinct from Religion." He found odd the old man's "anxiety to have been always consistent . . . in view of the extraordinary changes in opinion which he always seemed to be having."[151]

In noting Harry's third birthday, Morgan wondered whether four children was a big enough family. He recalled that the Morgan children called the seven Vivian Smith children the Oysters because in *The Walrus and the Carpenter*, "thick and fast they came at last and more and more and more."[152]

1904

In January 1904, the younger Morgans came over to New York for a brief visit. That fall they leased, furnished, the Prescott Hall Butler house at 22 Park Avenue, between Thirty-fifth and Thirty-sixth streets, just around the corner from the Morgan, Sr., house at Madison and Thirty-sixth Street.[153]

Jack kept in touch with his London office at J. S. Morgan & Co. by cablegram. Several business concerns interested him particularly. He was not happy with the results of the management of United Collieries, which had borrowed £100,000 from the Morgan firm.[154] The firm was also financially involved in the construction of the Transandine Railroad in South America.[155]

He reported that his colleague Dawkins was off taking the waters at Bad Homburg, a spa favored by Edward VII.[156] Later in the year, the Morgans had a house-party weekend with the Dawkinses, which was very pleasant. Fellow guests included Sir Rennell and Lady Rodd, newly returned from Rome, where he had been British minister, and now on their way to the legation in Stockholm, and the Stanleys—one of Lord Derby's eight sons and his wife. Also in the group was a brother of Lord Antrim of the McDonnell clan.[157]

1905

The whole family was ill with influenza in January 1905, a recurring theme. News from New York was that Morgan, Sr., had bought the Phelps Stokes house at 231 Madison Avenue, next door to his own at 219 Madison, and was letting the junior Morgans have it for the winter.[158] The family came over and occupied the new house early in 1905. They turned the stable into a squash court—a change that Satterlee observes reflects an outlook unlike that of the senior Morgan, who never exercised.[159]

Jack maintained his usual close touch with London. He asked the London office to offer bonds in American railroads, the Chicago Traction Co., and Chicago Burlington & Quincy Railroad to their friendly competitors the Hambro firm.[160]

He cabled the butler at 12 Grosvenor Square that he would return to England on the *Baltic*, sometime on April 26.[161] One of the big events of the 1905 London season was the state visit of the king of Spain, culminating in a gala performance at the opera. Back in England again after the New York stay, the Morgans attended the performance and found it a brilliant affair, with "everyone in uniform and all the women in their very best clothes and more diamonds and pearls than I have ever seen at one time." In the royal box, Queen Alexandra in a diamond crown "looked very pretty and about 40, in spite of her 60 odd years." The young king of Spain—Alfonso XIII, not yet twenty in 1905—looked "precisely like a picture by Velasquez of one of the Philips," but when he smiled his face lighted up and he looked "like a jolly ordinary boy—and rather a nice one."[162]

Morgan, Sr., and Anne, who had replaced her sister as her father's travelling companion following Louisa's marriage to Herbert Satterlee, were reported to be in Paris, but inconsiderately failed to write and tell when they planned to be in London so the younger Morgans could adjust their schedule accordingly.

On June 14, the Morgans drove to Paddington Station and took the uncrowded special train that took the invited guests to Windsor for the royal garden party in honor of the Princess of Connaught and her Swedish fiancé. "The royalties processed down the steps and through the crowd at after 5 o'clock—nearly ¾ of an hour late, delayed as usual by the queen, I was told—and then everyone was free to wander about and talk . . ."[163]

Pierpont Morgan and Anne arrived that week. The younger Morgans dined with them at 13 Princes Gate and found the house

"a perfect picture for Father has got the new French rooms furnished properly and they are most entirely satisfactory." These
included the room with the four Fragonard panels depicting the
Progress of Love painted for Madame du Barry, which are now in
the Frick Gallery in New York. Morgan, Sr., was on an art-buying
spree. Later in the week found "the Princes Gate party up to their
eyes in work and fuss, with dealers and their wares everywhere."[164]

Later that day, they drove out to Knole near Sevenoaks and
wandered for some time through that ancient house before dining
with the Sackvilles. Jack wrote, "the pictures, the plate, the furniture, the tapestries all in such a wonderful setting and mostly in
the places they were made for altogether made up an ensemble
which with the house beat anything I've ever seen. . . ." The rest
of the week continued very social, ending with a garden party at
the earl of Jersey's Osterley, an Adams-designed house outside of
London.[165]

A Taste of Responsibility: The Proposed Russian Loan

The younger Morgan had been working obscurely in London
during the period when his father was organizing the United
States Steel Corporation (1901) and was ordering important affairs
at the home office in New York. He was, however, reported to
have played an important part in two of these concerns. One was
the reorganization in 1902 of the ill-fated International Mercantile
Marine Corporation.[166] The other was the final liquidation in
April 1904 of the French company organized to dig a ship channel
across the Isthmus of Panama, an action that was essential before
the United States could undertake the Panama Canal project.[167]

The business of negotiating a loan to the Russian government
took Morgan to St. Petersburg in October 1905. For Morgan, this
mission was the greatest responsibility for the firm with which he
had yet been entrusted by his father. But far more important to
Morgan were the stirring events that took place during his visit.

Russia was in a state of turmoil in 1905. The defeat in the war
with Japan combined with hard times and socialist activity to pro-
mote revolutionary outbreaks among workers and peasants. This
forced the granting in the summer of 1905 of a new consultive
assembly, or duma, which liberals hoped would become a real
legislative body. The restoring to the universities of the autonomy
they had been recently deprived of led to their emerging as foci of
extremist agitation. Strikes and peasant uprisings followed. The

tsar felt compelled to call upon Count Sergei Yulievitch Witte, the industrializer of Russia, to take the reins of government in the crisis.

In October 1905, it was proposed that the London banking house of Baring Brothers and the Morgan firm help underwrite an issue of Russian 4 percent consols.[168] Morgan senior cabled his son, "Think it will be necessary for you to go to Petersburg." Count Witte, the chief minister, and his finance minister agreed that the only American firm they would do business with was the Morgan firm. Two days later, the elder Morgan directed his son to go with Baron Revelstoke of Baring's to Paris and there meet George W. Perkins of the Morgans' New York office, who was sailing for France on October 10.[169] From Paris, young Morgan proceeded to Petersburg.

The son asked his father how much of the Russian syndicate he was authorized to subscribe for J. P. Morgan & Co. and at what terms. The father cabled back that the Russian deal was off; it would be impossible to float a Russian loan in the United States at this time. Would Jack please tell this to Witte and his people. An added complication was the united opposition to the loan of the American Jewish community.[170]

Young Morgan and Perkins found themselves in a hideous position. They conferred with Witte and the finance minister, who were in despair. They would not have gone this far with the loan if they had known that Morgan would not participate, as he had given them to understand he would. Jack and Perkins together urged Morgan to reconsider. They listed the generous terms of the loan and said it need only be a token subscription. Morgan, Sr., and Charles Steele cabled back that an unsuccessful sale of Russian bonds now would prejudice the sale of future Russian bonds that they wished to underwrite and asked that their deep regret be expressed to Witte.[171]

The younger Morgan and Perkins continued to press for participation, introducing a series of arguments. There was an exchange of cablegrams back and forth throughout the day on October 23. Finally, the following day, the older man capitulated completely and authorized a loan of a hundred million French francs.[172]

Morgan was with a group of financiers at the finance minister's office when that official was called to the telephone. The call concerned a royal proclamation. One of the party was able to translate the minister's end of the conversation. "Oh, so it's being printed, is it? And Witte remains in full charge?—and the constitution too? It means the end of the old autocratic monarchy of Russia!" That night, according to Morgan, just past midnight, "I heard a triumphant shout from the street and found some people reading the proclamation, who told me in German what it was. For almost an hour the whole town as far as I could see it in the time was shouting and cheering. The people cheered even the Cossack patrols and the policemen!"[173]

Witte, essentially a supporter of autocracy, saw that it was too late to hold that position, so in the face of a general strike he forced a constitution on the unwilling monarch. At Witte's instigation, Nicholas II issued the October Manifesto on October 30, 1905. Witte's document promised civil liberties, extension of the franchise in new elections to the duma, and authority of the duma to approve all laws. On October 31, 1905, Morgan and Perkins cabled Pierpont Morgan, "We have seen the death of old and birth of new Russia."[174] The following day they left for Stockholm at noon by ship.

The political upheaval in Russia postponed further discussion of the proposed loan. Morgan only hoped that Count Witte could hold on and remain in power. He wrote of Witte: "It's many years since any one man has seemed so entirely important to a whole nation—and he a man who isn't trusted by either party. You see, the reactionaries think him too liberal and the others think him reactionary. . . ."[175]

The younger Morgans enjoyed their English tour of duty, and Morgan remained spiritually attuned to the way of life of the British landed gentry. But the senior Morgan was getting older, and it was time for Jack to return to the United States, closer to the seat of power of the Morgan firm. The permanent move came at the end of 1905, when all six of the Morgan family arrived from England on the *Oceanic*.[176]

Ironically, Jessie Morgan, who had bitterly resented having to leave home for a foreign land in 1898, was equally unenthusiastic about leaving her British social circle to return to this country in 1905.[177]

PART II
1906–1943

CHAPTER IV

The Return

1906–13

THE YOUNGER MORGANS REMAINED IN NEW YORK FOR THE REST OF the winter of 1905–6 and went back to England in the late spring for a month.[1]

The Russian-loan question was reopened in April 1906. This time, the Morgans were again at odds over the desirability of making the loan, but the sides were reversed. Pierpont Morgan cabled enthusiastically from Europe advocating the loan. Jack and the New York partners cabled back vehemently that the issue would be a failure.[2]

The week following Morgan's second visit to Petersburg, on April 18, 1906, the city of San Francisco was almost totally destroyed by an earthquake and the resulting fire. The younger Morgan, now back in New York, cabled to London on May 3 that the San Francisco banks were still closed and the bank vaults were still too hot to be opened, but no panic was anticipated.[3]

Witte was not able to remain in office. He became president of the first ministry in the new constitutional government and raised a large loan in France, which made the administration independent of the legislature, but he was dismissed in 1906.[4] Morgan called on him in Paris in November 1907 and reported that he was "looking much better than he did in Russia at the moment when he had all the power there was in the country." Morgan felt that he did not regret stepping down.[5]

As we know, the shortsighted failure of the liberals and moder-
ates to support Witte and the implacable opposition of the social-
ists, who wanted only a socialist state, caused constitutional re-
form ultimately to fail.[6]

The Morgan family returned on the *Celtic* on July 8. Also on
the ship were William Waldorf Astor, his wife, the former Nancy
Langhorne, and Joseph Pulitzer. To newspaper reporters who
swarmed around him on the ship's arrival in New York, Morgan
denied that he was coming back to the United States to take over
his father's affairs.[7]

The Panic of 1907

The economic decline of 1907 was slow to develop, but matters
worsened considerably in the fall, while Jack was in London. Jack
wrote to his mother on October 28 that it had been a tremendous
week of anxiety for all and the constant cables had kept him
posted on developments. "One thing, however, has made it all
easy to get on with—that is Father's splendid actions and position.
One man writes, Such general recognition and praise have come
to several generals and a few politicians but not to financiers!" He
continued, "I wish very much I had been there to watch and to
help in any way I could! But after fifty years of hard work to have
established such a reputation for fair dealing and sound conduct
that at a moment of real and great danger the whole country turns
to you must be a real reward for all the years."[8]

A few days later he was sent to Paris "to help along Father in his
work of keeping things from going smash." He enjoyed "going
about and seeing all the head people financially on this side, meeting them as an equal and hearing them say nice things about
Father."[9]

Jack's assignment was to arrange a loan of gold from the Banque
de France to stabilize the American financial situation. But the
French would only lend on the guarantee of the United States
government, which that government was not legally able to give.
Negotiations dragged on through November and finally petered
out.[10]

The role of Morgan, Sr., in alleviating the financial upheaval of
1907 was clarified by T. W. Lamont many years later.

> As to the elder Mr. Morgan: surely neither he nor anybody

else nor any group of men were "successful" "in stemming the ebb tide of business in 1907."

In America the serious crack began in the autumn of 1907 and took at first the form of banking difficulties in New York City. Several of the trust companies had inadequate reserves, the public became alarmed, and violent runs started on several institutions. Mr. Morgan, the elder, . . . gathered together the heads of the leading New York City banks, and formed a consortium to provide credit to the banks that were inherently sound but whose assets needed time for conversion into cash. This pooling of resources for the common good under Mr. Morgan's leadership finally rescued that particular situation, and he gained credit for his leadership. . . . But the action of the elder Mr. Morgan neither could nor did stem the business ebb. That went on pretty steadily, and business was "spotty" for several years. . . .

. . . In fact, the curtain of depression was not completely rolled up even in America until World War I was well under way and our industries became swamped with war orders from the Allies.[11]

The Archer-Shee Case

The business affairs of Frances Pell Archer-Shee, an American married to Maj. Martin Archer-Shee, an Englishman, were handled by J. P. Morgan, Jr. In the fall of 1908 young George Archer-Shee, age thirteen—son of the Morgan client, and a cadet at the Royal Naval College at Osborne—was falsely accused of forging a postal money order. It took two years and great perseverance to get the case into court, even longer than that to get the case before the House of Commons and for the Admiralty to admit to error, and still longer to get any sort of recompense for the expense incurred. Until the government's case collapsed about his ears, the solicitor-general to the Crown, Sir Rufus Isaacs (later the Marquess of Reading, who subsequently became a close friend of the younger Morgan), opposed the unhappy child's position all the way.[12] Morgan wrote to the father on November 27, 1908, "Do you want any introductions or anything of that sort to McKenna or anyone at the Admiralty? Anything that you would like that *anybody* here can do or get for you, you have only to ask for." He ended the letter, "With much sympathy for you in your anxiety."[13]

Increasing Responsibilities

The younger Morgan's influence in the firm increased following the Russia mission of 1905 and the Paris mission of 1907, even though both were unsuccessful. Continuing the Anglicizing of the London firm, the father deferred to the son's judgment in admitting Charles Whigham to partnership in J. S. Morgan & Co.[14]

The younger Morgan was in large measure responsible for maintaining liaison between the New York and London offices. He approved the London house investing in London Electric Power in 1908, but urged that the risk be diluted by entering into a joint venture with Baring Brothers and Sir Ernest Cassel, the king's financial advisor.[15]

Both the New York and London Morgan houses were interested in Latin-American government financing, a highly competitive field for international bankers. Jack Morgan entered into the spirit of controversy energetically and acted to make sure that no outside firm, specifically Speyer & Co., was going to come in and cut the Morgans out of the extension of the Mexican 5 percent, external-loan bonds.[16]

In Argentina, the firm frequently did business in an uneasy association with Baring Brothers. Morgan expressed the instability of that association by observing cynically in 1908, "Barings have no idea of dropping us out of the Argentine business, and I don't suppose that they would have such an intention unless the opportunity was very good."[17]

As anticipated, hostility developed between the Morgan and Baring firms over the sale of Argentine bonds, and young Morgan and John Baring, Lord Revelstoke, had a very disagreeable exchange. Morgan wrote about it with a vigor that reflects his increased stature in the firm, "I don't care how we fight him, but am quite ready to fight him when we need to."[18] Ill feeling between the two financial houses became so acute that Frank Vanderlip of the National City Bank intervened, and matters calmed down.[19]

Along with increased responsibilities in the firm, the younger Morgan gradually received more public recognition. On May 24, 1909, Judge E. H. Gary cabled Pierpont Morgan to recommend that Jack replace H. H. Rogers on the board of the United States Steel Corporation.[20]

In July, following his attendance at the twentieth reunion of the class of 1889, he was elected overseer of Harvard College for a six-year term.[21]

J. S. Morgan & Co. became Morgan, Grenfell & Co. at the close of 1909.[22] The winding up of the affairs of the old firm and the formation of the new was an important concern of the younger Morgan in the years 1909–11. The procedure was to liquidate the older firm completely and to start out a new firm with capital supplied by J. P. Morgan & Co. and Drexel & Co.[23] It was Morgan's intent "to endeavor to bring all the houses closer together with more mutual information as to the condition, plans, and investments of each."[24]

The pressure of the new responsibilities that were piled upon him caused young Morgan to have a partial breakdown in 1910 not unlike those suffered by his father in 1871 and 1876. He was put in the care of Dr. Austen F. Riggs and became a supporter of Dr. Riggs and his work for many years afterwards. For rest and relaxation following this illness, Morgan visited his London associates the Hambros at their shooting box in Scotland. He took to the Scottish scene and to the camaraderie of formal, organized grouse shooting at once.[25] In the fall of 1914, he was able to join the Hambro shoot at Gannochy owned by the Earl of Dalhousie and recently given up by old Sir Everard Hambro.[26] Morgan assumed Sir Everard's lease and entered into an arrangement with his son, Sir Charles Eric Hambro. Morgan took care of the expenses of the shooting, while Hambro paid for the lodge.[27] Morgan derived great satisfaction for many years from his visits to Gannochy (pronounced "GANnochy"), "walking and riding about on the moors is heavenly. Wherever one goes, there is a lovely view with hills with the heather just turning brown and cloud shadows chasing each other across them."[28]

In 1910 and 1911, the younger Morgan was active in the early plans for converting the Equitable Life Assurance Company to a mutual company.[29]

There was a flare-up between the Morgans, father and son, over how hard to push to have a Morgan-financed company be the first American security to be listed on the Paris bourse. Pierpont Morgan thought it of the utmost importance to be first.[30] The son, supported by Charles Steele, disagreed. They saw nothing untoward about the prior listing of American Telephone & Telegraph by another company.[31] The Morgans were soon able to get the Santa Fe Railroad listed at the bourse.[32]

The following spring, the younger Morgan was busy organizing a syndicate to underwrite a new issue of Interborough Rapid Transit bonds. Sales went well, and he could soon cable to Davison that the book had been closed and everyone was satisfied.[33]

International Mercantile Marine

The International Mercantile Marine Company was one of the older Morgan's consolidations that never quite worked out. Incorporated on June 6, 1893, as the International Navigation Company, it changed its name and expanded its scope on October 1, 1902.[34] The British management was constantly at odds with the Morgans.[35]

Throughout the year 1912, the younger Morgan represented his father in the affairs of the International Mercantile Marine. Morgan's troubles with the company reached a climax with the sinking of the White Star liner *Titanic* on April 15, 1912. Morgan wrote, "I have been so burdened with grief and excitement over this terrible 'Titanic' disaster. . . ."[36] The subsequent congressional inquiry led him to an outburst of exasperation and wishful thinking. He wrote H. P. Davison in London, "The investigation of the *Titanic* disaster which has grown from bad to worse since you left, has, I think, raised a general feeling that Legislative investigations must be controlled in the future, unless Congress wishes to make itself the laughing stock of the world."[37] He was incensed that Ismay, the head of the company, was blamed for the disaster,[38] and he himself served on the committee to raise money for the widow and daughter of Captain Smith.[39]

Morgan engaged P. A. S. Franklin to be chief executive of the company. Morgan had a high regard for Franklin "for his splendid conduct during the terrible time following the *Titanic* disaster. If anybody ever had an excuse for losing his head it was Franklin at that time and he never lost it for a moment and met the whole thing as a strong man and as a gentleman."[40]

As time went on, Morgan became more and more frustrated and exasperated by the company and its vicissitudes. He and Charles Steele finally resigned from the board in 1926. The reason given for the resignations was a conflict of interest, since their London house, Morgan, Grenfell & Co., was representing Furness, Withy & Co., who were negotiating to buy the ships that the company wanted to dispose of.[41]

Family Matters

While Jack was participating more actively in the affairs of the home office, the family continued to live in town during most of the year, with summers spent partly in England and partly in rented houses in the New York suburbs. The last place they rented was at Glen Cove on the northern or Sound side of Long Island.

Small-boat sailing became one of Morgan's favorite sports. In the summer of 1908, he wrote to Vivian Smith: "I have set up a small sail boat which is in the same class with a large number of others in the neighborhood and Junius and I, either together, or, when that is impossible separately, spend all of our spare time in racing her in Long Island Sound. So far we have had mostly calms and no very conspicuous success, but no doubt shall gradually learn our business and in the meantime the fun of it is enormous."[42] This enthusiasm persisted, and on the eve of World War I, Morgan was chairman of the New York Yacht Club's fifty-foot one-design class committee.[43]

The relationship between the younger Morgan and his mother was a very agreeable one, as we can gather from their long correspondence. This does not mean, however, that all was perfect harmony between them. He wrote to her companion, Mrs. Meredith, "Mrs. Morgan and I do not agree about certain points, and my point of view, on those points, worries her more than any satisfaction which she gets from me on other points."[44]

J. P. Morgan, Jr., sent his two sons to Groton School, the establishing of which had been so bitterly deplored by his old St. Paul's headmaster, Coit. But he was not an easy parent to the school administration. He addressed Endicott Peabody, the headmaster, writing as an "irate parent" (his expression) on the subject of "some wretched football game or other" that kept the boys at school on a day that seriously inconvenienced all boys and parents concerned. He concluded with expressions of personal affection, but noted "in spite of that my indignation still seethes."[45] Earlier in the year, he had written with his own brand of wry humor: "I am sorry to hear that your thumb has gone wrong; I hope it will be strong enough at the end of the holidays to keep the boys properly under it."[46]

Football aroused the Morgan ire. In a strongly worded letter, he declined to give Harvard money for football: "I cannot too em-

phatically say that nothing would induce me in any circumstances
to do anything that would further the game of football in any
manner. I have a complete and supreme dislike for the game in
every aspect, and, had I any power in that direction, I should use
whatever I had to stop the game being played at all as being (1st)
immoral, (2nd) dangerous, (3rd) brutal."[47]

Morgan's irascibility was not directed only at education institutions in these prewar years. He wrote H. P. Davison on one occasion, "I do not know exactly what you think I do over here that
you send me a mass of papers of a complicated description and
then telegraph me for an opinion the second day after I could
possibly have received them."[48]

A month later he wrote to Worth, the Paris couturier, accepting
on behalf of Mrs. Morgan the "least bad of the three" dresses
received, which were made with complete disregard, he said, for
the instructions. He concluded, "It is needless to say that I consider . . . that the whole matter has been treated with too much
carelessness and not as a first-class house should have done it." A
year later, he flatly refused to pay Worth 1500 francs for what he
regarded as a charge "far in excess of anything that could be justified" for alterations to a broadtailed lamb coat.[49]

In the early summer of 1910, great festivities attended the
awarding of an honorary LL.D. by Harvard University to J. P.
Morgan, Sr. A number of the family, including Jack, went up to
Boston by train on June 27. The next day, Thursday, June 30,
they watched the Harvard-Yale boat races from the deck of *Corsair*.[50] This boat-race visit was a custom that the younger Morgan
was to enjoy in later years, when he had inherited *Corsair*.

In April 1909, Morgan bought the Lawrence Jacob property,
which he had been renting at Matinicock Point on East Island near
Glen Cove, Long Island.[51] The following year he began to build
a house on the place. The architect was his longtime friend
C. Grant LaFarge of the firm Heins & LaFarge. But Jessie Morgan
was not happy with the arrangement and let the architect go. She
preferred to continue with her own ideas, working closely with
the general foreman, S. J. Stammers, with whom she had established a rapport.[52]

The house was greatly influenced in design by Denham Place,
Uxbridge, Buckinghamshire, a house built in 1692–1700, during
the reign of William and Mary, for Sir Roger Hill, whose father, a
lawyer, had been a successful member of Cromwell's government.[53]

The house at Matinicock Point is a solid, two-story, dormered-roof building in dark red brick with white trim. Decoration is restrained. There is a classical cornice below the eaves all around, and the front door is flanked with engaged Roman Ionic columns, surmounted by a broken pediment, and approached by a short balustraded stair and entrance stoop.

The family moved to their new place on the shore, and Morgan could write on June 2, 1911, to his mother at Camp Uncas, the family place in the Adirondacks, that while there were still workmen around, "We are really very comfortable and it's entirely charming being out on the point where there's so much more to see and where the air is fresher than at the back of the island."[54]

A burglar broke into the town house at 231 Madison Avenue on January 26, 1912, and stole a quantity of Morgan's smaller belongings—watches, wallets, pipes. He even smoked some of Morgan's expensive cigars.[55] The burglar was apprehended in September, but the affair was not closed; the burglar's wife appealed to Morgan for support, since her husband had gone to jail for burgling his house! He sent her fifty dollars.[56]

The Pujo "Money Trust" Hearings

The story of the Pujo Committee "Money Trust" investigation of 1912–13 primarily concerns the career of the elder Morgan, but its effects on the younger Morgan were so great as to make it essential to summarize those events. The panic of 1907 led to agitation for legislation to correct the monetary and banking ills faced by the country. A monetary commission was created by Congress in 1908, and its report was referred to the Banking and Currency Committee of the House, resulting in House Resolution no. 429. This called for an investigation to get "full and complete information on the banking and currency conditions of the United States for the purpose of determining what legislation is needed." As early as February 1, 1912, mention of the forthcoming investigation by the Senate Committee on Banking and Currency began to appear in Jack Morgan's cablegrams, but his warnings were not taken seriously.[57]

The senior Morgan's trusted lieutenants were Charles Steele, G. W. Perkins, Thomas W. Lamont, and Henry P. Davison. The younger Morgan might well have envied these men their close association with Pierpont Morgan in this time of large affairs. He did not. Perhaps closest to the elder Morgan was Davison. When Davison went to Europe, Jack urged him to go to Aix-les-Bains to visit his father, who took the waters there annually. He wrote to his father at the same time: "There are many things I want him to talk over with you—questions of broad policy and wide-reaching matters which are impossible to do by cable or mail."[58]

By April 25, he had cabled his father in Venice that Samuel Untermyer had refused to become counsel for the financial investigating committee unless a more drastic resolution was passed by the Senate, and that the Senate had passed such a resolution! He remarked, "Investigation will probably proceed now on as unpleasant lines as can be arranged."[59]

The serious fact-finding purposes of the original resolution were transformed by the investigation called for by House Resolution no. 504, introduced on April 22, 1912, by Congressman A. J. Pujo of Louisiana. The new resolution identified a villain, the New York banking community, and implied that its purpose was to prove its villainy.

Pierpont Morgan and Davison cabled from Aix that the firm should stand firmly on its legal rights with the committee and at the same time should enlist public opinion by hiring "in a confidential way best publicist available." The younger Morgan cabled back that the business community was terrified and was incapable of forming a united front, fearing to antagonize the committee.[60]

Samuel Untermyer, counsel for the Pujo Committee, was no academic radical, but a highly successful corporation lawyer. His motives appear to have been mixed. He seems to have had a genuine concern about the unfairness of the inequality of economic opportunity, but the purity of his motives in the Pujo hearings is open to question. There had long been hostility between Untermyer and the Morgan firm.[61] To business rivalry and political frustration, was added a personal motive for wanting to put down the elder Morgan. Two of his admirers, George Wheeler and Henry F. Pringle, tell of his becoming miffed at losing to Morgan entries in the Collie breed competition at a dog show![62]

Untermyer was a man with a thesis to prove: that the financial control of the United States rested in a few hands in New York City, and dominating these was J. P. Morgan. He employed the catchphrase "money trust"—though he explained that he spoke figuratively—to describe the concentration. Proof of his thesis was claimed to be found in the body of statistics produced, which showed that a number of Morgan partners or directors of banks believed to share a community of interest with the Morgan firm— George F. Baker's First National Bank, James Stillman's National City Bank, the Bankers Trust Company, and the Guaranty Trust Company—held among them 341 directorships in 112 major American corporations with total resources or capitalization of more than twenty billion dollars.[63] This was the spider-web theory of centralized control. It was an ingenious theory, but no witnesses were brought in to show that there was an agreed-upon body of corporate policy uniting these numerous companies into concerted purpose and action or that specific firms on the periphery had been compelled to carry out directives originating at the center of the web. It is odd, too, that there was not an upsurge of grievances to ventilate, evidence to present, and lawsuits to press by the victims of such alleged discrimination or unfairness.

Morgan partner Thomas W. Lamont wrote some years later to Henry Steele Commager to present and explain the case against the theory:

> The spider-web thesis works like this: if a Morgan partner sits on a board of, say, 25 directors, he, single-handed, "controls" the other 24. These 24, for the sake of the theory, figure as mere puppets. In practice I can assure you that the boards of our large corporations are made up of highly vigorous personalities, and anyone who is stupid enough to treat them as dummies would quickly learn his mistake. But the theory does not end with the triumph of one individual against 24. The 24 puppets are found on the boards of a number of other corporations where no Morgan partner sits, and the spider-web notion pictures all these other corporations, where no Morgan partner sits, as brought back under the Morgan thumb. The 24 puppets, we are asked to believe, serve as conduits for the flow of Morgan "control" to corporations with which no Morgan partner has anything to do, in which often no Morgan partner has any stock interest, and about which in many instances no Morgan partner knows anything.[64]

Still, the validity of this theory was to become accepted as fact—or, perhaps, as gospel—by several generations of critics of the economic system.

The hearings opened in May 1912 and lasted until January 24,

1913. The high point of the hearings was the testimony of J. P. Morgan, Sr. He comported himself with poise and dignity, did not allow himself to be shaken, and declined to admit to the dominant role in American finance that Untermyer hoped to establish.

The senior Morgan—together with his daughter and son-in-law, the Satterlees—left for Europe on January 7, 1913, after his appearance at the Pujo hearings. On February 13, in Egypt, he fell ill. His daughter Louisa relayed the doctor's diagnosis to her brother: "General physical and nervous exhaustion resulting from prolonged excessive strain in elderly subject."[65]

Jack immediately cabled back that he would come to his father's bedside at once if needed. Louisa replied that the father was touched by the son's offer: "But he is anxious you should remember how much [he] depends upon your being on the spot in New York—how many interests are in your hands. He is too weak [to] make decisions; he wishes [to] leave it [to] you. I am afraid he will worry at your absence from the helm."[66]

This is the first clear statement we have that J. Pierpont Morgan regarded his son as his successor in the firm. Ten days later, the same idea was conveyed again when Louisa cabled that it only upset the senior Morgan to see messages on "office matters": "He . . . wants you to decide in all such matters."[67]

Jack seems to have been unaware of the gravity of his father's condition. He wrote to Charles Steele on March 4, "All seems to be going on all right in Cairo, and Father will, I expect, sail next week for Italy. There has not really been anything the matter with him except blues and nervous dyspepsia. He is still very much in the dumps, but the doctor's reports are first rate."[68]

One of Jack's great concerns during his father's illness was how to prevent the older man from returning to the United States, where he (mistakenly) feared there might be a number of lawsuits and investigations by members of a public that had tasted blood at the Pujo hearings.[69]

Jack Morgan was quick to perceive the need to recognize the pressure of public opinion generated by the Pujo hearings and to reduce the bank stock holdings of J. P. Morgan & Co. Morgan wrote James Stillman of the National City Bank:

> The Untermyer enquiry and the press generally have indicated a feeling on the part of the public that J. P. Morgan & Company ought not to have large stock-holding interests in

our financial institutions . . . we all feel that it behooves us to pay more or less attention to public feeling of that kind, particularly as our relations to our friends do not depend on our stock-holding interests. Our idea is that we should reduce all our bank stocks to very manageable amounts.[70]

Morgan explained the current mood: "We have to thank one man more than any other for the state of the public mind, which I believe to be based on envy, fundamentally."[71]

The Pujo-Untermyer hearings undoubtedly undermined the elder Morgan's health, but at the time there was almost a conspiracy on the part of the firm and the family to suppress this view, even though Morgan's physician, Dr. George A. Dixon, recognized the connection in a press release. Writing to his brother-in-law Herbert Satterlee about that release, Morgan said:

> The statement might have been improved in one particular, which would have been not to refer to Pujo as one of the causes of Father's illness. We have all here maintained the note which he struck so well in Washington that he was much too big to be annoyed by miserable little things like that. The admission that it was vexatious called further attention to the feeling which we all know existed, but which the public throughout the country did not know of, and the statement was to that extent unfortunate. . . .
>
> There is no use in letting that little rascal Untermyer smile a happy smile and say "I brought it off after all." It is not a very important matter, but I thought I might just as well speak about it.[72]

Morgan was moved from Egypt to Rome, where he died on Monday, March 31, 1913.

Thomas W. Lamont held the Pujo hearings directly responsible for the death of Pierpont Morgan. He wrote,

> I was a witness to Mr. Morgan's growing amazement and indignation to find himself not taking part in a careful, factual inquiry, but being made the subject of innuendoes, charges, and the like by a lawyer acting like a district attorney, whose object never seemed to be to gain the truth but to try to trump up some justification for a thesis all of his own which, flying in the face of clear testimony,—if one takes the trouble even to skim it carelessly—he embodied in a report, every word of

which he wrote himself; the Congressmen who throughout
the hearings had hardly ever asked a single question of their
own simply attaching their signatures. The effect of all this
upon Mr. Morgan's physical powers was devastating. Within
three or four months, out of a seemingly clear sky, his health
failed and after a two weeks illness, from no particular mal-
ady, he died.[73]

Unlike counsel for subsequent congressional investigations,
Untermyer did not write a book claiming to have made his case.
That task was undertaken by Louis D. Brandeis. Brandeis wrote a
series of articles for *Harper's Weekly* in 1913 and 1914, which appeared in book form in 1914 under the title *Other People's Money and
How the Bankers Use It*.[74] This served to keep the conclusions of the
Pujo Committee alive and provided a convenient compilation for
later reference. The book was largely directed against J. P. Morgan & Co. Morgan saw the development from the hearings of a
body of dogma that was accepted with almost blind faith by a
generation of anti-business critics—ideas that were to be dormant
for twenty years and then emerge as essential tenets of the New
Deal.

Untermyer, whom Morgan held responsible for his father's
death, and Brandeis, who continued the anti-Morgan vendetta,
were both Jewish. Morgan's distrust of Jews—a sentiment which
does not appear in the earlier correspondence—dated from the
Pujo hearings.

On the death of his father, John Pierpont, Jr., became senior
partner of J. P. Morgan & Co. in April 1913.

CHAPTER V

The Succession

1913–14

FREDERICK LEWIS ALLEN EXPRESSED THE GENERAL UNCERTAINTY
about the new senior partner:

> When old Pierpont Morgan died, men had wondered wheth-
> er the supremacy of the banking house which he had built
> would come to an end. If character were the secret of financial
> influence, as the old man had argued at the Pujo inquiry, per-
> haps the great days of the Morgan house were over; for J. P.
> Morgan the younger, who now at the age of forty-five became
> the senior partner, had given no evidence of any such colossal
> personal force as his father had radiated. He was an attractive
> young man, by reputation solid and reliable; he inherited his
> father's patrician spirit and tastes, his father's scorn of the
> common herd, and his father's blinding temper; but his capac-
> ity for personal leadership had not been tested.[1]

The new senior punctiliously observed the amenities attending
the death of a famous and distinguished father, remained with the
family in seclusion for a few days, and then went right back to
work, which is exactly as his father would have wished. He came
down to the office before his father's body reached this country.
He was at his desk at 23 Wall Street on Monday morning, April 7,
1913, attended the partners' meeting, and then busied himself at
once with answering his correspondence.[2]

There was never any serious question as to who was to be head of the banking house of J. P. Morgan & Co. Partners Thomas W. Lamont and Henry P. Davison had been closer than young Morgan to the firing line and more active in the consolidations and battles of the firm under the elder Morgan, and there was some speculation as to the succession, but the transition was smooth— so far as the outside world could tell—and John Pierpont Morgan, Jr., was recognized immediately as the senior partner. He promptly dropped the *Jr.* from his name.

When the partnership agreement of J. P. Morgan & Co. became a matter of public record, it was learned to what degree the new Morgan dominated the firm. He had the power to fire a partner at any time. He was the sole and final arbiter of disputes between partners. On the departure of a partner because of death or withdrawal, Morgan determined the value of the firm's assets and the amount due the departing partner or his estate.[3]

The pressures on Morgan upon his succession were formidable. Davison cabled, "Am thinking much of you, hoping you are not overburdened, being very fearful you are."[4] The decisions to be made related to both major policy matters and minutiae–including such items as finding out what had happened to the family's Covent Garden opera tickets and deciding that the Fragonard murals should be taken from the walls of the London town house at 13 Princes Gate and shipped to the United States immediately.[5]

The Equitable Life Assurance Society

Morgan gave an impetus to the plan to convert the Equitable Life Assurance Society to a mutual company. He had inherited 502 shares of the 1,000 shares outstanding. On April 22, 1913, he was quoted in the press as being willing to sell the stock below cost in order to carry out the mutual plan. Two years later, he and the other big stockholders turned over their shares to Gen. T. Coleman du Pont as trustee for the conversion. The final changeover to a mutual company took place in 1917.[6]

The New York Central Bond Issue

Morgan's first important public statement was made at a hearing on June 24 before the New York State Public Service Board in connection with the proposed merger of the New York Central and the Lake Shore & Southern Michigan railroads. Morgan testified again before the Interstate Commerce Commission on September 9 as a representative of his firm, the fiscal agents for the New York Central, and said that the consolidation would improve operating efficiency and the new 4 percent bond would be a better and more standardized security than the original 3½. The *New York Times* observed in its news columns: "It was the first time Mr. Morgan had appeared as a witness before any Federal investigating body. The impression he created was favorable." The new refunding and improvement loan was approved. J. P. Morgan & Co. headed the syndicate to underwrite the issue.[7]

The New Haven Railroad

When Morgan was elected to fill his father's place on the New Haven board, he found the road in bad financial shape and undergoing an investigation by the Interstate Commerce Commission (ICC). The trouble was that Charles S. Mellen, the railroad executive brought in from the Northern Pacific by the elder Morgan to strengthen and unify the transportation network of New England, went about establishing New Haven control regardless of legal or financial constraints, and the results were disastrous for the railroad. There were shocking train wrecks (referred to humorously in Clarence Day's *Life With Father*) and serious money troubles. A critical report from the ICC was published on July 9, 1913, and within a week Morgan was able to oust Mellen and to install Howard Elliott as president.[8]

A new outburst of anti-Morgan sentiment over the railroad broke out in early 1914. Intemperate and inflammatory attacks were made in the United States Senate in late January. J. P. Morgan & Co. released a detailed report of all their transactions with the New Haven for the previous twenty years. The report was published on March 9, 1914, and showed that, far from looting the railroad, the Morgan firm had provided financial services—floating securities issues to the value of more than $333,000,000—at a profit of only one tenth of one percent! Pierpont Morgan's memory was extolled, and the firm was praised for its services to the transportation industry in a *New York Times* editorial of March 9, 1914.[9]

The railroad itself was sued by the U.S. Department of Justice for violating the Sherman Act by combining in restraint of trade and seeking to monopolize New England transportation. The

New Haven did not defend the suit, but entered into a consent decree on October 17, 1914, divesting itself of steamship and trolley-car lines.[10] Ironically, within a few years after the ICC had castigated the New Haven's control of the Boston & Maine, the commission itself found in favor of William Z. Ripley's plan for grouping the New England roads along the lines of the Morgan plan, for greater efficiency and economy.[11]

The Latter Half of 1913

Morgan was able to get some relaxation during the summer of 1913. He took a few short cruises on *Corsair*, including a day trip up the Hudson to show the visiting Lord Haldane the military academy at West Point. But his greatest pleasure was yacht racing on Long Island Sound in *Grayling*.[12]

His days were crowded with board and committee meetings in addition to the day-to-day business of the firm. His calendar shows him at meetings of the New Haven Railroad, National Bank of Commerce, New York Central Railroad, National City Bank, United States Steel Corporation, Northern Pacific Railroad, Western Union, and International Mercantile Marine.[13]

On September 16, Mr. and Mrs. Morgan and their two daughters sailed for England on the *Kaiser Wilhelm der Grosse*. One purpose of the trip was to continue the settling of his father's estate in England. Among other assets, the senior Morgan had left, with their contents, his London town house and the country place (actually suburban now that London had pushed out its old boundaries) Dover House, Roehampton.[14] Morgan commented tersely on this part of his trip in a cable to Davison, "Breaking up of houses unpleasant."[15]

But the visit to Britain was not all work. Morgan spent considerable time being a country squire at Wall Hall, dropping in at the Morgan London office for an hour or two from time to time, or going through his father's papers at Princes Gate and Dover House. There were shooting parties at Wall Hall or at Six Mile Bottom and house parties at the country houses of his friends. In November, he visited Lord and Lady Buxton at New Timber, spent several days shooting with the Duke of Sutherland at Lilliesfield, and was the guest of Sir Everard Hambro at Milton Abbey.[16]

The Morgans returned from Europe on the *Lusitania* on December 19, 1913. The violinist Mischa Elman occupied the stateroom next to Morgan, and fellow voyagers reported that the banker "was surfeited with violin music" on the crossing![17]

1914

The New Look at J. P. Morgan & Co.

The new J. P. Morgan was a different man from his father. Having disposed of the immediate pressing problems or put them in capable hands, he acted to put his own imprint on the firm. B. C. Forbes wrote: "On his accession he had notified his partners that the amalgamation and concentration of banking institutions and resources had gone far enough and that the house would confine itself strictly to attending to its regular business. He outlined a conservative policy."[18]

On the first business day of 1914, J. P. Morgan startled the financial community by announcing that he was resigning from the boards of directors of eighteen corporations, most of them companies in the New York Central and New Haven railroad systems. Four of his partners also resigned a number of their directorships. The Morgan firm gave up a total of thirty places. Morgan accompanied this drastic step by a public statement noting that this was in response to a change in public sentiment.[19] The resignations were spontaneous decisions and symbolized the new Morgan's quiet but effective transformation of J. P. Morgan & Co. to reflect his own temperament and conception of the role of the firm in the New York financial scene. He saw the firm as a commercial bank engaged in lending money on security and an investment bank concerned with floating high-quality security issues. Besides, mergers—so interesting to the elder Morgan—were now out of fashion.

Plans had already been drawn during the elder Morgan's lifetime for a new and improved home for the firm. The cornerstone at 23 Wall Street was laid on December 30, 1913. On November 11, 1914, J. P. Morgan & Co. moved into their new and handsome banking offices.[20] The Corner was grandly modernized by the new building, which continues to house the successor company, Morgan Guaranty Trust. The *Times* reported: "J. P. Morgan was busy receiving callers all day. His office was banked with roses sent by friends, and there was a life-size painting of the late J. P. Morgan." Frederick Lewis Allen gives us a more intimate view:

"The private offices on the second floor of 23 Wall Street were islands of modesty and quiet in the splendor and uproar of Wall Street. Their atmosphere was subtly British and old-fashioned. Wood fires burned in the fireplaces on chilly days; the well-worn easy chairs and couches were restful; a financial discussion there was like a chat in a gentleman's club."[21]

The Need for Cash: Sales of Art Works

Morgan moved rapidly in 1914 on his program to put his house in order. The next move was to raise cash. While the younger Morgan had inherited a vast fortune from his father, the bulk of the assets were in works of art, not all of them paid for, and against these there were considerable cash bequests to pay out and $3,000,000 in inheritance taxes to pay. J. P. Morgan, Jr., needed capital to conduct the international banking business.[22]

On January 26, 1914, a front-page story in the *New York Times* announced that some 4,100 objects from the senior Morgan's vast art collection would be put on exhibition at the Metropolitan Museum of Art for about a year, after which time many of the items would undoubtedly be sold. This created a great furor in the press and among art enthusiasts all over the world because the elder Morgan had intended to leave the paintings, sculptures, and other works to the Metropolitan Museum outright.[23]

By the middle of February, the Morgan Exhibition was installed. The spectacular works were the salon decorated by Fragonard for Mme. du Barry, the mistress of Louis XV, and Raphael's *Colonna Madonna*. There were paintings of the English eighteenth-century school, a Lawrence and a Turner, and period furniture, tapestries, bronzes, enamels, Greek vases, and Della Robbia and Donatello sculptures in relief.[24]

The liquidation of the Morgan art collection was revealed by Morgan on February 8, 1915, with the announcement that the Chinese porcelains that had been on view at the Metropolitan Museum for some twenty years had been sold to Duveen Brothers.[25] The *New York Times* took the position editorially that, while the dispersion was a serious cultural loss to the city, the community had been fortunate to be able to enjoy it for twenty years. They then expressed a remarkably sympathetic view of the economic realities.[26]

A fortnight after the Chinese porcelain sale, the art market was again stirred by the sale of the Fragonard panels. Henry Clay

Frick, the coke and steel magnate, had bought the room for his palatial new house on Fifth Avenue at Seventieth Street.[27] In April 1915, Duveen Brothers bought for an estimated three million dollars the collection of eighteenth-century French furniture and decorative art on exhibition at the Metropolitan.[28] The following year, in February 1916, Morgan presented the Metropolitan Museum of Art with works of art valued at more than a million dollars, including the celebrated Raphael *Colonna Madonna*.[29] Two months later, he sold bronzes, Limoges enamels, and Majolica pottery to the Duveens for a figure reported to be between $3,500,000 and $4,000,000.[30]

The publicity given to the sales obscured the fact that a very sizable number of items remained on loan to the Metropolitan Museum. On December 17, 1917, Morgan gave the museum all the materials on loan, with the single exception of a bronze figure of Eros from Boscoreale. This comprised a collection of objects with an estimated market value of $7,500,000. The bulk of the material was European decorative arts. There were also paintings, Egyptian antiquities, Renaissance sculptures, and armor. This generous act must have been a source of chagrin to all those individuals who had publicly wrung their hands or had criticized Morgan for parsimony when he was trying to bring order out of an estate filled with frozen assets.[31]

Meanwhile, Morgan's other business and private concerns proceeded in normal, unspectacular fashion. He continued to begin almost every working day with a visit to the library he had inherited and had come to cherish. He attended to J. P. Morgan & Co. business. He maintained his schedule of board and committee meetings, corporate and philanthropic. Morgan limited the number of public, non-profit organizations that he served because of his resolve to work for them actively, not merely lend his name. In 1914, he was active in the New York Trade School, the America's Cup yacht syndicate and New York Yacht Club, the Peabody Education Fund in England, the American Museum of Natural History, Cooper Union, the corporation and vestry of St. George's Episcopal Church on Stuyvesant Square, the Harvard University Board of Overseers, the Episcopal Church Fund, the Lattingtown Chapel Committee (which was working to establish St. John's Church at Locust Valley on Long Island), the Murray Hill Association, the Union Club, New York Public Library, and the Advisory Board of the Federal Reserve System.[32]

He met with various people of greater or less prominence. Thomas Fortune Ryan came to see him at the library on January 26. He attended the dinner U.S. Steel's Judge Gary gave for Sir Hugh Bell on March 27 and dined with President Lowell of Harvard on April 13.[33] He welcomed visitors from England—Sir Hercules Read of the British Museum and Fairfax Murray, his advisors on the art sales—in May, and he took the English banker Maurice Glyn and his wife on a cruise of Chesapeake Bay on *Corsair* later in the month. June was a month of activity. *Grayling* won several races.[34] There were the polo matches. On the fifteenth, at the Harvard commencement, Morgan attended the twenty-fifth reunion of the class of 1889 and saw his elder son, Junius Spencer Morgan, Jr., graduate from Harvard College.[35] Following the festivities in Cambridge, the Morgans went down to New London and watched the Harvard-Yale crew races from *Corsair*. Ten days later Morgan resigned from the boards of three large New York banks, First National, National City, and National Bank of Commerce, as required by the Federal Reserve Act.[36]

Morgan failed to make his European visits in only three years during this century, 1914, 1917, and 1918. He did take several vacation trips in 1914, however. The first was to Climax Lodge, North Carolina, for the shooting in February. At the end of October he spent a fortnight at Camp Uncas in the Adirondacks, and in mid-November he returned to Climax, taking Henry Clay Frick as a guest.[37]

While Morgan served on the Metropolitan Opera board and owned a box, there are few records of his actually attending a performance, although we do know that he went on December 9, 1914, to the American premiere of Richard Strauss's *Rosenkavalier*. Morgan was a conscientious funeralgoer. One of his partners, Temple Bowdoin, died December 2, 1914, and Morgan attended services for him on the fifth.[38]

A recurring felicity within Morgan's circle was their exchange of presents. Often these gifts were of game or fish. On July 13, 1914, Morgan wrote to James Stillman of the National City Bank to thank him for the "glorious salmon." Morgan hoped "he was as much fun to catch as he was to eat." The day after Christmas that year, he thanked railroad man James J. Hill for the Christmas present of apples.[39]

A custom of the elder Morgan's continued by the younger until the Second World War was the giving to friends or the wives of friends presents of chests of Chinese tea. These were usually sent in time for Christmas, but not invariably—as often with Clarence H. Howard of St. Louis, head of the Commonwealth Steel Company, with whom he exchanged presents at various times for many years. The tea was "Mandarin Mixture," and Morgan, Sr., and one or two other New Yorkers for many years bought up the whole year's output and gave it away.[40]

The Pre-War Depression: Government and Business

Morgan had felt that President Theodore Roosevelt was worse than useless in the financial crisis of 1907.[41] He also opposed Roosevelt's trust-busting activities. Morgan was apprehensive about the breakup of the large companies prosecuted for restraint of trade under the Sherman Anti-Trust Act of 1890.[42] When the Supreme Court did order their dissolution, however, Morgan found that the results were not so disastrous after all.[43]

Regarding the United States Steel Corporation investigation of 1911, the younger Morgan wrote, "the enquiry is evidently not to be a real one into real things but a fishing expedition to see if some anti-administration capital cannot be made out for the next campaign." He added, "it seems to be turning into an enquiry into the panic of 1907."[44] He became more exasperated as the hearings proceeded, and as the newspapers suggested that Morgan, Sr., had created the panic for selfish ends.

The agitation resulting from the depression led Congress to create a Commission on Industrial Relations to "inquire into the general condition of labor" and "seek to discover the underlying causes of dissatisfaction in the industrial situation and report its conclusions thereon."[46] Chairman was Frank P. Walsh, a Missouri politician.

As is standard practice in government inquiries, the commission sought to achieve a maximum of publicity by subpoenaing prominent men whose presence would give "news" value to the proceedings. Morgan was summoned to testify, along with John D. Rockefeller and Andrew Carnegie. Morgan was called upon to appear on February 1, 1915. The greater part of his testimony was restrained and tells a great deal about his views on labor. He took the position that day-to-day operations of a company were the responsibility of management, not of the directors. Morgan was not anti-labor union. There were cases in which he favored actions taken by unions, but he was opposed to the closed shop and to outside union organizers entering the plant and soliciting union membership on the company's time.[47]

Only once in the course of the hearings did he allow his natural repugnance for the whole investigation to show. B. C. Forbes, editor of *Forbes Magazine*, described the episode.

> While Mr. Morgan, in common with almost every one else, viewed Walsh as a notoriety-seeking mountebank, he did not proceed to the examination room with battle in his eye. . . . The moment he took the witness chair, however, "movie" machines began to click-click all around him. . . .
>
> This riled Morgan. . . . He considered that the Commission was subjecting him to unfair, unnecessary, and undignified treatment and that, therefore, he was not obligated to lend himself more than he could avoid to its far-from-judicial tactics.
>
> Hence, when he was asked if he considered $10 a week a proper wage for a longshoreman and replied, under pressure, "If that's all he can get and takes it, I should say that is enough," the public was not afforded a picture of the real Morgan, but of a citizen righteously indignant and angry.[48]

While he was trying to show that he did not take the proceedings or the chairman seriously, what he succeeded in doing was to appear callous and unfeeling toward the employees of his companies. In this he played right into the hands of his detractors of the political Left, who sought to further their own ends by portraying him as a symbolic figure of rapacious capitalism. Morgan's failure to realize that he was not a private person and his consequent refusal to make the effort to be forthright, let alone gracious, in public statements misrepresented not only his own views on humanitarian questions, but those of the entire business community and of the economic order in which he believed—to the detriment of them all.

Woodrow Wilson was elected president of the United States in 1912 on an anti-business platform. Like so many from academic life, he did not fully comprehend the operation of economic forces, and he deplored the rewards received by successful men of affairs. Sustained by a comforting conviction of moral superiority, he held that material success could only result from evildoing, and in his first term he pushed through a broad program of legislation that regulated and restricted business and reduced its profitability.

Congress did not need the self-righteous, quasi-theological rhetoric of Calvinist Wilson to support the always politically attractive appeal to popular envy. The business community, for its part, had invited this campaign by tolerating with characteristic short-sightedness the secrecy and restrictive practices that they should have corrected long before. Nobody emerged from this encounter looking entirely devoted to long-run public interests except the architects of the Federal Reserve System. Morgan did endorse the establishment of the Federal Reserve System. He was gratified to be appointed to the Advisory Council of the Federal Reserve Second District.[49]

The success of the president in getting his program enacted produced a feeling of deep pessimism in J. P. Morgan. Nor did the prospect of an electorate expanded further by women voters reassure him. He wrote that "woman suffrage . . . would only help to complete the ruin of the country already hurt by universal manhood suffrage."[50] Morgan believed realistically that, human nature being what it is, voters with nothing to lose would proceed with fine egalitarian principles to vote themselves benefits that were to be paid for by the provident and successful. Morgan's vehemence and scorn were heightened by the fact that he felt that government policies were adding to the difficulties of recovery from the prevailing depression.[51] As we noted earlier in discussing Pierpont Morgan's role in 1907, it was only the stimulus of rearming Europe that brought the United States out of that slump, just as it was the rearming of the Western powers again in the early 1940s that would bring the country out of the slump of the 1930s after the New Deal's endless money-spending, "pump-priming" efforts had failed.

Radical movements flourish in times of depression. One pre–World War I radical movement was the revolutionary IWW (Industrial Workers of the World, nicknamed "Wobblies") agitation. Their demands and threats of violence were naturally uncongenial to J. P. Morgan, but Morgan did not allow his private views to affect his humanitarian convictions. He was a major contributor to the University Settlement Society, 184 Eldridge Street, New York, a shelter directed by the Rev. Robbins Gillman. When the papers reported that Gillman must be in sympathy with the aims and methods of the IWW because he had fed and cared for them at the shelter, Morgan wrote and asked mildly if this were the case. Gillman replied that he had indeed looked after the IWW men, though he did not approve of their violent methods. Morgan wrote back, "Of course . . . I was delighted to have the place arranged so that the men could be sheltered there, and equally of course, I had no idea that you should enquire as to the political views of the men benefitted. . . ."[52]

CHAPTER VI

World War I
1914–18

1914

J. P. MORGAN'S PLACE IN HISTORY WAS ESTABLISHED BY THE FIRST World War. Under his leadership, the firm took the dominant role in financing the Western Allies in their struggle with the Central Powers and in providing the Allies with the materials of war and in the process developed the United States as an arsenal to meet its commitments when it entered the war on the Allied side. When the war was over, Morgan took the lead in financing the reconstruction of the war-torn or war-impoverished nations.

On June 28, 1914, following a long period of nationalist seething in the Balkan states, a Serbian fanatic murdered the heir apparent to the Austro-Hungarian throne. A month later, after a series of colossal diplomatic blunders and miscalculations, Austria attacked Serbia on July 29, thus involving Germany on the side of her fellow Germans and Russia on the side of her fellow Slavs. On August 1, Russia declared war on Germany. The following day Germany invaded France. On August 4, Germany invaded Belgium, whereupon Britain honored her guarantees of Belgian independence and declared war on Germany.

For a few hours following the Austrian attack on Serbia, there was some optimism that the hostilities would not spread. A meeting of bankers at J. P. Morgan's office on Thursday afternoon, July 30, was attended by Morgan; H. P. Davison, of J. P. Morgan

& Co.; Francis L. Hine, president of the Clearing-House Association; Charles H. Sabin, vice-president of the Guaranty Trust Co.; Benjamin Strong, Jr., president of the Bankers Trust Co.; A. Barton Hepburn, chairman of the board of the Chase National Bank; H. G. S. Noble, president of the New York Stock Exchange; and William C. Van Antwerp, a member of the board of governors of the Exchange. It was decided that the New York Stock Exchange would remain open for trading.[1]

After further discussions early on Friday morning, July 31, at Morgan's office, however, it was decided to close the New York Stock Exchange, following the lead of the other exchanges in Europe, and Morgan issued a statement of cautious optimism. Perhaps war could be averted.

The French Credit and Prohibition of a Foreign Loan

Within the week, the Morgan firm had negotiated with the French government an arrangement whereby the French government deposited $6,000,000 with the Morgans' Paris house, Morgan, Harjes & Co., and simultaneously the Morgan firm credited a like amount to the French ambassador in the United States. This transfer permitted the French to make necessary purchases in this country and at the same time provided funds for the aid of Americans stranded in Europe by the outbreak of the war.[2]

In the midst of all this turmoil, Jack's sister Anne Morgan sent one of the most irrelevant cablegrams on record, "Atmosphere most thrilling."[3]

Events moved with great rapidity. Before another week went by, private interests in France asked the Morgan firm to consider floating a $100,000,000 loan for the French republic. The firm promptly asked the U.S. State Department if the administration had any objections to their making such a loan. The State Department ignored the Morgan inquiry, but in response to a similar question from the Swiss government, Secretary William Jennings Bryan declared loans by American bankers to any foreign nation at war to be inconsistent with the true spirit of neutrality.[4]

New York City Financial Crisis

An early result of the international financial uncertainty was the threat to the solvency of New York City. In 1914, the city borrowed operating funds in anticipation of tax collections. To realize more favorable terms, New York borrowed abroad and therefore had a short-term debt payable in pounds and francs at a time when those currencies became scarce. There was talk of defaulting, but J. P. Morgan and H. P. Davison intervened personally, invited Kuhn, Loeb & Co. to go along with them, and were able to enlist the support of almost all the banks in New York to float a note issue and to accumulate adequate gold supplies to rescue the city's credit. For their efforts as syndicate managers, the Morgan and the Kuhn, Loeb firms charged no fee.[5]

1915

There were two principal areas in which the Morgan firm was able to come to the aid of the Allies, one was in supplying money, the other—unexpectedly for a bank—was in supplying the actual materials of combat.

The British Commercial Agency Agreement

The Allies needed access to American industrial and agricultural production, and access included money with which to buy those products. Any idea of a direct loan was shelved (as has been seen) because of the neutrality policy of the Wilson Administration. The two remaining sources of Allied funds for purchases in the United States were gold shipments and the sale of American securities owned by investors in the Allied nations.

Before the time seemed ripe to reopen the issue of loans, however, the Morgan partners became interested in facilitating the flow of supplies from the United States to Britain and her allies. On November 26, 1914, at Morgan's request, H. P. Davison left for Britain to discuss with the government the whole question of aid to the Allies.[6] The result of Davison's conversations with Prime Minister Herbert Asquith and Munitions Minister David Lloyd George was that on January 15, 1915, the British Commercial Agency Agreement was signed, under which J. P. Morgan & Co. became the purchasing agents for Great Britain in the buying of war supplies in the United States. Later, a similar agreement was worked out with France.

Directed by the organizing genius of E. R. Stettinius, Sr., the Export Department of J. P. Morgan & Co. was created, and for two and a half years it supplied an increasing volume of war supplies for the Allies.[7]

The term "military-industrial complex" became popular in the

United States following its use by Dwight D. Eisenhower in a public address at the end of World War II. Unfortunately for subsequent American military preparedness, Eisenhower gave it a prejudicial connotation by seeming to suggest some sort of conspiracy between the Pentagon and big business, possibly for unnecessary arms purchases. Actually, the expression has validity as a factual description of the need of the military for matériel and the problems of securing supplies from civilian manufacturing concerns. At the time of the Morgan agency agreement, sources of equipment to supply the military were very limited. J. P. Morgan & Co.—acting through Stettinius in developing sources of armaments for the Allies from unenthusiastic and reluctant American industrialists—created the military-industrial complex in this country almost unaided. Following the close of the war and until the very end of his life, Morgan might be loosely referred to as a continuing participant in this complex, as a member of both the board of directors and the finance committee of the United States Steel Corporation, but it is difficult to attach any particular significance to this fact.

Allied Credits

During Davison's meetings with the British officials in December 1914 that led to the signing of the Agency Agreement, the subject of loans had come up. Davison was in no position to commit the firm, but he was encouraging to both the British and the French government officials.[8] The firm agreed to set up a $12,000,000 credit in New York, against which the Russian government could draw in making purchases. Morgan—at the American end of the negotiations—had to be down in Washington on January 18 to preside at a meeting of the Advisory Board of the Federal Reserve Board, and he was able to have a fifteen-minute talk with President Wilson to seek official sanction for the Russian credit. This was a very significant meeting and may have marked the reversal of the administration's position on neutrality.[9]

Following the meeting with Wilson, Morgan went on holiday to Jekyl Island, Georgia, faced the Industrial Relations Committee,[10] and then in mid-March sailed for Europe to clarify the agency arrangement with England and to discuss a French loan. In England, he talked with the leading political, military, and business leaders: Sir Edward Grey, Winston Churchill, Lord Kitchener, Lloyd George, Montagu Norman, Governor Cunliffe of the Bank of England, H. H. Asquith, and Walter Runciman, President of the Board of Trade.[11] The following month, in April 1915, J. P. Morgan & Co. issued a one-year loan of $30,000,000 for the French republic.[12]

Upon his return to the United States in May, Morgan resumed his customary methodical routine of board and committee meetings, punctuated by brief, relaxing changes of scene.

Morgan's life followed a series of slowly shifting patterns. The day usually began with a visit to the Pierpont Morgan Library next door. There followed meetings with the partners. Afternoons usually found him at a board meeting or committee meeting of one or more of his charitable or public-interest organizations or business corporations.

In mid-May, the family regularly moved out to Matinicock Point at Glen Cove, Long Island, and Morgan commuted to Wall Street by automobile or steam launch until time for the summer visit to Britain. In late November, the family moved back to town to 231 Madison Avenue, southeast corner of Thirty-seventh Street. From time to time, Morgan would take a brief holiday from the office and shoot quail at Climax, North Carolina, or play indifferent golf at the Jekyl Island Club in Georgia, or loaf at Camp Uncas in the Adirondacks in upstate New York.

In the years between the wars, his schedule included a long annual stay in Britain divided between Wall Hall in Hertfordshire and Gannochy in Scotland for the grouse shooting. The return to New York took place later and later in the fall as Morgan became less and less involved with the management of the firm.[13]

Although the war itself was running against the Allies, American public opinion in the spring of 1915, while generally pro-Ally, was not greatly aroused. During the week of Morgan's departure, the newspaper-reading public had been titillated by such items of absorbing interest as the reopening of the case of Harry K. Thaw, who had shot and killed the architect Stanford White over an affair involving Mrs. Evelyn Nesbit Thaw that had taken place long before she became Mrs. Thaw, as well as the prospect of another farewell tour by French actress Sarah Bernhardt, who had recently had one leg amputated.[14] Even at the offices of J. P. Morgan & Co., domestic business continued to dominate the firm's concerns. They were the syndicate managers of a group of railroad bond and note issues that included $10,000,000 Erie one-year 5 percent notes; $27,000,000 New Haven one-year 5 percent collateral gold notes; and the largest corporate securities offering yet made in this country, the $100,000,000 New York Central 20-year 6 percent convertible-debenture bond issue.[15]

The American public was shocked out of its inward preoccupation by the news that on May 7 a German naval submarine had torpedoed and sunk without warning the British passenger liner *Lusitania* off the Irish coast, with the loss of 1,198 lives—more than 100 of them American.

By this time, the rate of gold shipments from Britain and British possessions was increasing and so was the conversion of Allied-held American securities. This last made it possible in June for J. P. Morgan & Co. to arrange a loan of more than $30,000,000 to the Rothschild banking firm of Paris, the proceeds to be made available to the French government for purchases in the United States. The loan was secured by Pennsylvania Railroad and Chicago, Milwaukee and St. Paul bonds exchanged by private French owners for French war bonds.[16]

This was a week filled with large headlines in the papers. There was a great clamor in the British House of Commons about the agency agreement with the Morgan firm.[17] Nearer home, Samuel Untermyer was advocating legislation to restrain the power of the New York Stock Exchange with shrill denunciations of "the carnival—I would almost say orgy—of corruption and swindling that has marked its history."[18]

Morgan made his statement about the Rothschild loan on Tuesday, June 22, and left for Boston for the Harvard commencement the following day. The day after that he was at New London on *Corsair*, to attend, as was his yearly custom, the Harvard-Yale boat races.[19] Upon his return to the city, Morgan plunged into the affairs of the Murray Hill Association, of which he was the newly elected president. This group of property owners in the area comprising approximately the area of Madison and Park avenues between East Thirty-fourth and East Thirty-eighth Streets was to fight a losing battle over the next fifteen-odd years to preserve the residential character of the neighborhood, which theoretically had been assured by a restriction in 1847.[20] Commercial building encroached steadily, while the association lost in the courts and with the Board of Estimate to real-estate interests marching—in the words of architecture-critic Lewis Mumford in another context— under "the soiled banner of progress." Morgan himself gave the coup de grace to the residential flavor of his own block in 1927 with the building of the Pierpont Morgan Library Annex. But the Morgan garden remained and was a source of pleasure to passersby, including Arthur Guiterman, the writer of light verse, who published a few years later in *The New Yorker* this pleasant appreciation:

LETTER TO MR. MORGAN

Dear Mr. Morgan: Sir, I beg your pardon,
But I must thank you for your lovely garden
That so delights me (walking toward Eleventh Street),
On Madison near Thirty-seventh Street.
Remember, I don't covet it one particle;
What could I do with such a costly article?
Besides, as possibly some other few do,
I get more out of it, I think, than you do.
I'd never steal it, should some chance abet me
And your nice-looking private sleuths should let me,
For how could I preserve it, green and pretty,
An ornament to our barbaric city
With sculptured seats from Florence, Rome, or Venice?
I greatly fear I'd use the space for tennis
Instead of making it my bounden duty
To have it kept a little plot of beauty
By some accomplished landscape chiropractor
As you do. You're a public benefactor;
And that is why I write to you to say
Your crocuses were up St. Patrick's Day.
Don't thank me, Sir! I saw them all aglow,
And sort of thought that you would like to know.
                                        Arthur Guiterman[21]

Morgan was charmed by the thought and wrote Guiterman a graceful response.

The climax of an eventful week was reached on Saturday. On July 3, 1915, a mentally deranged German sympathizer made a murderous attack on J. P. Morgan and narrowly missed killing him with two pistol shots in the lower abdomen.[22]

From the very outset of World War I, Morgan was strongly pro-Ally and particularly pro-British. From what we have seen of his life in Britain and his many ties with that country, this was not remarkable. He was, in effect, an Anglo-American and frequently spoke his mind on the subject. He wrote from London to James Stillman of the National City Bank: "Of course everyone who counts at all in New York is doing his best to show his sympathy with the allied cause, and to give it every assistance in his power. I hope that the people over here realize that there is no likeness between the official attitude of our Government and the state of mind of individual citizens. Certainly we are all trying to show them so."[23]

The Morgan assassination attempt proved to be only one part of a larger conspiracy intended to hamper American aid to the Allies. The assailant, "Frank Holt" of the Cornell University German Department, turned out to be Erich Muenter, a former Harvard instructor who had disappeared from Cambridge after having been indicted for poisoning his wife in 1906. Following the Morgan episode, evidence was produced to connect Muenter with the dynamiting of the Capitol in Washington on July 2 and with the explosion and fire at sea in July on board the steamer *Minnehaha*, which was carrying munitions to the Allies. Muenter, alias Holt, committed suicide in the Nassau County Jail, Mineola, New York, on July 6.[24]

Morgan was very modest about the murderous attempt on his life. He wrote to a French well-wisher, "I am ashamed to be included among 'les blessés de la guerre' as my wounds were very slight and promptly healed." To his friend Owen Wister, the writer, he wrote with some understatement, "the experience was a very disagreeable one."[25] The attack was the overt expression of a hostility that had produced a flood of threatening letters from German sympathizers, but it aroused considerable sympathy and good will for him. The crowd that gathered outside 23 Wall Street at half-past four to see Morgan get into his limousine at the close of his first day back at work applauded him as he left the building and hurried across the sidewalk to the curb.[26]

Following the attack, a system of guarding Morgan by relays of armed bodyguards, all former marines, was organized to look after him and his family while they were in the United States. This protection continued the rest of his life, and the detailed account of his whereabouts at any given time that is to be found in the Secretary's Diary volumes is explained in part by the logistic demands of this guarding.[27]

The Anglo-French Loan of 1915
The loans and credits granted to the Allies up to this time were merely preliminaries to the $500,000,000 Anglo-French, five-year

5 percent external loan of 1915, which had underlain the conversations between Morgan and Davison and the British and French government officials for so many months. The loan was issued on October 14, 1915, but it was preceded by a month of negotiation between the British commission, headed by Lord Reading, Lord Chief Justice, and the Morgan firm, represented by Morgan, H. P. Davison, and T. W. Lamont.[28]

In the course of the negotiations, the Morgan partners conferred with the principal bankers of the United States. At length, on September 25, it was agreed that J. P. Morgan & Co. would try to form a syndicate to underwrite the $500,000,000 bond issue. The British and French governments were jointly committed to repay the bonds, which bore interest at 5 percent and matured in five years—at which time they were convertible to longer-term 4½ percent bonds. The underwriters were given a two-point spread: the issue was bought at 96 and was sold to the public at 98.[29] The greatest tasks were lining up the syndicate and distributing this enormous issue. Morgan had just returned from a fortnight's vacation when he was stricken with appendicitis, and he underwent surgery on Wednesday, October 17, 1915. He was back at his office on December 2.[30]

Meanwhile, the investment banking business of J. P. Morgan & Co. continued active. The firm bought $10,000,000 in Santa Fe railroad preferred stock on November 26 for resale and took up $20,000,000 additional Interborough Rapid Transit first and refunding 5 percent bonds of the 1913 mortgage. A few days later they bought $2,000,000 in New Haven equipment trust certificates. In the closing days of 1915, it was announced that the Erie Railroad would issue a new series of convertible bonds between $15,000,000 and $20,000,000 and the Morgan firm would head the underwriting syndicate.[31]

Morgan picked up where he had left off in his regular attendance at company and institution meetings. This time he added a new responsibility, one to which he was earnestly devoted: the Church Pension Fund to provide income for retired Episcopal clergymen.[32]

1916

In mid-January 1916, Morgan spent a fortnight shooting at Climax Lodge, North Carolina. He returned to New York on the twenty-third, went the next day to the Morgan Library, and dined that evening with Joseph Choate at his home at 8 East Sixty-third Street. On the twenty-fifth, there were United States Steel Corporation meetings lasting almost all day long, culminating in the resumption of dividend payments at the rate of 5 percent.

He was abroad all of February and the greater part of March—most of the time in Britain clarifying the agency agreement, although he spent a few days in Paris—and was back in New York on March 19.[33]

Interborough Rapid Transit Company: Thompson Committee Hearings

A recurring theme in the financial and political history of New York City has long been the subway system. The Interborough Rapid Transit Company was financed by August Belmont & Co. in 1901; J. P. Morgan & Co. participated in subsequent financing.[34]

In 1915 the Thompson Legislative Committee was set up to investigate charges of impropriety in the granting of contracts for the extension of New York subway lines.[35] Morgan testified at length on June 15, 1916, and again on June 19 that he knew of no wrongdoing in the management of the Interborough. He told why he had got into subway financing in the first place: "The only reason I bothered with the matter at such a tremendous expense of time and trouble was because I wanted to see the city get the subways." When interrogated about J. P. Morgan & Co.'s $250,000 charge, he explained that this was for keeping in readiness for more than a year the sum needed for financing the Interborough, an amount that reached $105,000,000. The other charge of a quarter of a million dollars was for personal services of the Morgan firm in holding daily conferences with Interborough officials advising them on their contracts and negotiations. Morgan was asked, "Do you mean to say that you charged $250,000 merely for conversations?" "Yes sir, and well worth it too," he replied.[36]

French and British Loans

The Morgan firm and Brown Bros. & Co. worked out an arrangment—announced on July 13, 1916, but reported, appropriately, in the press on the fourteenth of July—for a loan to France of about $100,000,000. The lending syndicate issued $94,500,000 in three-year 5 percent gold notes, due August 1, 1919. Collateral to secure the loan consisted largely of securities of neutral countries held by a company formed for the purpose: American Foreign Securities Company, Robert Bacon, former American ambassador to France, president.[37]

On September 1, 1916, J. P. Morgan & Co. headed a syndicate that issued $250,000,000 United Kingdom of Great Britain and Ireland two-year 5 percent gold notes, due September 1, 1918. Unlike the larger Anglo-French loan of 1915, this issue was backed by American securities.[38] On October 25, another loan to Britain was announced. J. P. Morgan & Co. offered $300,000,000 in secured gold notes dated November 1, 1916.

On November 25 it was announced that the American Telephone & Telegraph Company had sold $80,000,000 in collateral trust 5 percent bonds to J. P. Morgan & Co., which was putting together a syndicate to market them.[39]

A footnote to history: On November 21, 1916, the Austrian Emperor Francis Joseph II (1830–1916) died. His nephew's assassination had precipitated the war.

1917

The announcement that Thomas Cochran would resign the presidency of the Liberty National Bank to become a partner of J. P. Morgan & Co. on January 1, 1917, caused the list of partners to be published. They were Morgan, "head of the firm"; Edward T. Stotesbury of Philadelphia; Charles Steele, "of uncertain health"; Henry P. Davison, "the closest associate of the late Mr. Morgan and of the present head of the house"; William Pierson Hamilton, William H. Porter—"away for five months recovering from a breakdown due to overwork, but . . . expected to resume his old duties in a few days"; Thomas W. Lamont; D. W. Morrow; Edward R. Stettinius; Arthur E. Newbold; and Horatio G. Lloyd.[40] It was noted that in the general moving up, Cochran would take the desk vacated by T. W. Lamont, who would move into the inner office with the senior partners, Morgan, Steele, and Davison. In addition, each partner had a private office on the second floor of 23 Wall Street.[41]

Morgan's first announced benefaction during 1917 was a gift of $150,000 to the million-dollar endowment drive of Trinity College, Hartford, of which he was a trustee. A month later it was announced that Morgan had agreed to help the American Academy in Rome by canceling a dollar of the mortgage he held on their property for every dollar they took in from their forthcoming endowment campaign. That mortgage was an inheritance from the elder Morgan, who had advanced money to the academy. Ten days later, Morgan gave $50,000 to the Wadsworth Athenaeum in Hartford, together with title to the collection of decorative arts from the Morgan, Sr., estate already on loan to that museum.[42]

On January 17, J. P. Morgan & Co., the syndicate managers, announced the issue of the $250,000,000 British secured-loan 5½ percent convertible gold notes to be dated February 1, 1917—$100,000,000 with a one-year maturity, the balance in two-year notes.[43] France had hoped to borrow from American investors, too, but the market decline following the German memorandum of January 31, 1917, announcing unrestricted submarine warfare was so great that it would have been impossible to sell the securities. The market improved during February and was helped greatly by the Federal Reserve Board statement on March 8 modifying its earlier position on the purchase of the securities of belligerents. Accordingly, the Morgan firm announced the formation of a syndicate to handle the $100,000,000 Government of the French Republic two-year 5½ percent secured-loan convertible gold notes, dated April 1, 1917, and on March 21 listed the collateral.[44] This was the last of the great war loans negotiated and managed by J. P. Morgan & Co. During the remainder of the war, however, the firm issued ninety-day British Treasury bills almost weekly.

In March 1917, Morgan took out the largest life-insurance policy ever written. It was for two and a half million dollars and was designed to offset the anticipated drain of death duties on his estate.[45]

As tensions between the United States and Germany increased, Morgan made two moves to help the country's preparedness effort. In company with a number of other supporters of the Naval Reserve Committee on Enrollment of Yachts, he offered the *Corsair* as a naval auxiliary to the United States Navy Department in the event of war.[46] This was the third of four steam yachts to bear the name *Corsair* (*Corsair*, 1881–91; *Corsair II*, 1891–98; *Corsair III*, 1899–1930; *Corsair IV*, 1930–40), and in the four years since he had inherited it from his father, he had got very little use from it.

When Congress failed to appropriate funds to meet the United States Army payroll in 1877, it was the elder Morgan who had lent the money to the War Department to tide them over; so in March 1917, forty years later, when Congress did not appropriate money to continue the buying of supplies for the army on the eve of inevitable war, the younger Morgan agreed to advance a million dollars without interest to enable the depot quartermaster at New York to contract and pay for urgently needed supplies. Before the money was advanced, however, the Federal Reserve Board stepped in and relieved the situation.[47]

The United States at War

On April 6, 1917, the president signed a formal declaration of war with Germany, following a vote of both houses of Congress. Morgan wrote to an English friend: "Of course, I personally am still much ashamed that America is so late in the fight, which is the only slight cloud on my joy in really being in it at last."[48]

The financing and the supplying of the Allies were most properly taken over by the United States government, now committed to the support of its allies in a joint effort to defeat the Central Powers. A headline on page one of the *New York Times* of May 4, 1917, reads, in part: "ALLIES TO BUY THROUGH WASHINGTON, TO HANDLE MONEY ALSO: government thus will displace J. P. Morgan in both activities."

The anti-business bias of the Wilson Administration prevented it from taking advantage of the great experience and the technical competence and organization of the Export Department of J. P. Morgan & Co. which under Stettinius's direction had supplied England and France with the materials of war so effectively since early in 1915. This same prejudice made it very difficult for Morgan people to find jobs of real importance in war work.

Morgan accepted the situation without bitterness. He offered his services to Wilson and made every effort to be useful in the prosecution of the war.[49] In April, he conferred with the Treasury Department on the issuing of United States war bonds.[50] To Morgan's daily schedule there were now added meetings of Red Cross and Liberty Bond and French War Orphans committees.[51]

In the midst of all the pressures and major events, Morgan maintained the personal touch. He congratulated Waldorf Astor on the birth of a son in April 1917. Morgan was present on the evening of Thursday, April 19, 1917, at a special meeting of the New York Yacht Club. The purpose of the meeting was the striking from the club's membership roll of the names of Wilhelm II, the German emperor, and his son, the crown prince—a petty gesture![52]

When the United States entered the war in 1917, the Morgan firm urged the Allies to abandon the agency agreement and deal directly with the United States government for munitions supply. The Balfour Commission, sent over by the British government to negotiate supply and related matters, ignored the years of efficient service by the Morgan firm in providing material and loans and snubbed the Morgans. Morgan was furious at the implication conveyed to the public that Britain was dumping the Morgans because they had been prodigal or dishonest. He cabled the London office and asked that Prime Minister Lloyd George be requested to do something about his people. The London office cabled back the following day that any ignoring was unintentional; the mission had taken their cue from the anti–Wall Street Wilson Administration. After a few weeks, Morgan could cable back: "Our relations with British Mission were most cordial and satisfactory. Change seemed to come about immediately after our cables to you."[53]

The war was coming closer to the family circle. H. P. Davison's two sons in the Naval Aviation Group had serious plane mishaps in the summer of 1917. Junius was in the navy receiving special training at Annapolis, and Morgan's daughter Frances's husband, Paul Pennoyer, was admitted to officer candidates' school at Plattsburgh, New York.[54]

Morgan's reflections on Germany and the peace of Europe are worth recording in the light of later events. In the summer of 1917 he wrote: "Thank Heaven everyone seems to see that peace without reasonable security will be useless and that the only way such security can be had is by thoroughly licking Germany and the German people till they won't want to try it again. Even then it may be necessary to lick them again five or less years from now if they show signs of gathering themselves together for another attack on the civilized world."[55]

The imminent collapse of Russia disturbed Morgan very much. He believed that the only solution would be a temporary dictatorship in the hands of someone who would "not be too much affected by scruples about coercion."[56]

Morgan partners were active in promoting bond sales. In the first big Liberty Loan campaign of early June 1917, the firm subscribed $50,000,000. Morgan was present at the loan rally on the floor of the New York Stock Exchange; he had long held a seat on the Exchange, but nobody remembered his ever having been present before.[57]

Morgan commuted between his house on Long Island and his office in lower Manhattan on his fast, new, Herreshoff-built power cruiser *Navette*. The Navy had accepted the offer of *Corsair*, which was converted to a submarine chaser and was on duty in the Atlantic. At his office, he was kept busy running the banking business. The Morgan firm organized a syndicate that submitted the winning bid to take the entire offering of $55,000,000 worth of New York City bonds at the controller's sale on July 12. Other issues in which they participated that summer and fall included the $100,000,000 Dominion of Canada two-year 5 percent gold notes; the $15,000,000 General Electric Co. three-year 6 percent gold notes; the $15,000,000 Chicago & Western Indiana Railroad one-year 6 percent collateral gold notes; the $15,000,000 New York Central two-year 5 percent notes, and the $14,500,000 New York City revenue bills.[58]

While J. P. Morgan and his associates were employing great energy and administrative and financial skills toward aiding Britain and France and their allies, the gloomy fact was that the Central Powers were winning the war. Matters did not improve for the Allies in 1917. America's entry in April gave a lift to morale, but that was an intangible offset to failures on the western front in Champagne and at Ypres, the defeat and defection of Russia, and the Italian rout at Caporetto. There was improvement in coping with the submarine danger, and a few victories were won far from the main theatre of war, in the Near East and Africa, but the outlook was not bright for the Allies.

1918

In 1918, Morgan continued conscientiously to do his part, directly and indirectly, to help the war effort by contributing to the strength of the economy, supporting government regulations and fiscal measures, and directing the firm in the sale of short-term British treasury notes, as well as in countless other ways.

The securities underwriting business of J. P. Morgan & Co. got off to a promising start in the first week of 1918 with an offering of $40,000,000 American Telephone and Telegraph Co. one-year 6 percent notes by the syndicate that the firm headed. This was a preliminary to the telephone company's $50,000,000 seven-year 6 percent convertible gold bonds sold during the summer.[59]

On Sunday, January 13, Mr. and Mrs. Morgan gave a luncheon for seventeen at 231 Madison Avenue for the duke of Devonshire, who was the governor general of Canada. In addition to members of the Morgan family and the duke's aides, others present included Wilson intimate Col. E. M. House, Senator Elihu Root, Morgan partners T. W. Lamont and Charles Steele, Henry Clay Frick, Columbia University President Nicholas Murray Butler, C. A. Coffin of General Electric, and Ambassador Myron T. Herrick.[60]

In the midst of all these activities, Morgan did not neglect the cause of scholarship and historic preservation. In March, he and Archer M. Huntington, of the transcontinental railroad fortune, financed the American Museum of Natural History archaeological exploration of Aztec ruins in New Mexico.[61]

A major factor in winning the war was the food supply. In the spring of 1918, the Montana Farming Corporation was organized, with Morgan serving as a director, to undertake the cultivation of a great tract of arable land on four Indian reservations in the north-central states.[62] The attempt at large-scale, mechanized agriculture in Montana failed in three years. Morgan wrote to the organizer, T. D. Campbell, in 1921, "Hard luck all around."[63]

A fortnight after the announcement of his participation in the wheat-growing company, Morgan received his first honorary degree, the LL.D. from Trinity College, Hartford. Former President Theodore Roosevelt received the Doctor of Science degree at the same time.[64] The following January, when Morgan learned of Roosevelt's death, his conventional obituary statement was: "He would have been a great man had he been able to construct—or turn his mind to construction when the tearing down had served his turn. Also had he been less egotistical and able to allow others to work when in his company. He was certainly in some ways a man of genius—and geniuses are difficult contemporaries!" His private, off-the-record comment was, "At last! The Lord and I see eye to eye!"[65]

The fall of 1918 found the tide of war turning toward an Allied victory. Morgan was able to write, "It's such a pleasant thought that the Germans are just beginning to get the dose of the medicine they have been serving out for the past four years."[66]

The fourth Liberty Loan campaign opened in October. Morgan

was active in the drive as a member of the blue-ribbon New York Stock Exchange Fourth Liberty Loan Committee, along with such well-known figures as B. H. Borden, James C. Colgate, Henry Clay Frick, Gates W. McGarrah, Seward Prosser, Jacob H. Schiff, Benjamin Strong, and Frank A. Vanderlip.[67]

The End of the War

The war officially ended on November 11, 1918.

Morgan cabled congratulations to King George V, ending with "God Save the King!" To this, the British monarch replied "Glorious victory to which your great country has so materially contributed."[68]

Shortly after the armistice, Morgan took a two-week vacation at Climax Lodge, North Carolina, followed almost immediately by another bird-shooting visit to Gardiners Island as the guest of Clarence Mackay.[69] With the strains of war eased, Morgan set about returning to normal living. He ordered a new suit of sails for *Grayling*.[70] He began to agitate for the return of *Corsair*.[71] At the annual meeting of the New York Yacht Club on the evening of December 19, he was elected commodore to replace George F. Baker, Jr. Upon its return, *Corsair* became flagship of the club squadron.[72]

To wind up the year 1918, Mrs. Morgan planned a gala Christmas party for December 27, with champagne from Louis Sherry.[73]

CHAPTER VII

The Postwar Years
1919–23

1919

THE MORGANS SAILED FOR ENGLAND ON THE *Mauretania* IN THE first week of 1919. The vessel was described as looking "tired" after four years as a troop transport. Morgan read Strachey's *Eminent Victorians*, a bon-voyage present from his mother, on the way over as a change from his usual shipboard diet of detective stories.[1]

It was a sad visit. Word reached Morgan of the death of his niece Betty Hamilton when he was "in the midst of mourners." He explained, "Everyone has lost their dear ones what between the war and this pestilence of influenza. Everyone tries to go about and do the work that has to be done and take up life again but the shadows will remain of course for years. . . . Everyone here is feeling the strain and curious let downness of changing from a War to a Peace basis of living."[2]

He also observed, "It's wonderful to see how the dancing craze has struck London—like New York some years ago. Elderly men on their way home from the City stop somewhere and have a few turns—and the young people dance as if it were the chief joy of life."[3]

While Morgan was abroad, he was promoted to the rank of commander in the Legion of Honor in company with his partner Henry P. Davison and Herbert Hoover. On this same visit, he discovered that Maurice Bosdari, who was in prison for having forged the elder Morgan's name to some bills of exchange, was elderly and ill, so he wrote to Edward Shortt, the British Home Secretary, and asked that Bosdari be released.[4]

In late January, Morgan was rotated off the advisory council for the Federal Reserve Board after having served a four-year term. He had attended the monthly meetings in Washington with the same conscientiousness that he went up to Boston every month for the meetings of the Harvard Overseers.[5]

A close associate of the Morgan firm during the Allied munitions-purchasing days had been Rear Admiral Sir Guy Gaunt. Morgan learned that now that the war was over, Gaunt had left the navy and turned to farming in England. Morgan offered to lend him up to £4,000 to get started.[6]

As an expression of British appreciation of American wartime help, the Goldsmiths' Company of London voted to give Morgan the "honorary freedom and livery" of the Company. He felt greatly honored, particularly since they were "in . . . our sort of business." The only two other honorary members were King George V and Foreign Secretary Arthur Balfour.[7] The drawback was that he had to give a brief talk. He wrote, "I am still suffering from having to make a speech on next Wednesday—ridiculous nonsense to feel that way about it!" Morgan expressed his appreciation of the honor by sending an Elizabethan gold salt to the company.[8]

Morgan was not happy about the state of the Paris house, particularly since the new move to the Place Vendôme, across from the Ritz Hotel. He told Herman Harjes that Edward R. Stettinius would be coming over to advise the office. Stettinius wanted to make drastic changes. He was supported by Lamont.[9] Stettinius was convinced that the French office under the direction of Herman Harjes and J. Ridgeley (Jack) Carter was slack and needed reorganizing. He thought that Morgan felt the same way, and Morgan seems not to have disabused him of that belief. But when he tried to do something about tightening up the procedures of the Paris office and establishing a closer connection between it and the home office at 23 Wall Street, he encountered hostility and passive resistance in Paris and received not only no support but even opposition from J. P. Morgan. He felt that he had been let down.[10]

We get more than a hint of Morgan's temperament and how his changing moods could affect the entire emotional climate of the firm from a single revealing passage from a letter Stettinius wrote

to H. P. Davison in 1921, when Davison was dying at Magnolia
Plantation in southern Georgia:

> I want to tell you how happy I have been since you had a
> visit from Jack. When I heard that he was going down to see
> you, I was a little apprehensive, not because I feared that any-
> thing unpleasant would develop, but only because I feared
> that you might be apprehensive yourself. I am delighted that
> the visit was a source of pleasure to you both. He is, as you
> yourself saw, in the finest possible form, and when I say that
> he is and has been himself, I am saying everything that I can
> say by way of making clear that everything and everybody
> here has been, and is, happy and contented.[11]

Late in February, pending T. W. Lamont's return from the Paris
Peace Conference, J. P. Morgan became temporary chairman of
an international committee of American, British, and French
representatives to protect holders of Mexican securities and explore the entire problem of Mexico's national debt and capital
requirements.[12]

Morgan had gone abroad in early January. He returned on February 28 on the *Aquitania*, along with 5,000 returning American
soldiers. When reporters asked Morgan what the outlook for
American business in Europe was, he observed that it would be
prudent to see if there were any money to pay for orders before
accepting them.[13]

Morgan wrote to employees of J. P. Morgan & Co. in the armed
services and war work offering to help them be demobilized so
they could return to work as soon as possible.[14]

The flooding of the labor market with returning servicemen put
added strains on the United States Employment Service just at
the time when Congress failed to appropriate money to operate it.
J. P. Morgan & Co., veteran observers of a long series of congressional blunders, once again came to the rescue and advanced
$100,000, with the observation that they would like to be repaid,
but realized that there were no guarantees. Congress specifically
excluded reimbursement to the Morgan firm in the next appropri-
ations measure.[15] Morgan then declined to renew the credit to the
Employment Service.

The postwar demands of the banking business were numerous
and varied. The Morgan firm was engaged in January 1919 in
organizing a syndicate to convert $150,000,000 of British 5½ per-

cent notes to twenty-year 5½ percent bonds. Of the original $250,000,000 issue, $100,000,000 had been paid off by February 1, 1918.[16] In February 1919, the firm offered to sell something over $28,000,000 worth of bonds of that same British issue not reserved for conversion. Between these two announcements, the firm stated that on April 1 they would redeem the French 5½ percent notes due that day.[17]

In April of 1919 began the long, drawn-out, and discouraging attempt by Morgan to do a generous thing for the United States. He offered his father's London house at Princes Gate for use as a residence for the American ambassador to Britain. He first consulted Senator Henry Cabot Lodge as to the proper approach, then made the formal offer on May 24.[18] He pointed out that the house, the London home of his grandfather, Junius Spencer Morgan, and his father, was suitable for a residence, but not big enough to serve as embassy as well. Nobody in official Washington had the courtesy to reply to this offer.[19]

Finally, after two years of prodding, the Senate Foreign Relations Committee on January 20, 1921, authorized its chairman, Henry Cabot Lodge, to draft a Senate resolution accepting the house at Princes Gate. The House Foreign Affairs Committee reported the measure favorably, but not unanimously, to the House, which passed it as an amendment to the Diplomatic and Consular Appropriation Bill on January 29. More important as a policy matter was the appropriating in the same bill of $150,000 to buy an embassy in Paris.[20] Morgan had shamed the Congress into recognizing the United States's new role as a world power.

Flushed with the success of the Russian Revolution, radicals elsewhere in the world made a special effort to cause disturbances on May Day 1919. More than twenty prominent Americans were singled out to receive identical bombs through the mail on that day. J. P. Morgan found himself in the company of such diverse individuals as Supreme Court Justice Oliver Wendell Holmes, John D. Rockefeller, Mayor John F. Hylan of New York, Judge Kenesaw Mountain Landis. Most of the bombs, which had all originated in New York, were intercepted in the mails by post office authorities.[21]

The fifth and final Liberty bond ("Victory Loan") issue was on May 20, 1919. Morgan was active in preparation for floating the issue.[22]

Headline-seeking by politicians began again at the national level and with the usual rhetoric in early June 1919. On June 9, members of the Senate Foreign Relations Committee, inspired by their chairman, William E. Borah of Idaho, allowed themselves to become upset about the proliferation of copies of the supposedly secret text of the peace treaty with Germany. Senator Borah muttered darkly about "great international bankers from New York." Morgan was called upon to testify; he made it clear that he had not seen a copy of the treaty. In response to questioning, he stressed the need for the American banking community to help the war-ravaged nations to get on their feet economically: "America can only sell to Europe if they can get paid for what they sell, and that payment has got to be arranged for until they begin to produce. There has got to be a time arranged for between the time they begin to produce and the time they begin to send goods over here. That has got to be arranged with the banking interests all over the country."[23]

After school was out in June of 1919, Morgan took his son Harry with two young friends for two days sailing on *Grayling* on Long Island Sound, "a very jolly and harmonious party." Unseasonable fog and rain set in after two good days, so the cruise was given up.[24]

There was some postwar confusion around the Morgan office, but by June, Morgan could say that business was "not quite as mixed up as it was for a time after Davison's return [from heading the American Red Cross]. It's a very great comfort to have Lamont back too [from the Paris Peace Conference] and we are now pretty well manned again, and I can plan to be away with a fairly easy mind."[25]

We saw that after his return to the United States from his long tour of duty at the London office, Morgan had regularly gone to England and Scotland in the late summer, before the war. He resumed this schedule in 1919, now that the war was over.

The summer of 1919 was a time of world-wide labor unrest. Morgan's August crossing on the *Lapland* was delayed by strikes in Britain, and a wave of strikes—including the New York subways—plagued this country. Morgan's comment was, "I am sorry for the families of the working people whose providers are misled into foolish actions by a lot of demagogues."[26] A nation-wide strike of steelworkers took place in late September, and there was some violence. The chief issue was union membership. Judge Elbert H. Gary, chairman of the board of the United States Steel

Corporation, had introduced into the industry improved working conditions, profit-sharing, and shorter hours, but had held firm to the idea that union membership should be optional, not mandatory, for the company's employees. He resisted the union demands for a closed shop. Morgan, long a director of the corporation, cabled Gary from London on September 22, the day the strike was called: "Heartiest congratulations on your stand for the open shop, with which I am, as you know, absolutely in accord. I believe American principles of liberty deeply involved and must win if we all stand firm."[27] He was gratified by Governor Calvin Coolidge's putting down of the Boston police strike.[28]

In October 1919, the Morgans went to Paris for a fortnight. Morgan reported to his mother on his meeting with his youngest sister, Anne. He and Anne had very little in common. She was a dedicated Francophile and spent most of her life in Paris. He found her nervous tension and rapid pace quite tiring and warned their mother: "Be sure you don't let yourself be put out of your way by her—it won't do for you and you must not risk it."[29]

From Paris in 1919, Morgan wrote, "I also had the great honor of being given 5 minutes of his very precious time by Clemenceau and that was perfectly delightful. Certain things about him such as the feeling of vigor and aliveness and being entirely attentive reminded me rather of Father which was extremely pleasant."[30]

There was work to be done at the office, but the Morgans managed to get off on a visit to the battlefields and to Lille and Bruges. On Friday, October 24, they lunched with the Herman Harjeses and there met Marshal Pétain and his aide, Colonel Duchesne. Morgan said of Pétain, "His chief charm was a sort of gentle quiet humor which I could understand and be amused by all the time. His most gentle and civil way of teasing Mrs. Harjes who is a great friend of his and whose cantines have helped him considerably was most charming."[31]

The following week, Morgan received an honorary degree from Cambridge University. The Morgan party went up from London in a special director's car provided by the Great Eastern Railway. On arrival, they were driven to Emmanuel College, whose master, Dr. Giles, was vice-chancellor of the university. They were met by a group of thirty or forty people. Morgan wrote: "After lunch we were walked or carted off to the Senate House where there were some quaint ceremonies and we stood one after another before the V. Chancellor, who, after the public orator railed a lot of Latin about us (much of which I understood!), took us by the hand and while the undergrads in the gallery made a great row said over us the necessary formula. It was soon over but it was great fun and a great delight to have such a splendid honor given to one." After the ceremony, they went over to Christ's College and had tea with Dr. Shipley, the master. Then they went back to Emmanuel to call on the Gileses and be shown over John Harvard's College, which Morgan found especially interesting on that account.[32]

Morgan had his portrait painted in November 1919 by William Orpen. He explained: "Jessie likes his work and wants it done and he doesn't take an impossibly [long] time like lamentable Boco Flor. Also, what he produces looks to me like a picture and not an attempt at a photograph."[33]

Morgan returned from England on December 6, 1919, on the *Lapland* after a three-month visit. He told reporters that the re-establishing of normal economic relationships depended entirely on the signing of the peace treaty.[34] The peace-treaty issue was the most controversial question of the day. On June 29, President Wilson had been one of the signers of the Treaty of Versailles between the Western Allies and a defeated Germany, but for the treaty to be valid and binding for the United States it had still to be ratified by the United States Senate.

Morgan favored the creation of the League of Nations and was exasperated at President Wilson's ineptitude in "selling" the idea to the American public or even in informing them adequately.[35] In signing the treaty, Wilson had compromised his principles of self-determination of peoples and acceded to an unrestricted reparation bill against the defeated Germans in order to bring about the existence of the League of Nations. There was a strong body of public sentiment in the United States against giving up as much national sovereignty as unqualified acceptance of the League would demand. It is thought that if Wilson had been willing to agree to certain reservations, the Senate would have ratified the treaty. As it was, Wilson rejected a proposed compromise, urged the Democrats in the Senate to defeat the compromise resolution when it came to a vote on November 19, and unwisely made ratification a partisan issue. The Republicans won out, so the treaty was never ratified by the United States—which remained technically at war with Germany—and the United States never joined the League of Nations. And the inequities in the Versailles treaty, which Wilson was sure would be corrected by action of his cherished league, remained to fester and contribute to the start of another world war more devastating than the first.

On November 13, 1919, the papers carried the announcement that J. P. Morgan & Co. had organized the Foreign Finance Corporation to purchase the securities of foreign companies. This company is not to be confused with the ill-fated Foreign Commerce Corporation, another Morgan venture, which was to start operations a few weeks later and which was being organized at the same time as the Foreign Finance Corporation.[36]

1920

On January 1, 1920, it was announced that three new members had been admitted to general partnership in the Morgan banking house of J. P. Morgan & Co., New York; Drexel & Co., Philadelphia; Morgan, Grenfell & Co., London; and Morgan, Harjes & Co., Paris. All three represented a new generation of the Morgan "family." They were Junius Spencer Morgan, Jr., elder son of J. P. Morgan, Elliot Cowdin Bacon, son of former Morgan partner Col. Robert Bacon, and George Whitney, nephew of former Morgan partner E. F. Whitney.[37]

The usual pattern of board and committee meetings continued until midsummer of 1920, when it was interrupted by the annual departure for Britain.[38]

In the spring of 1920, Morgan's duties as commodore of the New York Yacht Club put him in the midst of all the activities connected with the America's Cup races. He cruised on *Corsair* up to Newport on June 9 to watch the trials between *Resolute* and *Vanitie*. The traditional course of the America's Cup international yacht races had been between New York City and Sandy Hook, New Jersey. Morgan convinced Sir Thomas Lipton, the indefatigable challenger, that the races should be moved to Newport, Rhode Island.[39]

The Postwar Depression: General Motors

A serious economic dislocation and depression developed after the war. Its causes were various and differed between areas and industries, but their cumulative impact was very great. It is surprising how quickly this depression would be forgotten in the succeeding boom and the even greater depression at the close of the decade.

The automobile industry was one of the first to feel the economic downturn. Theirs was a boom-and-bust situation. General Motors Corporation had been able to profit enormously in 1919 from the pent-up public demand for consumer goods—particularly automobiles—generated by the unavailability of those products during the war. Carried away by the euphoria of sudden riches, the management expanded production capacity on the assumption that good times would go on indefinitely. Capital outlays were financed in 1920 by the sale of stock. The du Ponts, the Morgan firm, and other interests bought blocks of stock at this time and were able to name a number of directors to an enlarged board. With unexpected suddenness, the demand for automobiles slowed down, and by the summer of 1920 it had virtually stopped. General Motors shares on the New York Stock Exchange declined abruptly. It was then discovered that William C. Durant, president of the corporation and the man most responsible for its success, had got his personal finances into a mess by optimistically buying General Motors stock and borrowing the money to buy it by putting up additional General Motors stock as collateral. The creditors were on the point of selling the collateral when it was realized that this would force down General Motors shares still further and might create a financial panic that could demoralize the entire market. At this point, the du Ponts and the Morgan firm stepped in and rescued the company. Since E. R. Stettinius was the Morgan partner who represented the firm on the expanded board of directors, he became their representative in the rescue operation.

No episode illustrates more clearly the nature of the Morgan partnership than this situation in which Morgan was able to go off on vacation with complete confidence that his partner Stettinius had matters in hand. He wrote to Davison two days before sailing: "I think you will be, as I am, very pleased with the General Motors situation, and perfectly delighted with the way Stettinius is handling it. A man of reasonable age always, I think, enters a marriage with some apprehension, and I know that I had some apprehensions about the marriage between JPM&Co and the General Motors but those doubts are all cleared up now, and I am entirely satisfied and very much pleased."[40]

The Morgans sailed for England on the *Adriatic* on August 14, a party of four with young Harry Morgan and Mrs. Morgan's brother Ned Grew. There was a great deal to attend to at Wall Hall. A new superintendent, John Fleming, had been engaged to take over direction of the farm earlier in the year. Morgan wanted to set up a club for the villagers at Aldenham, to be run by the locals themselves. To this end he bought the Chequers public house and converted it to community uses.[41] Morgan noted that he intended to keep the pub's liquor license because his "enthusiasm for prohibition had been somewhat abated by seeing its effects over here." The following year he could report: "The men's club has moved into the remodeled public house and has had a great success already . . . the men run it all themselves." He also noted: "The women who belong to the Women's Institute have also a right to use parts of it and it really seems to be in a fair way to fill a want which exists and has existed always. . . . Village life in winter is rather hard and dull and this gives them something to talk about and arrange for. There is a small hall for cinema shows and dancing—and it's really going to make a difference to a good number of honest, hard working and powerfully dull men and women."[42]

His sense of freedom from responsibility while on his shooting holiday in the Highlands in 1920 was complete. He wrote, "I hear from the office how everything goes on—not by way of consultation but by way of information. . . ." Not the least of the freedoms was the absence of the armed bodyguard thought to be necessary at home but not in Britain.[43]

This pleasant state of relaxation was rudely disrupted. Morgan was at Gannochy when word reached him of the murderous Wall Street explosion of September 16, 1920. Apparently an explosive device was placed in a horse-drawn wagon and went off at noon when hundreds of office workers in the financial district were in the street on their lunch hour. At least thirty people were killed and scores injured in the blast. The Morgan premises at 23 Wall Street were severely damaged, and two employees were killed; William Joyce (son of Thomas W. Joyce, a longtime Morgan officer) died instantly and James A. Donohue died in the hospital later. Junius S. Morgan, Jr., was injured by shards of flying glass. The bomb was filled with chunks of cast iron identified as broken-up window sash weights and had the same effect as a shrapnel artillery shell. The outrage seemed utterly pointless; the papers pointed out that if it was supposed to be a Leftist threat or gesture against capitalists, it failed woefully of its purpose because the victims were office workers in modest circumstances.[44]

Back in Scotland, the 1920 shooting season ended in the last week of September. Morgan reported that he was "in the very top of condition" and the season's bag had totaled 4,000 grouse.[45] After the close of the shooting season, the Morgans returned to Wall Hall.

Morgan had been elected to membership in the Athenaeum Club, London, in the spring of 1920. He wrote of his first visit following admission: "It is a most respectable place to which all the Bishops and most of the learned and wise belong—I was quite shy about going there. However, Sir Hercules Read took me and showed me round so now I know I'm all right."[46]

The Morgans crossed over to Paris in October 1920. In the course of their visit, they made a very brief motor tour to Tours and the Loire Valley.[47]

Morgan's last day in Paris in the fall of 1920 was exhausting. He wrote, "When I got through with seeing the President, the Prime Minister, the Finance Minister, Tardieu and Loucheur and a lunch of the Amis de la France there was not much strength left in me!" He commented: "All the officials feel that France is really well started on the road to recovery from the material losses of the war, and that they can point with satisfaction to very real progress made. . . . They want help of course, and some of them in that wish seem to forget that there are other troubles in other nations, but they don't *need* help nearly as much as they *wish* for it."[48]

Where some people are unfortunately accident-prone, Morgan was almost the reverse; he experienced a series of lucky accidents. Entirely without previous planning on his part, he seems to have been on hand at a number of important moments in world history: Ladysmith and Mafeking nights, Queen Victoria's funeral, the promulgation of the Russian October constitution. In November of 1920, he was in London on the occasion of the funeral of the Unknown Warrior, who was buried in Westminster Abbey. He wrote: "The idea did not appeal to me at first at all—it seemed rather forced and even somewhat neurotic. But carried out as it was, it was wonderfully impressive and almost intolerably emotional."[49]

At home, the American political campaigns were reaching a climax with the coming of election day. The Democratic candidate for the presidency was James M. Cox, a supporter of the League of Nations. His running mate was Franklin D. Roosevelt. Warren G. Harding was the Republican. Both men were Ohio newspaper publishers. Morgan wrote Davison: "The political situation is almost amusing to me, if it were not so painful. I cannot vote for a pro-German Ohio editor, who justified the 'Lusitania,' just because his views on the Peace Treaty are somewhat better than the other fellow's and I do not like to vote for the kind of jelly-fish the Republicans have put up."[50] Harding was elected and proceeded to justify Morgan's misgivings.

It was in 1920 that Morgan engaged an undercover agent, one Charles Blumenthal, to try to discover if there was, as he had come to suspect, an organized anti-Morgan conspiracy within the American Jewish community. Blumenthal reported periodically through the next two years.[51] Morgan was mistaken, of course, but he conceived the idea from the attacks of Samuel Untermyer upon his father and himself, the attacks of Louis D. Brandeis, and the activities of James Speyer of the competing firm of Speyer & Co.

Morgan also lived at a time in American social history when Jews, along with other recent immigrants—Irish, Italian, and other—were generally looked down upon by the descendants of earlier immigrants. This prejudice was less a matter of racial or religious bias than of class-consciousness, and it diminished markedly as these ethnic groups became absorbed into the general pattern of American life. It was usually the lower orders who came to America because, except in the case of political émigrés and younger sons, the others enjoyed a comfortable status where they were and had no reason to leave home. Earlier arrivals either feared the competition of the newcomers or, having risen higher on the socioeconomic ladder, looked with distaste on their coarser speech and manners and their uncomfortably foreign appearance and ways. At the same time, educated or well-born or highly placed visitors of the nationalities of the despised groups often received embarrassingly fulsome welcomes to this country. Because of their business acumen, many lower-class Jews rose in the economic ranks more rapidly than in the social scale, so Morgan became aware of them on trans-Atlantic liners, in the more expensive hotels, and in business meetings.

Morgan observed in one letter that his trans-Atlantic passage in the summer of 1924 was highly satisfactory because there were, "no Jews and no one on board travelling with anyone else's wife."[52] Morgan's class consciousness applied to other ethnic groups as well. He spoke of Ferdinand Pecora, the inquisitor in the New Deal investigation of the investment-banking business as a "dirty little wop,"[53] but he enjoyed a warm friendship with Achille Ratti, the Vatican librarian who became Pope Pius XI. He was suspicious of American Catholics, most of whom were of Irish or southern-European peasant stock—although (as just noted) he enjoyed his association with the pope.

Morgan opposed the appointment of Jews and Catholics to the governing board of Harvard University, saying, "I would base my personal objection to each of these two for that position on the fact that in both cases there is acknowledgement of interests or political control beyond and, in the minds of these people, superior to the Government of this country—the Jew is always a Jew first and an American second, and the Roman Catholic, I fear, too often a Papist first and an American second."[54]

It would be a mistake to seize upon these events and infer that Morgan was fundamentally anti-Semitic. Against the account of the Blumenthal investigations and his dislike of such individuals as Samuel Untermyer and James Speyer should be set the long record of anonymous support to promising Jewish students whose education at the Harvard Medical School he helped to finance year after year through his friend Dr. Franklin Dexter. Dexter administered the granting of small loans and sometimes outright gifts of cash to needy medical students—many of them Jewish, as Dexter's reports show—from a fund supplied by Morgan in increments of $500. In the spring of 1917, Morgan gave $5,000 to Dr. Dexter's fund.[55]

Morgan had many Jewish friends and business associates, and he believed that Paul Warburg's appointment to the Federal Reserve Board in 1914 was an excellent choice.[56] In thanking Mortimer Schiff for a copy of the newly published biography of Jacob Schiff, his father, Morgan wrote, "Your father was a kind friend of many years standing for whom I had a very great respect."[57] J. P. Morgan & Co. and Schiff's firm of Kuhn, Loeb & Co. were closely involved in countless large syndicates organized to float security issues. Morgan enjoyed a long association with the marquess of Reading and sent a Christmas gift of tea regularly to Lady Reading. There were also his joint undertakings with the

Guggenheims in Kennecott Copper and in the Alaska Syndicate.[58]

Morgan did not regard himself as actively hostile to Jews. He wrote to a friend: "I . . . regret to see your anti-Semitic feeling coming so strongly to the surface." He was shocked by Hitler's treatment of the Jews. He wrote: "As you know I am not very enthusiastic about Jews, but I must say that my heart is full of sympathy with those unfortunate people in Austria who suddenly find themselves outcasts after being respected and useful citizens, and outcasts deprived of all their property. It is more wicked than I thought anybody could be."[59]

1921

The first postwar *Corsair* cruise was to the Caribbean in January and February of 1921 and began at Charleston, South Carolina. It was a party of six, the Morgans (with valet and maid), the Grenfells (with maid), Miss M. E. Williams, and Amory Gardner of Groton, Massachusetts. *Corsair* sailed to Nassau and on to Haiti, then to San Juan, Puerto Rico, St. Thomas, St. Eustatius, Guadaloupe, Martinique, and Barbados, thence north to Jamaica, Santiago de Cuba, and on to Brunswick, Georgia.[60] The Protestant ethic troubled Morgan ever so slightly in his pleasantly relaxed state: "I am so well and having such an ideal time that it makes me a little ashamed at not being at work. Not enough so, however, to make me think of going back for a while yet."[61]

Upon his return to New York, Morgan went first to the Library. He was back at 23 Wall Street on Monday, March 7. In less than a week he was off again. He went to Thomasville, Georgia, to visit his partner Henry P. Davison.[62] H. P. Davison had not been in good health since he left the chairmanship of the American Red Cross, and Morgan was concerned about him. Morgan finally was able to arrange for Davison to make a cruise on *Corsair* and on the way to pick up Dr. Austen F. Riggs in whose gifts as a specialist in mental health Morgan had great confidence. Davison, of course, was dying of a brain tumor, but nobody knew that yet. Morgan had long been a supporter of Dr. Riggs and his sanitarium in the Berkshires. When Riggs's affairs became involved, Morgan bailed him out. Morgan was also a longtime patient and backer of Dr. William Howland Wilmer, the eye specialist of Johns Hopkins University.[63]

Private Ventures

Upon his return to the office, Morgan was caught up in the usual series of corporate meetings. He also attended meetings of smaller companies in which he was personally involved. In contrast with the larger, publicly owned corporations on whose boards and committees he sat, these lesser concerns were usually not very successful. This is not an unusual pattern for the peripheral business interests of financiers.

One such concern was the Carrie company, which manufactured gyrocompasses. Morgan had become interested in the company at least as early as March 1919 and continued to confer with them for several years.[64] Another company was the Submarine Signal Co. Morgan was a substantial investor, as was Maj. Henry L. Higginson of Boston, the "angel" of the Boston Symphony Orchestra. Morgan wrote to F. L. Higginson, Jr., in Boston in March 1921 to inquire about rumors that the concern was being mismanaged and that there was a move afoot to force it into receivership.[65] This was one of the inventions-inspired companies that proliferated during the war. Another war-related company was a small electronics firm called American Radio & Research Corporation. This concern was particularly active in adapting scientific discoveries and inventions to practical use, particularly during World War I. Although the company had become profitable toward the end of the war, it came upon hard times with the close of hostilities and the stopping of military purchases. The American Radio & Research Company finally went bankrupt.[66]

Morgan also had a considerable interest in the publishers Harper & Brothers in the early 1920s.[67]

On a very modest scale, Morgan authorized John Callahan, the caretaker of Camp Uncas, to start a fox-breeding business on a shared expenses and profits basis. Uncas already provided firewood and vegetables for several Morgan houses, but this was a commercial venture. The quality of silver fox skins produced by John Callahan at Camp Uncas was high enough to have them cured and dressed by C. G. Gunther's Sons in New York. Losses in 1925 came to $1,156.83, so an attempt was made early in 1926 to improve the product. A pair of foxes to improve stock were bought for $1,700. The Uncas fox farm lost money again in 1928. It made a profit of $525 in 1929, the last year recorded; half of this was turned over to John Callahan. People apparently stopped buying silver fox furs after the 1929 stock market crash.[68]

Postwar Foreign Loans

In the fall of 1919, J. P. Morgan & Co. became the financial agents in the United States for the Belgian treasury. The firm headed the syndicate that offered Belgian securities. The first Belgian loans were the $30,000,000 twenty-year 8 percent sinking-fund gold bonds and the $4,270,000 external-loan 6 percent gold notes due in 1925.[69]

The firm also enlarged its activity in the South American field with a Republic of Chile issue of $24,000,000 twenty-year 8 percent sinking-fund gold bonds.[70]

The most important reconstruction loan of 1921 was the $100,000,000 French twenty-year external-loan 7½ percent gold bonds. The market for the French loan did not flourish, and in mid-June a bonus was offered to stimulate sales. Syndicate participants recieved an extra ½ percent to 1 percent commission above the original percentage.[71]

It was through the Morgan bank that the German reparations payments to England and Belgium were sent.[72]

In 1921, there was a spate of interest in the revived China Consortium organized the preceding October. Thomas W. Lamont was the spokesman for the American bankers involved in this government-endorsed plan for lending money for the modernizing of China. Hopes for bringing China's economy and communications into the twentieth century were high, but results were disappointing.[73]

Sailing

The Morgan family were very active on the water in the spring of 1921. They raced *Grayling* successfully from late May to early July. At the close of the first half of calendar 1921, Morgan reported to the Collector of Internal Revenue his ownership of *Corsair*, 304 feet overall; *Navette*, 114 feet overall; *Grayling*, 72 feet overall; and four *Corsair* tenders under five tons.[74]

Following his annual attendance at Harvard commencement and the crew races at New London, Morgan was back racing *Grayling* on Long Island Sound. He came in second behind his future son-in-law George Nichols. He was rapturous. "It's wonderful what intense pleasure it is to get, after five years, into a sailing race again and to have the old feel of the boat coming back. It almost makes one forget there has been a war."[75] The 1921 annual cruise of the New York Yacht Club took place as usual in

July. As commodore, Morgan had to be along the whole time, but he hoped to enter *Grayling* in seven races.[76]

The Postwar Depression: Banks in Trouble

With the 1929 disaster still in mind, it is difficult to think of the business slump of 1921 as a full-fledged economic depression, but it was felt acutely at the time. Morgan spoke of "these hard times." The Morgan firm was active in a number of rescue missions to save foundering concerns. Morgan wrote in July of 1921, "Business still continues to be in a large measure listening to the troubles of others and trying to see if we can help wisely and safely. So far we have been able to do so in a good lot of cases—but I suppose that there will soon come along some of the sort that no one can help except by the painful process of bankruptcy first, and then rebuilding."[77]

The papers reported that J. P. Morgan planned to sail for Europe on Saturday, August 6, 1921. On August 7, however, the *Times* noted that he took his wife and younger son Harry down to the White Star Line pier at the foot of West Eighteenth Street, saw them safely on board the *Cedric*, and then left them. "Private business," was the reason given for his last-minute canceling of his passage.[78]

The casual reader might have been startled to learn that Morgan stayed in New York in order to prevent the possible collapse of the Guaranty Trust Company, which would have had far-reaching effects on the whole financial structure. The postwar depression was both sudden and capricious. In worldwide commerce, sugar was a commodity on which the economies of a dozen countries depended. As was the case also with automobiles, the war-inflated prices of sugar had led to increased production and to increased borrowing to make that expanded production possible. When the world price of sugar fell sharply, the growers and refiners could not sell the product to pay off the credits, and a chain reaction was started. The lesser banks and trading companies could not meet their loan payments to the next larger banks, which, in turn, could not meet their own obligations. The case in point involved the Guaranty Trust Company of New York, which was the largest stockholder in the Mercantile Bank of the Americas and its largest creditor. The Mercantile Bank of the Americas was deeply involved in sugar loans. It was clear that the first rescue effort could not raise enough money to save the Bank of the Americas, so the

Morgan firm entered the picture, and a new plan was agreed to on August 8. On August 12, J. P. Morgan made a reassuring public statement. E. R. Stettinius took charge of the revised plan on behalf of J. P. Morgan & Co., and the slow process of bringing the Bank of the Americas and, in consequence, the Guaranty Trust Company, back to health was begun.[79]

A second reason for Morgan to delay his departure for Europe was the brain surgery performed on his partner H. P. Davison. He finally sailed on the *Olympic* on August 13, after the operation had been pronounced successful.[80]

Britain

The approach of the grouse season in Scotland acted like a tonic on Morgan. He wrote in July 1921, a month before his scheduled departure, "My mind is singing a little song of joy in the back of my head all the time at the thought of the delights of that month up there!" Morgan went to Gannochy immediately upon reaching Britain and remained there from August 22 to October 2, with only one brief visit to London.[81]

The farm at Wall Hall had begun to operate as a working farm by the fall of 1921 under the skilled management of John Fleming. Morgan could write, "I think now that within a year or so we shall be really producing here enough of milk and pigs and eggs to keep the whole place and all the people who live on it and work for it going well on a paying basis. Though what rate of interest we shall earn on the investment remains to be seen. If we don't earn a fair rate, one year with another, it will mean that we have not been successful."[82]

Both of the Morgans took most seriously their duties as landed gentry. He wrote in the fall of 1921, "Jessie has been so busy working at the Women's Institute and all the other activities at Wall Hall that she has done away with some of the good that Scotland did for her. . . . It means endless conversations with all sorts of people in the neighborhood and much planning and arranging.[83]

The Morgans went to Paris on October 12 and from there motored through the South of France, returning to Paris on November 2.[84]

Morgan had a realistic outlook on old age and death. In the fall of 1921, when Louisa and Herbert Satterlee were concerned about the failing health of Satterlee's mother and were making a great effort to have her kept alive, Morgan wrote, "Of course it must be done but one does wonder a little what she is being 'kept for.' However, it would be quite impossible not to do all they could to keep her, so there it is."[85]

Morgan very definitely believed in the Christian concept of life after death. A few weeks later, on the death of a relative, "Folly" Rhett, he wrote, "She has had a hard time the past few years and for her one can only feel happy and at ease for the new life must open before her with a wonderful prospect."[86]

The Morgan family had deep roots in the London financial community. Morgan wrote on the last day of October 1921, "I dined in town one evening with the 'Society of Merchants Trading to the Continent,' a very pleasant Society of which I have been a member for many years and of which Grandfather was also a member for the 1860's. It was quite a numerous gathering of what is really the best in the City. . . ."[87]

Morgan was back at his desk on December 7, 1921. He promptly got into the routine of meetings. He began by attending his first International Mercantile Marine finance committee meetings in almost two years.[88]

His term of office as commodore of the New York Yacht Club ended on December 15, when Harold S. Vanderbilt was elected the new commodore. The following evening, Vanderbilt gave a dinner for Morgan, the retiring commodore.[89]

1922

January 1922 was a long round of almost continuous board meetings. Asked to serve on another committee, Morgan refused with a most explicit account of his working day: "Beginning at nine-fifteen, I have eight or nine hours, or more of work every day when I am in this country, and it is one thing after another, absolutely continuous occupation. I am trustee and on the committee for a great many different kinds of things. . . . Could I get rid of the two museums [Metropolitan Museum of Art and American Museum of Natural History] and the [New York Lying-In] Hospital, it might give me time to undertake a new thing, but I really cannot get rid of them."[90]

Occasional alleviations in this routine were the visit to the Library of Henry Ford, and a luncheon at 23 Wall Street for Chilean ambassador to Britain Edwards. Dean Le Baron Briggs of Radcliffe

College met with Morgan at the library on January 21, a visit that was to bear fruit a year later with the announcement of Morgan's $5,000 gift to the Radcliffe endowment drive.[91]

Jessie Morgan required oral surgery early in 1922. The Morgans left on February 6 for Jekyl Island, Georgia, where she had a painfully slow convalescence. One of the recent blights has been the pollution of beaches by crude-oil leaks, spills, or discharges from tankers. The same disgusting mess affected the beaches of Jekyl Island in February 1922, to the distress of man and waterfowl. Morgan's vacation reading included a biography of Lord Ripon, S. E. Morison's *Maritime History of Massachusetts*, and *Enchanted April* by the author of *Elizabeth and Her German Garden*.[92]

March found Morgan back at 23 Wall Street and the usual routine. One unusual visitor was Nikola Tesla, the Serbian inventor and electrical genius. Tesla had received financial help from Morgan over a considerable period of time before World War I until, at the beginning of 1915, Morgan had had to tell him that he could not go on indefinitely putting money into his electrical researches.[93]

Another break from the usual schedule was a trip to Hartford to attend the Aetna Insurance Co. board meeting. Morgan had long been a member, but it was not often convenient to get up to Hartford.[94]

Morgan played duffer's golf casually during most of his life, especially in England during his holiday. Following the winter vacation at Jekyl Island, he played more golf at home. During the early spring of 1922, he played a number of times at The Links golf club at Garden City, Long Island. Morgan entered The Creek's Initial Golf Competition and Founders Competition tournaments in July 1924. He had not been officially handicapped, but he played in the upper 90s or about 100 for eighteen holes.[95]

This mild interest continued for years, but he enjoyed playing and used to joke about his game. He wrote to the Reverend Edgar Stogdon at the Vicarage, Harrow, early in 1929 that his game had improved greatly and the vicar could not possibly beat him this year![96]

Morgan broke his right ankle in July 1932 while playing his ball out of the rough. In the summer of 1935, he wrote: "I . . . have an idea that I should be able at least to carry my own weight as things have been rather looking up for me lately on the golf course." A year later he wrote Charles Steele, "I am trying . . . to play occasionally but my game even now has not reached the point of being golf at all, and it seems to be getting worse instead of better."[97]

German Reparations

A cloud of uncertainty hung over European finance from the unsettled question of German war reparations. The Reparation Commission struggled to reconcile the economic realities and the provisions of the Versailles treaty. In 1921, the German financial situation was so precarious that Germany asked for a postponement of the 1922 reparations payments due dates. A provisional moratorium was granted, and the commission appointed a Committee of Bankers in April of 1922 to explore the possibility of a German loan abroad for repayment of the capital of the reparations debt.[98]

Morgan served on the bankers' committee. His departure on the *Olympic* on May 13 followed a tiring week. Henry P. Davison died on the sixth; the funeral was on the ninth. On the tenth, Morgan received the honorary degree of Doctor of Commercial Science from New York University at a private ceremony in the Pierpont Morgan Library.[99]

The Committee of Bankers met in Paris in late May. The *Commercial and Financial Chronicle* reported that Morgan was given the seat of honor on the chairman's right and observed: "The Paris dispatches made it clear that the representatives of all the other nations are counting more upon Mr. Morgan than any other individual for a practical and comprehensive plan."[100]

The conference failed, and the meetings broke up on June 10, 1922. For Germany to float a loan abroad, her credit needed to be strengthened. This would have required Germany's debts to be scaled down. In response to an inquiry from the bankers, three of the four members of the Reparation Commission favored the idea. France refused even to discuss changes in the reparations payments.[101]

Following the breakdown of the conference, Morgan wrote Joseph Grew, "I have not seen Tardieu's article on the Policy of France, as yet. As far as I am concerned, I have pretty well concluded that that policy is controlled neither by imperialism, militarism or avariciousness but almost entirely by funk. I believe that, in the back of his mind, Poincare has known all along that Germany could not pay on the scale that he claimed to desire, but that what he really wants is to ruin Germany—and I am afraid he has pretty nearly got that now." [102]

Morgan remained in Europe throughout the summer and fall. He was asked how the Allies' debts to the United States should be treated. He replied:

> Those debts should be canceled. As a practical proposition they can never be paid, but they should be canceled for another reason. This money was loaned our allies after we entered the war, at which moment we pledged all our strength and resources to winning it. When we entered the war in April, 1917, we could not send soldiers because we did not have them ready. We sent dollars in the form of loans to our allies. While we were sending dollars, our allies were sending soldiers until ours got there. I look upon these loans as being the same sort of contribution to victory as our sending 2,000,000 troops. [103]

The Morgans returned to Britain on June 11 and remained until September 27, with a scant week's visit to the Continent in late July. [104] Grouse shooting for Morgan was not an end in itself but an excuse for walking and climbing over the Scottish moors and hillsides. "The birds . . . have been quite sufficient to give us good sport, and as long as there are enough of them to draw us all out to the hills, and make us walk about the heather and see the views, it is quite the same to me if they get many or comparatively few." [105]

Morgan had a surprisingly limited acquaintance with Europe outside of Britain and Paris. He planned to visit Rome in the fall of 1922. Jessie had never been, and he had not been there himself since 1877, when he was nine years old. [106] The Morgans looked forward to the Roman visit and conscientiously boned up ahead of time. Morgan wrote, "All our time is spent with guide books and Roman history is our daily diet. . . . Oh it is going to be such a spree!" [107]

Their arrival in Rome on October 19 coincided with the completion of the publication of the facsimile edition of the Coptic manuscripts assembled by the elder Morgan. The work of restoration, compilation, and editing had been done in the Vatican Library when the newly consecrated Pope Pius XI—then Achille Ratti—was Vatican librarian. Morgan planned to present him with the first copy of the work. On the eve of this visit with the pope, Morgan reflected on his career and concluded that he was content with being a banker. He wrote, "My special job is the most interesting I know of anywhere. More fun than being King, Pope, or Prime Minister anywhere—for no one can turn me out of it and I don't have to make any compromises with principles."[108]

The Morgan visit took place at the same time as Mussolini's march on Rome. The timing was another of Morgan's historical lucky accidents. Morgan was not displeased by the Fascist take-over. He was relieved to have order restored in the turbulent post-war Italy and the Communists put down. He later wrote to Dr. Dexter in Boston, "We had the great satisfaction of seeing Mr. Mussolini's Revolution."[109]

Morgan's state of intellectual indigestion following a brief but intense visit in Rome must be familiar to any visitor to the Eternal City. He wrote: "My head is such a jumble of statues, pictures, ruins, churches, Popes and Emperors, Fascisti and Poets and many other things that it will take me many weeks to get clear ideas about anything."[110]

The Morgans arrived back in New York on the *Adriatic* on December 3, 1922, the day after an attack by Untermyer on the Morgan firm as the alleged protectors of trusts.[111]

On Saturday, December 16, Morgan met with a group of the partners at the Pierpont Morgan Library to discuss the possibilities of a loan to Germany. The following Tuesday, J. P. Morgan & Co. issued a statement in regard to a German loan.[112] This followed a call by Morgan upon Secretary of State Hughes in Washington. The firm stated that for such a loan to be made, the total amount of reparations that Germany would have to pay should be fixed, so that the lenders would know where they stood, and Germany would have to put her own financial affairs in order.[113] But the German loan was not forthcoming for almost two years, not until October 1924. Meanwhile, Germany in 1923 sustained the vindictive and economically unproductive French military invasion of the Ruhr industrial area and the disastrous inflation of the mark.

1923

The year 1923 opened on an academic note. On January 3, the $5,000 gift from Morgan to Radcliffe College was announced.[114] That same day, he wrote to E. C. Grenfell in London, offering to help out his closest friend in English university circles, Sir Arthur Shipley, the master of Christ's College, Cambridge, whose house-guest he had often been. Shipley was compelled to give up his entire patrimony of £13,000 to save his brother from bankrupt-cy. To rescue Shipley from financial disaster, Morgan offered £20,000—from which half of the income was to go to the master, half to the fellows of Christ's.[115] A few days later, on January 7, he was listed along with several of his partners and Endicott Peabody of Groton as a member of the committee appointed to consider ways and means of cementing closer relations between Harvard and Emmanuel College, Cambridge, John Harvard's college.[116]

The arbitrators of the proposed merger of the Northern Pacific and Great Northern railways, J. P. Morgan, George F. Baker, and Arthur Curtiss James, met at the Library on January 4. The fol-lowing week, a syndicate headed by J. P. Morgan & Co. were the successful bidders for the $50,000,000 5½ percent thirty-year Cuban bond issue.[117] The Morgan firm had long been interested in Cuba. Of all the partners, D. W. Morrow was the most inter-ested in Latin-American affairs, and he was ultimately to leave J. P. Morgan & Co. to become U. S. ambassador to Mexico. Mor-gan had great respect for Dwight Morrow. He said of him, "He is a rather wonderful person I think and has one of the most beau-tifully working minds I have ever known. It's a constant pleasure to me to see it work and to watch the effect of its working on other people."[118]

The Austrian Loan

The $130,000,000 postwar reconstruction loan to Austria was the largest of its kind to be managed by the firm in 1923. The loan was floated in the form of twenty-year 7 percent guaranteed-loan sinking-fund gold bonds. The issue was offered to the public of nine nations simultaneously on June 11. Morgan commented in the press:

> The importance of the Austrian loan which is being issued today lies in the fact that the attitude of American investors to this loan will show that they are interested in helping those nations of Europe which are prepared to help themselves to-ward the re-establishment of their credit.
> Last year at the bankers' conference held in Paris, I stated that it was my opinion that if the security to be given was

clearly good, and the investors of other lending nations would cooperate to the extent that they felt themselves able to do, I believed that the American markets would participate to an important extent in the rehabilitation of the European financial situation. At that time these conditions could not be satisfied. Now, however, for the first time a loan is offered which fulfills both conditions.[119]

The first half of 1923 was marked by a number of vacations. Morgan was at Climax, North Carolina, in January and at Jekyl Island for the latter half of February and part of March. In early May, there was a week's *Corsair* cruise on Chesapeake Bay, ending at Washington with a visit to Mount Vernon.[120]

Around the edges of his arduous meetings schedule, Morgan found time for a few rounds of golf. He began the season on the last day of March, was at The Links on April 7—moving day for the Morgans from 231 Madison Avenue to Matinicock Point—and played on weekends through April and May.[121] That June, Harvard University awarded the honorary Doctor of Laws degree to Morgan to add to his earlier degrees from Trinity College (Hartford, Conn.), Cambridge University, and New York University. In conferring the degree, President Abbott Lawrence Lowell read the citation: "John Pierpont Morgan, a son of Harvard, heir to the power and responsibilities of a great financial house, he has used them with courage in a dark crisis of the World War and at all times with uprightness, public spirit and generosity." W. L. MacKenzie King, prime minister of Canada, received the LL.D. at the same time.[122]

The *Corsair* party for the Harvard crew was given early this year—not on the day after commencement, as was customary. It was a busy time in the family. Morgan received his honorary degree on June 21; his son Harry graduated from Harvard the same day and then was married on June 26 to Miss Catherine Adams. Between commencement and the wedding day, the family cruised up to Manchester on *Corsair* to visit the Crosbys.[123]

On June 30, 1923, Russell Cornell Leffingwell joined the Morgan firm, the first new partner to be elected since the death the year before of Henry P. Davison. Leffingwell had been a lawyer with the Cravath firm. The partners were now: J. P. Morgan, Edward T. Stotesbury, Charles Steele, William H. Porter, Thomas W. Lamont, Horatio G. Lloyd, Dwight W. Morrow, Edward R.

Stettinius, Thomas Cochran, Junius Spencer Morgan, Jr., Elliot Cowdin Bacon, George Whitney, Thomas S. Gates, and Leffingwell.[124]

Morgan sailed on Saturday, July 23, on the *Homeric* for his annual summer visit abroad.[125] While he was at sea, President Harding—the "jelly-fish" of Morgan's preelection comments—died in San Francisco under peculiar circumstances.

The Morgans went directly to Wall Hall upon landing. Under the direction of John Fleming, the Wall Hall farm had developed into an active, going concern. Following a sale of Morgan pigs, the *Farmer and Stock-Breeder* magazine asked for a photograph of Morgan. He wrote to Fleming, "I do not know whether they want a photograph of me to compare it with the photographs of the pigs; I could suggest that Mr. Wilson's photograph might meet the case more satisfactorily than my own picture, he has come to look so like his charges."[126]

Before returning to New York at the end of his annual visit to Britain, Morgan paid regular business visits to his partners abroad to show the flag. "I have found it pays very well for me to settle into both the London and Paris office for a short time every autumn—it keeps me in touch with their activities better than any other arrangement—and it's quite important for me to be in touch—it makes cables to be much more informative." After a stay at the Paris office, Morgan planned a trip to the South of France starting at Toulouse, going on to Pau, and winding up at Biarritz.[127]

Morgan returned from his long visit to Europe on the *Majestic* on December 10. As usual, he declined to be interviewed.[128]

As we will see in the chapter that follows, the year 1924 is an appropriate year for a digression from a strict chronological account of Morgan's life to examine his interest in books and in the Morgan Library.

CHAPTER VIII

Morgan
the Book Collector

For more than twenty-five years preceding his death, Morgan, Senior, had been assembling that splendid, if miscellaneous, collection of books and manuscripts with which everyone interested in book collecting is familiar. In 1906 the first Morgan Library building was completed. It was still "Mr. Morgan's Library," a private, personal collection, even though a few scholars were allowed to use it.

We saw the younger Morgan converting into cash the greater part of his enormous inheritance of works of art. But he held on to the library and the books and manuscripts and drawings and graphics (etchings and mezzotints) that it contained. More than that, he became an active book collector in his own right.

No formal acquisitions policy seems to have been laid down. There continued to be only a general understanding of what the younger Morgan and the staff were trying to do. A letter to the heritor of another collection tells us something of Morgan's aims to fill out the library collections. "I am endeavouring to complete as far as possible the undertaking that my Father began, of gathering in this Library, as full as possible a collection of incunabula."[1]

On November 12, 1919, Morgan wrote from London to the librarian, Belle da Costa Greene, about the copy of Shakespeare's poem *Venus and Adonis* coming up at auction for an estimated £10,000. He observed, "I believe we shall do better to spend the money we have available—which is not an unlimited amount—in continuing our policy of filling in with special manuscripts and with printed books before 1520, than we shall by scattering it about in buying Shakesperian items which seem to me to be higher priced than one can justify."[2]

John H. Plummer of the Pierpont Morgan Library has a very reasonable explanation of the ill-defined acquisitions policy prevailing under the Morgans, father and son. He suggests that they were carrying on the tradition, with which both were familiar, of the British nobleman's library where attention was paid to collecting individual works of excellent quality rather than to organizing a purchasing program directed toward completeness or specialization in specific fields. The biography of the Philadelphia bookseller Abraham S. W. Rosenbach gives some support to this concept of the discriminating amateur in referring to "the gentlemanly collector J. P. Morgan."[3]

The actual acquisition process was a very simple, logical arrangement: Booksellers and others with books and manuscripts and prints to sell would write or call either Mr. Morgan or Miss Greene. Sometimes Mr. Morgan or Miss Greene would just go browsing and shopping. Whichever of them received an attractive offer or located an interesting item would promptly get in touch with the other. They would discuss the item, possibly call in an outside opinion, and buy or reject the book or manuscript. Where considerable sums of money were involved, Morgan usually made the final decision. The result of this close collaboration was that selection was a joint matter, and it is difficult if not impossible to assign credit for purchases not specifically attributed to one or the other of them.

The younger Morgan's first important contribution to the collection was the present to his father of the manuscript of Thackeray's *Vanity Fair* in 1905.[4] What with the difficulties of settling his father's estate and J. P. Morgan & Co.'s involvement in financing and arming the Allies in World War I, he had neither the time nor the money, let alone the energy, to devote to serious collecting until after the war. His first major gift directly to the Library was the wartime purchase in 1915 of another Thackeray manuscript, *The Rose and the Ring* (1853), illustrated by the author.[5]

Mediaeval and Renaissance Manuscripts

A second wartime acquisition was the first of a series of illuminated manuscripts added to the collection. This was a book of *Scenes from the Old Testament*, French, thirteenth-century.[6] The actual purchase was made by Miss Greene in 1922. Morgan later wrote Miss Greene, "The book is certainly very wonderful, and I think would be quite sufficiently 'oh my' to 'épater' the [Roxburghe] Club."[7]

In the year 1919, the manuscript collection received a tremendous boost at the H. Yates Thompson sale. The London dealer Bernard Quaritch acted for Morgan in bidding in six items, most of them from the earl of Ashburnham collection, but including from the duke of Hamilton collection an eleventh-century Byzantine Gospel Lectionary, or collection of selections from Holy Writ to be read aloud in the church service as the day's lesson.[8]

In 1920, Morgan acquired a very handsome mid-tenth-century Byzantine herbal, Dioscorides, *De Materia Medica*. During this period, Morgan continued to subsidize the project that has already been mentioned as begun by his father: the photographing and restoring at the Vatican Library of the elder Morgan's collection of Coptic illuminated manuscripts from the eighth to the tenth century.[9]

In the spring of 1922, Archbishop Sophronios of Leontopolis, a prelate of the Greek Orthodox Church, needed money to continue his researches at the Bibliothèque Nationale in Paris, so the patriarch of Constantinople authorized him to sell thirteen mediaeval Greek manuscripts. Morgan in London conferred with Miss Greene in New York and wound up buying two, a Saint John Chrysostom tenth-century item and a sixteenth- or seventeenth-century psalter for the moderate price of 15,000 French francs.[10]

Later that summer, Lionel Cust offered Morgan a manuscript of the *Koran* in Cufic script. Morgan bought this Arabic manuscript at the urging of Miss Greene for £650.[11] It would be a mistake not to further our acquaintanceship with Belle da Costa Greene by quoting from a later and unrelated paragraph in her letter: "I am very glad to hear that my dear old (in age!) friend, the Comte de Laborde has been made a member of the Roxburghe Club. . . . Externally, he is mild, good and a bit dull. Actually, he is wild, bad, and very learned. Being such direct opposites we get along famously."[12]

The elder Morgan had bought an important collection of Babylonian cuneiform tablets, and the son financed their deciphering and publication. This scholarly work was put in the hands of Albert T. Clay (one wonders whether this savant's career was influenced by his name). Henry S. Morgan, younger son of J. P. Morgan, Jr., recalls that as a youth he was present when one of the clay envelopes protecting the small, pillow-shaped tablets, was broken to reveal a royal proclamation of the third millennium B.C.; the scholar read aloud, translating as he went. The document began: "Since things are no longer what they used to be. . . ."[13] Work on the tablets was nearly complete by the summer of 1923, and Miss Greene wrote that she was not in favor of adding further to the collection.[14]

In 1922 and 1923, Morgan took part over a period of several months in complex and absurd negotiations over the purchase of a collection of Greek manuscripts held by the Russian monastery of St. Andrew on Mount Athos. In May 1922, Archimandrite Metorphan wrote to Robert Blake, the Harvard Byzantinist and later library director, asking him to offer the material to "the gentleman desirous of acquiring our manuscripts" (i.e., Morgan) at 500,000 drachme. The letter began, "Your Devoutness: Most deeply respected Robert Karlovich [Blake's father was Charles Blake]! May the grace of God be with you!" and ended: "Calling down upon you and your family the blessing of God, we remain with true reverence for yourself." Morgan's response was to write to Blake in a rough parody of the archimandrite's high-flown style:

> To the deeply Shandian Karlovich
> May the grace of Rabelais be with you! Amen. . . .
> I regret to find the holy brethren of Athos are so deeply tainted with worldly wisdom and guile: after some secret communing, it has been revealed to me that our revered Father-in-Crime, the learned K. Lake [Harvard biblical scholar Kirsopp Lake], would counsel silence for a brief time.
> Surely it would ill become us of the sackcloth to lend ourselves willing victims to this holy larcency.[15]

Morgan did not buy the manuscripts.

At about this time, A. S. W. Rosenbach is said by his biographers to have gone to the Morgan Library to offer Miss Greene some books. "Miss Greene had just agreed that Rosy's enthusiasm about them was justified and that they belonged in the Morgan Library, when Mr. Morgan entered. He was not the wise man his father had been, and he was sometimes given to imperious moods.

He commenced an attack on Belle Greene for daring to consider a purchase without consulting him, an attack that embarrassed the Doctor greatly, for to him Belle was far more than a rich man's employee. Abruptly, he packed up the manuscripts and, telling Mr. Morgan he no longer wished to sell them, left the library. Dr. Rosenbach, for all his appreciation of the Morgan business, never forgot that it was the unimaginative younger J. P. Morgan who was said to have ordered the destruction of a number of Washington letters because of their bawdy contents. Belle Greene wanted the manuscripts in spite of the unhappy scene her friend had witnessed, and at her request they were sent back to her."[16]

Rosenbach seems to have been a generation late with the rumor he so readily accepted as fact. The younger Morgan wrote to the writer George Upshur: "You speak of some Washington letters which were destroyed. I do not know where you heard this, but Father always denied it. . . ."[17] It seems improbable that destroying Washington letters was a hereditary Morgan taint or compulsion.

The next important additions to the manuscript collection came with the private purchase of four items from the earl of Leicester in 1926. Perhaps the most exciting of the group was the *Berthold Missal* from the Abbey of Weingarten in Swabia, one of the great masterpieces of German thirteenth-century manuscript illumination.[18]

A year later, in 1927, Morgan bought six manuscripts from the estate of Sir George Holford. Among them were the *Reims Gospels* (ninth century), the late-thirteenth-century *Book of Hours*[19] for Yolande de Soissons, and the fragmentary early-sixteenth-century *Book of Hours* of Jean Bourdichon of Tours, miniaturist of the Anne of Brittany *Hours* in the Bibliothèque Nationale.[20] From Morgan's point of view the best of the lot was the twelfth-century English *Life, Passion, and Miracles of St. Edmund*.[21]

Throughout the remainder of the 1920s, Morgan and his librarians added to the manuscript collections, but at a slower rate.

Morgan became perhaps most widely known as a collector of mediaeval manuscripts for two that he did not keep: the *Psalter and Hours* of John, duke of Bedford, and the *Luttrell Psalter*. The Bodleian Library, Oxford, wanted the first, and the British Museum wanted the second. Morgan discovered that the museum lacked money in hand to buy the book. There was considerable feeling that England would be the poorer if this important item were allowed to go to the United States, so Morgan did a generous thing. He wrote to Sir Frederic Kenyon of the British Museum: "I should like to make you the following proposition: That the British Museum should go ahead and buy the Louterell [*sic*] Psalter as cheaply as it can at the sale. I will advance all the money that is necessary to buy it, lending the money to the Museum, without interest, for a year. At the end of a year from the sale, the Museum will repay me the money and keep the book as its own property, of course. If it does not do so, the book becomes my property and will be delivered to me by the Museum in payment of the debt."[22] In other words, he voluntarily gave up the opportunity to bid on the manuscript and advanced the money so the British Museum could have time to raise the purchase price without the risk of some outsider snapping up the prize. He made a somewhat similar arrangement with the Bodleian Library in the case of the Bedford *Hours*. He also contributed to the purchases.

Both Oxford and Cambridge universities honored Morgan with honorary degrees. Cambridge gave theirs on October 31, 1919— primarily, as we have seen, as an expression of appreciation for his part in J. P. Morgan & Co.'s supplying material and money for Britain in World War I. But his interest in books was not overlooked. In presenting Morgan for the LL.D., Sir John Sandys, the Public Orator, spoke of him as one "who, not unmindful of academic studies, not only collects books, but also reads them."[23] The Oxford degree Doctor of Civil Law, conferred at a special convocation on November 25, 1930, was more immediately a gesture of thanks for Morgan's saving of the Bedford *Hours* and the *Luttrell Psalter* for England.[24]

Early Printed Books

Morgan continued to buy early printed books throughout the postwar period. In 1919, he bought from Quaritch two incunabula that had been in the C. Fairfax Murray collection broken up in 1910: *A Mirror of Human Salvation*, printed in Utrecht in 1470, and a *Dance of Death* printed by Knoblochtzer in Heidelberg, 1488. From the H. Yates Thompson sale in that year, he acquired an *Aristotle* in Latin, printed in Venice in 1483. In November, Morgan wrote Miss Greene that he had directed Quaritch to bid in the Caxtons and Wynken de Worde books at the Britwell Court sale.[25]

The Library acquired the Ulm *Aesop* in 1925. The pace of collecting quickened in 1928. Acquisitions included Brant's *Das Narrenschiff* (*The Ship of Fools*) (Basel, 1494), thought to be decorated by Albrecht Dürer, and Antoine Vérard's *Roman de Tristan* (Paris, before 1496).[26] Nineteen twenty-nine was a good year, with the Vindelinus *Bible* (Venice, 1471);[27] the Ratdolt's 1494 *Graduale Romanum*, a music book for church choir; and the pseudo-Matthew *Infancia salvatoris* printed by William Caxton at Westminster c. 1477.[28]

Two more Caxtons were added in 1930: John Lydgate, *The Chorle and the Bird* [the churl, or peasant, and the bird], c. 1477, and by the same author, the better-known *The Hors, the Shepe and the Ghoos*, c. 1477.[29] Major accessions continued through the 1930s but tended to taper off after the 1938 purchase of the Caxton imprint of the anonymous treatise on diet and health—the only medical work Caxton printed—*Governayle of Helthe* (*The Governal of Health*), c. 1489.[30]

Bindings

In his first approximation to a policy statement on collecting, written in 1919, we saw that J. P. Morgan, Jr., was opposed to throwing money around on high-priced Shakespeare quartos. He added: "The same applies to the collection of bindings of which Pearson has written to me. Six or seven thousand pounds taken out of our available spending money for a lot of bindings collected by somebody else, does not appeal to me. . . . We have very good bindings, and I do not feel like adding to them in this wholesale way, though an occasional few may be very well when one has the loose change necessary. I hope you will agree with me about this."[31]

Among the few bindings acquired, presumably when the loose change was available, were a number of very handsome examples, particularly those discussed and illustrated in Howard M. Nixon's *Sixteenth-Century Gold-tooled Bookbindings in the Pierpont Morgan Library*. Several stand out. Among them is a binding for Marguerite de Valois, first wife of Henry IV, Henry of Navarre, of a work on astrology bound c. 1580–84 in limp white vellum decorated in gold with a marguerite (flower) and crowned *H*, for Henry. This was acquired from L. Gruel in 1919. Another one was done in

Paris in 1586 for the historian Jacques-Auguste de Thou (1553–1617). It is in red morocco with an overall design of alternating monograms and armorial bearings in gold. It was bought from A. S. W. Rosenbach in 1923.[32]

In 1938, the Library bought from the Mortimer Schiff sale at Sotheby's a Paris binding by Claude de Picques for Henry II, c. 1550, a copy of Theophrastus's *De Historia Plantarium*. King Henry II of France, the father of Marguerite de Valois, has been called the greatest bibliophile of his time, not excluding Jean Grolier, and the greatest collector of bookbindings of all time. The binding is in olive morocco over wooden boards in the style adopted by Francis I for his Greek texts.[33]

Morgan and his staff were not often the victims of error or deception, and little got past the penetrating eye of Miss Greene. She had for some time been skeptical of the authenticity of a binding attributed to Benvenuto Cellini and bought from the highly reputable Paris dealer Seligmann. Sure enough, her educated hunch proved correct. The binding turned out to be a polygot affair—most of the parts of German workmanship. Seligmann was mortified, and Morgan had to reassure him that he did not for a moment question his good faith.[34]

Literary Manuscripts, Autograph Letters, Modern Printed Books

We noted that Morgan began his serious book collecting in 1915 with the manuscript of W. M. Thackeray's *The Rose and the Ring*. A bill from the Rosenbach Company in 1915 lists the following additional purchases: an autograph manuscript of Keats, "On Looking into Chapman's Homer" (1816); Shelley, *Adonais* (Pisa, 1821), presentation copy to Severn; and Shelley, *Zastrozzi* (London, 1810), presentation copy to Dashwood. The total bill for $15,000 was paid August 26.[35]

When Morgan as an individual or the library as an institution got started collecting in a given area, an effort was made wherever possible to round out the holdings in that area, if only for tidiness. Miss Greene wrote to Morgan on May 29, 1922: "In regard to Rosenbach's Thackeray items . . . I have made him an offer of ten thousand dollars. . . . My only enthusiasm in the matter is that it *finishes* the Thackeray question in the Library, for all time, and *in so far as I know*, would make your Thackeray collection the finest known." Miss Greene asked him to cable whether or not she was authorized to pay Rosenbach the $10,000. A note on the copy of the letter says, "Cabled O.K. 6/7/22."[36]

This same conscientious point of view appeared two and a half years later at the Arnold sale at Anderson Galleries in New York. Miss Greene wrote, "In regard to the Tennyson items which, personally I loathe, it is a question of perfecting your already very large and fine collection of imbecilities." Morgan replied from London, "I reluctantly confirm that we ought to have the Tennyson idiocies. . . ."[37]

There were limits to Miss Greene's conscientiousness about rounding out special collections. Many years after the Tennyson episode, the Library was offered the manuscript of Dickens's *Life of our Lord*. She wrote, "This is an appalling product," and directed John Axten, Morgan's secretary, to reject it. She added: "Inasmuch as the lady states that the Dickens manuscripts are all in museums or private collections, it might be another pleasant blow to let her know that we have . . . complete original manuscripts of: *Battle of Life, Christmas Carol, Cricket on the Hearth, Frozen Deep* (with Wilkie Collins), *Holiday Romance, Hunted Down, Sketches of Young Gentlemen*, and over 500 autograph letters."[38]

Drawings and Prints

Miss Greene was interested in prints and nagged Morgan and the trustees to let her buy them. She wrote about the mezzotint portraits coming up at Sotheby's on November 12, 1924: "I rather fear that they may not interest you particularly." She went on to explain, invoking, as she tactfully almost never did, the departed but still strong presence of Morgan, Sr.: "Mr. Morgan had such a splendid and respresentative collection of mezzotints and, this Library 'being what it is,' as [Michael] Arlen says, I felt that you ought to cover the entire field of mezzotinting." Morgan authorized her to go ahead and bid.[39]

At ten o'clock on the evening of Tuesday, February 12, 1924, a little ceremony of financial and political importance took place in the Pierpont Morgan Library on East Thirty-sixth Street just east of Madison Avenue. It was the signing of the contract between Japanese officials and representatives of the syndicate of American bankers headed by J. P. Morgan for the offering of the $150,000,000 Imperial Japanese Government external-loan thirty-

year 6½ percent sinking-fund gold bonds. The loan was to provide money for the rebuilding of Japan after the disastrous earthquake of 1923, which had all but destroyed the cities of Tokyo and
Yokohama.[40]

Peculiar significance attached to the Japanese loan ceremony,
for within the week the library where it had taken place would
become one of the best-known libraries in the world, perhaps only
less famous than the British Museum and the Bibliothèque Nationale. J. P. Morgan gave the Morgan Library the great private
collection of books and manuscripts and drawings begun by his
father and added to by him, together with the building that
housed it, to a board of six trustees (of which he was president) to
administer as a public research library. He also provided a considerable endowment. The *New York Times* reported in detail the
opening press conference held at three o'clock on Friday afternoon, February 15, 1924:

> J. Pierpont Morgan at home showed himself to be the most
> simple and unassuming of men. There is nothing about him
> there that suggests the ruler of Wall Street's financial des-
> tinies, unless perhaps it is the sense of force conveyed by the
> erect and athletic figure, the strong face, the direct and pierc-
> ing glance of the eyes, and the sureness of movement and
> utterance. . . .
>
> Leading the party on a tour of the big room, Mr. Morgan
> immediately ceased to be the man of affairs and became the
> book collector, recalling with glee and delight many incidents
> connected with the acquisition of various volumes. Mixed
> with his own reminiscences were stories of his father's adven-
> tures as a collector. . . .
>
> It was noticeable that during the accounts that were given
> of the books and their acquiring, the words "my father" were
> many times on the lips of the present head of the house of
> Morgan. While he was showing his books he got to talking
> about the pleasures of collecting. Suddenly he seemed to think
> of something. He almost ran out of the room and asked an
> attendant for a key. He got it and returned to one of the cases,
> which he unlocked and from it took out what seemed to be a
> little silver box, less than the size of a half pound box of candy.
> He showed the outside of the "box," which was of silver fil-
> igree upon a gold back.
>
> "A year or two ago a man came here with this and showed it
> to me," he said. "He said, 'Mr. Morgan, you must have this in

your library.' I asked him why. Then he opened it up and there was this—see"—and Mr. Morgan showed on the fly-leaf the words, "Oliver Cromwell, Lord Protector." He pronounced the words almost gleefully.

"You see, it was Oliver Cromwell's prayer-book. That's what makes the fun about this, the things people bring to you and the things you find in unexpected places." . . .

The party then passed across the entrance hall and into the room on the west end. At the threshold they paused, so striking was the effect created by the setting. It is another two-story high room. The walls are in crimson tapestry. The ceiling is from an Italian palace. Priceless art objects adorn the tables and low bookshelves and the walls are rich in Italian masterpieces.

"The most beautiful room in New York," exclaimed one of the party.

"This is the room where my father literally lived," said Mr. Morgan. "I think it is probably the most peaceful room in New York. You never hear a thing in here except occasionally a bad automobile horn. I don't mind telling you"—this with a broad smile—"that this is going to remain the President's room."

In one corner of this room is a door with heavy bars and braces that gives the clue to the fact that it opens into what is in reality a vault. It is lined with bookshelves and on them rest the collection of original manuscripts and letters.

Mr. Morgan took from a shelf a little volume which he opened and showed. It was the original manuscript of Dickens's "A Christmas Carol."

"Scrooge and all the rest of them are in there," he said. "Isn't that nice?"

There was another book, "The Corsair," Byron's original manuscript.

"My father loved his yacht, 'Corsair,' you know," said the present owner of the collection. "It occurred to him once that he might be able to get Byron's manuscript. He looked around and found a man who located it. That's the way it came into his possession." . . .

In this room Mr. Morgan made use of a phrase that seems to be habitual around the Morgan library. Miss Belle da Costa Greene, the librarian, who becomes Director under the new administration, had made use of it in showing treasures earlier in the afternoon. The phrase is "'Oh, my!' stuff." It seems to mean features of the collection which readily excite expressions of admiration from the visitors. . . .

Almost the last thing he said was a question.

"Now what do you think of it? Have I done a good thing in making this gift?" he asked. He cast a glance about at the treasures which were no longer his in the sense that they had been his and his father's and there was almost a wistful note in his voice.[41]

Morgan appears here as a modest, even shy, man anxious for approbation.

After the transfer of legal ownership, the collecting process became less personal. As president of the trustees, Morgan continued to dominate the scene, but Miss Greene was under legal obligation to get authorization from the whole board. Morgan lived next door, and he liked to come to the Library every day and spend an hour or two in the West Room whenever he was in New York.

In 1928, a new west wing was added on the site of the elder Morgan's house at the northeast corner of Madison Avenue and East Thirty-sixth Street. The Pierpont Morgan Library had outgrown its original building. So Morgan had his father's house on the adjacent lot demolished and a library annex put up on the site.[42]

The Morgan Library lent books and manuscripts to other libraries and museums for exhibitions, but Miss Greene wasn't happy about it. Her misgivings were justified by the strange case of the stolen Scott manuscript. In the fall of 1932, the Morgan Library lent the manuscript of Sir Walter Scott's *Guy Mannering* to the library of Columbia University for an exhibition of Scott material. On October 25, it was discovered that the manuscript had vanished. The newspaper gossip columnist Walter Winchell, who made much of his underworld connections, printed a paragraph about it in the *New York Daily Mirror* and tried to help the Columbia authorities find out what had become of the manuscript. He was not successful.[43]

On April 17, 1933, President Nicholas Murray Butler of Columbia University wrote to Morgan of his relief upon learning that the manuscript had mysteriously reappeared.[44] It was never publicly explained, but Morgan learned from a friend of his who had been in contact with the underworld at the time of the

Lindbergh kidnapping (Anne Morrow Lindbergh, the child's mother was the daughter of Morgan partner Dwight Morrow), that the professional burglar who had stolen the manuscript had been unable to sell it and had since died. The friend's criminal connection wondered if the friend would like to have the item returned to Mr. Morgan. So it came back wrapped in plain paper.[45]

Morgan continued to make small presents to the library, including letters he himself had received from members of the British royal family, and to be interested in its affairs throughout the 1930s and into the 1940s, but the days of the great gifts were over, and the coming of World War II slowed down the whole process as had World War I a generation earlier. The last exchange that we have between Morgan and Miss Greene is in the summer of 1939. Miss Greene complained about the people who had come to New York for the fair and visited the library to see the special exhibition of books and manuscripts assembled on the occasion of the fair: "The visitors, few or many, are so d——— respectful, never speaking above a whisper, that I occasionally think of importing a hoodlum (I should say another hoodlum) to keep myself company." Morgan replied: "I do not think I should feel as badly as you seem to about the respectfulness of the visitors. They ought to feel that way whether they show it or not. . . . though of course I can quite understand your desire to have *some* hoodlumism around somewhere, for company's sake, now that I am abroad."[46]

CHAPTER IX

The Boom Years
1924–28

1924

LESS THAN THREE WEEKS AFTER THE 1924 OPENING TO A LIMITED public of the Pierpont Morgan Library, the Morgans sailed on the *Lapland* to join *Corsair* at Naples for the planned Mediterranean cruise.[1]

While the Morgans were away, several events took place. On March 12, the Morgan firm announced as fiscal agents of the French government that they had formed a group of banks to establish a credit of not less than $100,000,000 to the Bank of France. J. P. Morgan & Co. charged no fee to the Bank of France for their services in arranging the credit.[2] The day of the arrival at Naples, Mrs. Morgan's carnation display won first prize at the flower show in Grand Central Palace in New York.[3] On the international scene, the Dawes Committee on German Reparations was finishing their work of determining the precise amount of German obligations and how to meet them. The committee submitted its report on April 9.

The Mediterranean cruise was a great success. Morgan wrote to Dr. Dexter, "We had a glorious time in Greece and the adjacent isles and have returned not quite as wise as Ulysses after visiting the same places, but, nevertheless, with an added stock of health and interest." In writing to Sir Arthur Shipley, he observed of the trip, "We *were* a happy party, weren't we?"[4]

The German Loan

The great international issue of the summer of 1924 was still the German reparations problem. Could the newly proposed Dawes Plan be made to work? To make it work and enable Germany to meet her reparations obligations, there would have to be a huge loan to Germany. Could such a loan be floated? Only Morgan could answer that question.

When Morgan reached Paris on April 25, refreshed from a month's Mediterranean cruise, he immediately plunged into discussions with members of the Reparation Commission, who were anxious to get his advice on how to make certain of American participation in a German loan.[5]

Morgan returned to the United States for May, June, and July. He sailed for Europe again on the *Minnewaska* on July 26 and after a week in London left for Gannochy.[6] But Morgan's mind was not entirely on the game birds. "My mind's in a very soft and lazy state—in consistency rather like an overboiled cauliflower. However, I keep a few of the puzzling questions in the back of my head and don't think about them too much and solutions begin to emerge after a time."[7]

In mid-September, he left Scotland for London and wrote: "The German loan is the big business which has brought me down—and I hope very much that among us we can find a way of arranging it for it's of great importance. Only I am still rather doubtful about the possibility for the politicians have got things in such a state as to add greatly to our difficulties." Morgan explained some of the problems to Herman Harjes on the last day of September: "The point of difficulty is that, unless the Continent—both neutral and Allied markets—will take a reasonable share of this German loan, they will overstrain the English market, which is already very much chilled and is getting more so every day."[8]

At length the 1924 $200,000,000 German external-loan 7 percent gold bonds were floated, and the Dawes Plan was put into effect. The Reparation Commission approved the terms of the loan. The contract was signed in London on October 10, 1924, by Montagu Norman for the Bank of England, J. P. Morgan for the American underwriters, and Schacht and Luther for Germany. Morgan wrote:

It's the most important and responsible job we have had to tackle since the end of 1915, and as there were nine different markets in the same number of different countries to be cajoled or induced or driven into cooperation, and most of them did not at first wish to have anything to do with it, you can see how very confusing it has all been. However it's a real success and I have no doubts at all of the security and of the need of having the questions settled and giving to everyone an assurance of stability and quietness for a few years at any rate. In fact, disagreeable as it has been working for Germany, I've considered it as the last bit of our War work—and as important as any and so have not minded as much as I feared would be the case the interviews with the Teutons which have had to be.[9]

Before the German loan was finally approved, negotiations resumed on the project of floating a French loan in the United States. Morgan went from one conference table to the other.[10] Five weeks later, on November 24, the firm announced that they—in association with the First National Bank of New York, National City Company, and Brown Brothers & Co.—were heading a syndicate to offer on Monday $100,000,000 Government of the French Republic twenty-five-year 7 percent sinking-fund gold bonds at 94 percent and accrued interest, to yield approximately 7.53 percent.[11]

Meanwhile, an election had been taking place in the United States. Mrs. J. Pierpont Morgan, Sr., had come down from Bar Harbor, Maine, to her home precinct in New York to vote for Coolidge. Within a few days she was taken gravely ill. Her condition rapidly worsened. Her three daughters, Louisa Satterlee, Juliet Hamilton, and Anne Morgan, gathered, and her son cut short his European trip to take the *Berengaria* for home on November 15. Mrs. Morgan died on the night of the sixteenth. A funeral service was held on Friday, November 21, in Cragston, and a second service was held on Sunday morning at St. George's, Stuyvesant Square, in New York City. Morgan arrived in time for the second service. Burial was in the Morgan family plot in Hartford.[12]

With Mrs. Morgan's death, there came to an end a correspondence between mother and son that had extended back at least to 1878. The exchange was naturally sporadic, because for a great part of that time the two had lived next door to each other on Madison Avenue; when one was away, however, they wrote faithfully.

Morgan wrote to Charvet in the Place Vendôme and ordered six black heavy silk ties "suitable for mourning wear" with wing collars.[13]

Although Morgan himself invariably stayed clear of politics, in the November 1924 election, the firm was abused by partisans of both the Republican and Democratic candidates! The Republican Calvin Coolidge, who had succeeded to the White House on the death of Harding, was an Amherst classmate of Morgan partner Dwight Morrow. His Democratic opponent, John W. Davis, was one of the firm's lawyers. As early as August 1924, the Hearst papers had attacked Davis in an editorial that said, "The proud old Democratic party proposes to substitute the House of Morgan for the White House."[14] Before a Senate committee investigating campaign funds, Frank P. Walsh and old Morgan-hater Samuel Untermyer, now counsel for Progressive Senator Robert La Follette of Wisconsin, were active in trying to make it appear that Morgan and Morgan partners controlled the Republican Party with large campaign contributions. They were somewhat chagrined to find that Morgan himself had given nothing.[15] Coolidge and his running mate Charles G. Dawes of the Dawes Plan won the election handily, and the allegations of the anti-Morgan groups quietly died.

1925

Nineteen twenty-five opened with the election of three J. P. Morgan & Co. employees to a new category of limited participation in the firm. Arthur M. Anderson, William Ewing, and F. D. Bartow were given a peculiar status described by a representative of the firm: "While not a partnership, the offices conferred upon the three are the closest thing to it and might be described as a junior partnership."[16]

J. P. Morgan rarely made public speeches. A scant half-dozen of his addresses are recorded. One of these was the talk he gave on the evening of January 12, 1925, at the testimonial dinner of the New York State Bankers' Association for George F. Baker, age eighty-four, the New England–bred financier and principal donor to the Harvard Business School, on Baker's diamond anniversary with the First National Bank. The greater part of the speech was addressed to the courage and other virtues of Mr. Baker, but at one point Morgan made a statement about banking that expressed his own views on business morality. "Were I required to state an ethical code for our profession, I think that I would say the first rule should be: 'Never do something you do not approve of in order more quickly to accomplish something that you do approve of,' for there are no safe short cuts in piloting a business or a ship."[17]

March, April, May, and the first half of June in 1925 were months of almost continuous meetings, punctuated by such variations from the routine as games of golf at The Links.

That spring Morgan returned to sailing smaller craft in the Sound regattas. He bought back the old thirty-foot sloop *Phryne*, built in 1905 by Herreshoff, which he had owned and raced from 1910 to 1915.[18]

The spring of 1925 also saw the beginning of a series of postwar monetary stabilization loans and credits provided by J. P. Morgan & Co. or by syndicates that it headed. On April 28, a credit of $300,000,000 was established to facilitate Great Britain's return to the gold standard as announced by Chancellor of the Exchequer Winston S. Churchill. Two-thirds of the total credit was taken by the Federal Reserve Bank. J. P. Morgan announced the participation of the firm in the balance. Little more than a month later, the firm extended a credit to Italy in the amount of $50,000,000.[19] Large foreign loans were floated in rapid succession during the summer: the $45,000,000 Government of the Argentine Nation 6 percent external-loan sinking-fund gold bonds, issue of June 1, 1925, due 1959; the $50,000,000 Kingdom of Belgium thirty-year 7 percent external-loan sinking-fund gold bonds; and the $75,000,000 Commonwealth of Australia thirty-year 5 percent external-loan bonds.[20]

At the end of the year, the Italian credit was expanded into a loan offered on November 20, 1925, as the $100,000,000 7 percent external-loan sinking-fund bonds of the Kingdom of Italy and was promptly oversubscribed. The final stabilizing credit of 1925 was for improving the monetary position of Belgium. It was participated in by J. P. Morgan & Co., the Guaranty Trust Company of New York, and a group of British, Dutch, and Swiss banks.[21]

Meanwhile, tragedy struck the Morgan family. The death of Mrs. Morgan, Sr., in the fall of 1924 at the age of eighty-two had not been unexpected. But on Sunday, June 14, 1925, Mrs. Morgan, Jr., while returning from church services at St. John's, Lattingtown, was stricken with a sudden illness that was diagnosed as lethargic encephalitis, a relatively rare form of sleeping sickness distinct from the African variety transmitted by the tsetse fly. She soon lapsed into a coma.[22] Mrs. Morgan never regained consciousness. Her death came from cardiac arrest on Friday, August 14;[23] she would have been fifty-seven on September 30.

Jane Norton Grew Morgan had been shielded from the glare of publicity that beat down upon her husband, but she was a very real person in her own right. She managed households, town and country, very competently with the responsibilities of bringing up four children and entertaining. She directed the staff of gardeners at Glen Cove and won numerous prizes at flower shows on Long Island and in New York City. Shortly before her death, it came out that she had anonymously contributed to the archaeological work in Greece at sites the Morgans had visited on their 1924 Mediterranean cruise on *Corsair*.[24] Like her husband, she was a book collector. Her specialty was books in the general area of the arts.[25]

Mrs. Morgan was interested in the Pierpont Morgan Library and was greatly liked by the staff. Librarian Belle da Costa Greene was a clear-seeing, often hard-eyed, realist given to occasional sprightly but not effusive utterance, so it is very revealing to find evidence of the affection that both Mr. and Mrs. Morgan inspired to read her expression of devotion and compassion written from Siena shortly before Mrs. Morgan's death.

> I have written you four letters and destroyed them all, because I could not bear to intrude myself, and my unavailing sympathy upon your anxiety—and I shall not send this until I reach Paris, and there, I hope, learn that Mrs. Morgan is definitely improved.
>
> I did not believe that I could have suffered as much for anyone else, as I have for you during these dreadful weeks. Truly, there has not been one hour when I have not thought of Mrs. Morgan and yourself, nor one night when I have not prayed for you both.[26]

Morgan was one of the last of the old school in matters of social usage. He wrote on black-edged notepaper. From his London tailors, Henry Poole & Co. of Savile Row, he ordered two black mourning lounge suits and a black topcoat to be held until his arrival in late September.[27]

In the spring of 1926, Morgan wrote to the mayor of Glen Cove, Long Island, to tell him that he would present a park along the Sound for public use by Glen Cove and Locust Valley residents in memory of his wife. The expense of buying up this real estate was so great that he was unable to contribute to the New York Academy of Medicine as requested, explaining that the outlay "has left me practically completely dry."[28] The following year he planned another memorial. He offered $200,000 to the Neurological Institute of the Columbia University Presbyterian Hospital for a forty-eight bed ward for the study of treatment of encephalitis, the sleeping sickness that had caused her death. The gift was contingent on the institute raising $1,400,000.[29]

The day after the funeral, Morgan and his sons went on board *Corsair* and cruised up to Manchester, Massachusetts, where Mrs. Morgan's sister Rita Crosby and her family lived.[30]

Morgan went back to work upon his return from the cruise. He attended the usual meetings: First Security Corporation, United States Steel, Pullman Company. On Friday, September 11, he drove in from golf at The Links to greet Vivian H. Smith of Morgan, Grenfell & Co. upon his arrival on the *Berengaria* and take him out to the empty house at Matinicock Point for the weekend. A week later, on September 19, Morgan and Smith started for England on the *Olympic*.[31]

Upon arriving in England on September 25, Morgan immediately motored to Wall Hall. Wall Hall in Hertfordshire had been Mrs. Morgan's property, and she had bequeathed it to her husband.[32] He resumed his placid rural-English semimanorial existence. Not that being a country squire did not bring an assortment of problems peculiar to the situation. In response to the inquiry of a Miss Clark, Morgan had to send word that the fringe benefits of working on Wall Hall farm did not include funeral expenses.[33] The community club installed in the former pub raised issues of its own. The club was theoretically self-governing, but Morgan was the court of final appeal. There was a great to-do about whether it was right to play games on the Sabbath. Morgan's advice was followed, and games were permitted.[34] He arrived back in New York on the *Majestic* on December 1 and appeared to have benefited from his trip abroad.[35]

December 1925 was not unlike other Decembers of recent years, except in one important particular. Morgan had found a new place to go duck hunting. For several years he had been the guest of Clarence Mackay at Gardiners Island. He now joined a group that went shooting at Spesutia Island in the Chesapeake Bay. He and his partner Thomas Cochran spent two days there in December.[36]

1926

The year following his wife's death found Morgan restless. He was at his office less than half of the year. In mid-January he assembled his guests at Jacksonville, Florida, and set out on *Corsair* on the eighteenth for a cruise of the Caribbean. They put in at Nassau, Martinique, St. Lucia, Port of Spain, Trinidad, and returned to Brunswick, Georgia, by way of Jamaica. The cruise ended on March second. Ten days after his return to New York, Morgan became ill and was confined to the house for ten days more.[37] There followed an unbroken period of more than two months of work relieved by fairly regular golf.[38] He attended the familiar corporation meetings: Discount Corporation, First Security Corporation, United States Steel, Pullman Company, and those of the usual philanthropic organizations—New York Public Library, Cooper Union, Metropolitan Opera, Church Pension Fund, New York Trade School, Metropolitan Museum of Art, Pierpont Morgan Library, American Museum of Natural History.[39]

A frequent caller at the Library was Benjamin Morris, the architect of the new wing of the Pierpont Morgan Library.[40]

In January, Morgan acceded to the request of the Daughters of the American Revolution to be permitted to disinter the body of "Captain Mollie" Corbin from its grave on his late mother's place and to rebury it in the nearby West Point Cemetery. Margaret Corbin had replaced her husband in manning a cannon during the Revolutionary War battle of Fort Washington, Manhattan Island, on November 16, 1776, until she was wounded.[41]

In late April, Judge Elbert H. Gary, chairman, reported that at Morgan's suggestion the board of the United States Steel Corporation had voted to place its common-stock dividend rate on a regular 7 percent basis.[42] A day or so later, Morgan replied to an inquiry from the Indian Currency Commission, which was gathering testimony on the proposal that India circulate gold coins. There was one question on the Commission's interrogatory that he felt competent to answer: "Would a proposal by the Government of India to obtain such credits in New York for the purpose of carrying out the scheme referred to (for putting gold into circulation in India, concurrently with the sale of silver) be likely to encounter any such difficulty as would make it undesirable to contemplate that step?" Morgan stated emphatically that the opposition to the proposal would be very great and credits might well be unobtainable.[43] Montagu C. Norman, governor of the Bank of England, applauded Morgan's position:

> I gather that you have nailed the coffin of Indian Gold Circulation. In point of fact this country and Europe (and indirectly your country) were in real danger of trouble up to a month ago according to the extent to which each country was committed to gold.
>
> My object is to tell you that the alternative of gold coinage seems dead, thanks to your having your feet on the ground and saying that black and white are different! I am grateful.[44]

Long interested in the affairs of the American Museum of Natural History, Morgan gave the museum a collection of sapphires, which were put on exhibition on May 17. Carrying on his wife's interest in flowers, Morgan exhibited tulips at the summer show of the Horticultural Society of New York on May 22 and 23 and won a first prize. On the first of June, he went up to Camp Uncas for a brief visit.[45]

Crown Prince Gustaf Adolf of Sweden visited this country with his wife, Crown Princess Louise, in June 1926 to receive an honorary degree from Yale University for his scholarly work. Morgan led him on a tour of the Pierpont Morgan Library and took him up to New Haven on *Corsair* for the special convocation.[46]

The Morgan grandchildren were a great pleasure during this lonely time. In writing to Morris Whitridge, he spoke of them as "a constant source of delight and amusement."[47]

Morgan made one more *Corsair* trip to Manchester in July before sailing for Europe on the *Majestic* on July 17.[48] The summer in Britain followed the customary pattern: a stay at Wall Hall, off to Gannochy on August 13, a return to Wall Hall. There were two brief visits to Paris. The first, on August 23, was to attend Herman Harjes's funeral; the second was in mid-September.[49]

While Morgan was away, his gardeners kept up Mrs. Morgan's

tradition of growing flowers and exhibiting them. Morgan dahlias won—somewhat embarrassingly—the J. P. Morgan prize at the dahlia show of the Nassau County Horticultural Society on October 1.[50]

An economic manifesto advocating lowered tariff barriers was circulated in October of 1926 and was signed by a number of world figures in business, finance, and politics. It was reported that Montagu Norman conceived the idea. The document was published in London on October 19 over the signatures of J. P. Morgan; Albert H. Wiggins, president of the Chase National Bank of New York; Sir Arthur Balfour; Lionel N. de Rothschild; Sir Josiah Stamp; and many others.[51]

J. P. Morgan & Co. became particularly interested in the oil industry in the fall of 1926. They underwrote a stock issue for Marland Oil Company and were authorized by Standard Oil Company of New Jersey to sell $120,000,000 of twenty-year 5 percent noncancellable debentures to raise part of the money needed for the retirement of the corporation's $200,000,000 of 7 percent preferred stock.[52]

Morgan returned from abroad on the *Adriatic* on November 22. He was reported to have brought with him two brass-bound chests containing mediaeval manuscripts.[53] These would doubtless have included the four bought from the earl of Leicester for the Library.

Immediately upon his return to New York, Morgan set out again for a few days' shooting at Spesutia Island. Between shooting trips, Morgan went about his usual business at the office and attended the usual meetings right through December.[54]

Christmas was always a big event in the Morgan family. Mention has been made of the annual gifts of tea chests. Morgan's list of cash and other presents to the vast staff employed at his various establishments was a very long one. At Wall Hall, he remembered seven men and thirteen women employees, not counting postal workers and tradesmen. At Grosvenor Square there were six women and a man. At Camp Uncas he sent presents to a staff of sixteen and the local station agent. At his mother's old place, Cragston at Highland Falls, there were fourteen on the staff, with five spouses and another station agent. This accounting does not include the staffs at 231 Madison or at Matinicock Point, who were near enough to receive their presents in person rather than through the mail. In addition, there were presents of boxes of cigars to Grenfell, Whigham, and Michael Herbert in the London office and to such New York friends as Paul G. Pennoyer, James Gore King, C. Grant LaFarge, and the baggage master at Grand Central Station![55]

1927

Nineteen twenty-seven opened with the announcement that for the first time J. P. Morgan & Co. had admitted to partnership members of its own organization. Heretofore they had always brought in men with established reputations outside the firm. On the last day of 1926, the limited partners Francis Dwight Bartow, Arthur Marvin Anderson, and William Ewing were elected general partners. The same announcement by the firm recorded the close of the interest of two partners who had died within the year, William H. Porter and Henry Herman Harjes. In accordance with French law, the death of the latter had caused a change in name of the Paris house from Morgan, Harjes & Co. to Morgan & Cie.[56]

Morgan began the year with a visit to Spesutia Island. He returned to ten days' work and a number of dental appointments and then left for a week at Climax Lodge with his partner Charles Steele in a private railroad car. After two more weeks, more bouts with the dentist, and a meeting about the merger plans of the Northern Pacific and Great Northern railways, he went off again— this time to Jekyl Island for three weeks, stopping off briefly at Climax both going and coming.[57]

With his interest in shooting, Morgan always had dogs around the place. One of his great favorites in the middle 1920s was Juniver, of whom he wrote, "I take great comfort and pleasure in his society." A little girl in England wrote a letter addressed to Juniver. Morgan promptly replied to the child and sent the letter to Sir Malcolm Murray of Fort Belvedere, who raised dogs, to post. We do not know whether it was signed Juniver or J. P. Morgan. Morgan wanted a dog to be on hand to replace his beloved, aging Juniver, "because Juniver is such a dear." But he changed his mind and refused the offer of a young dog, lest old Juniver's feelings be hurt. He wrote, "I think it would break both Juniver's heart and mine to set up a rival to that gentleman in my house." Juniver died in December 1934, aged twelve years.[58]

J. P. Morgan moved to expand his investments in real estate

early in the year with the purchase through Flintlock Realty Company of the twelve-story Anderson Building at 12–16 John Street, valued at $700,000. This was reported to be the second important building in the downtown jewelry district owned by the Morgan family. He continued to trade in real estate during the first half of 1927. In May he bought the Hoyt house at 28 East Thirty-sixth Street, in the Murray Hill district, and in the first week of July he sold the four-story house at 135 East Thirty-sixth Street, at the northwest corner of Lexington Avenue.[59]

In April, Morgan took a party on a *Corsair* cruise to Bermuda. During his absence, Dow, Jones & Co. published comparative figures of bond offerings by investment banks or syndicate heads or participants during the first quarter of 1927. J. P. Morgan & Co. led the list with a total of $169,640,000, Kuhn Loeb & Co. came next with $161,803,000, and Harris, Forbes & Co. of Chicago was a poor third with $108,184,000.[60] At the end of the year, the Dow, Jones & Co. summary of new bond offerings in 1927 showed J. P. Morgan & Co. in the top position among syndicate heads with $502,590,000, National City Company second with $435,616,000, and Kuhn Loeb & Co. a close third with $423,988,000.[61]

Morgan had an exchange of letters with Harvard history professor Samuel Eliot Morison. The upshot was that he agreed to provide $200 a year for three years (1928–30) toward the cost of publishing the *New England Quarterly* which was just getting started.[62]

In April, Morgan wrote to congratulate George W. Wheelwright of Brookline on the engagement of his daughter. His letter shows us the heartfelt feelings of a parent: "There is no satisfaction in the world like having that worry off one's mind, and until the children marry, it is a worry that is ever before us."[63]

Morgan's pleasure in reading detective stories is a recurring theme in reports of his trips. In the course of correspondence with the Old Testament scholar Montague R. James of Eton, Morgan wrote in April 1927: "Your letter is of special interest to me in that you speak of your use of the time given by your holiday in Suffolk, and I note that detective stories are part of your curriculum. I am rather a victim myself, and delighted to find a person of much intellectual vigor as yourself also an addict."[64]

Newspaper reporters covering Morgan's frequent arrivals and departures on trans-Atlantic crossings often mentioned the supply of detective stories that inevitably accompanied him on these voyages. We rarely learn a specific title, but he had written Dr. Franklin Dexter in the summer of 1918: "*Jimmy Dale* was fine. I very much enjoyed it. Have you seen another by the same man called *The Wire Devils?* that also has some thrills." He also enjoyed John Buchan's thrillers.[65] Of an unnamed Sayers mystery, he later wrote Mildred Buxton that it "amused me greatly, Miss Dorothy Sayers has given as pleasant and, on the whole, most accurate impression of what I consider the British character, of anybody I have ever read. It is delightful."[66]

A week after his return from a visit to Bermuda, Morgan spoke at a meeting of some fifty active members of the clergy and laity of the Protestant Episcopal Church to commemorate the tenth anniversary of the Church Pension Fund. Under his stewardship, the fund had grown from $5,000,000 to $23,000,000.[67] Morgan's great contribution to the Episcopal Church, begun in 1927, was the underwriting of the publication of the revised Prayer Book.[68]

Mid-May was the regular time for the Long Island diocesan convention; it was also the time for the opening of the yacht-racing season. In the spring of 1927, Morgan owned, in addition to *Corsair*, the steam launch *Navette*, Captain John G. Greenlaw, and the thirty-foot sloop *Phryne*, Captain Edwin Nelson.[69] Styles in boat rigging shifted in the 1920s from gaff rig to Marconi rig, changing the shape of the mainsail from a quadrilateral to a triangle. *Phryne* was successfully converted to the new style in the spring of 1927. Morgan raced her a number of times in May and June.[70]

Early in June, he awarded the degrees at the Cooper Union graduation. Later in the month his entries, especially the roses, at the Nassau County Horticultural Society flower show won four first and seven second prizes. The week of the flower show, Morgan made his annual trip to Manchester, Massachusetts, on *Corsair* and attended the Harvard commencement.[71]

In 1927, J. P. Morgan & Co. bought a controlling interest in Johns-Manville, the asbestos manufacturing company. Morgan purchased a number of shares of the concern and distributed them among his family, explaining that the earning power of the company would be improved under the revitalized management, and the stock was bound to appreciate in value.[72]

On Wednesday afternoon, July 13, 1927, Morgan met with Hjalmar H. G. Schacht, the German financial expert, at the office of the New York Federal Reserve Bank. The following day he went on a brief midweek *Corsair* cruise.[73]

Morgan sailed for Britain on the *Mauretania* on July 27 accompanied by his daughter Mrs. George Nichols and her three children. The party reached Wall Hall on August 2. Morgan promptly assumed his familiar squire role. The country place in England was primarily a working farm, but there were flower gardens, and Morgan authorized his gardener Arthur Steward to enter a Wall Hall exhibit in a British flower show.[74]

As was his regular routine, he motored up to his Scottish shooting box at Gannochy for the opening of the grouse season on August 12. Although unseasonable rains spoiled the shooting for many, the Morgan party did very well and bagged 207 brace of grouse in one day's shooting.[75] But as Morgan was to write Belle da Costa Greene on another occasion, it really didn't make a great deal of difference about the shooting: "I am off to Scotland in a couple of days from now, and hoping for a really good holiday up there, though the reports of the grouse are not very encouraging. Still, not being a very blood-thirsty person, I don't mind as long as we have pleasant company and enough birds to keep us outdoors four or five days a week."[76]

On the last day of September, Dwight W. Morrow's resignation from J. P. Morgan & Co. became effective, and he began preparations to take up his appointment as United States ambassador to Mexico in mid-October. Morgan wrote, "We shall indeed miss Morrow, but every man must be allowed to do what he thinks is his duty, only I wish that he had not thought that this *was* his duty." Morrow was apparently on very good terms with the du Ponts (although Stettinius had been at odds with them over General Motors' dividend policy three years earlier), so Morgan felt it necessary to write to Pierre du Pont that Morrow's departure would not diminish the "feelings of friendliness existing between the partners of the firm and the members of all the du Pont family and business."[77] Harold Stanley was elected to partnership at the end of the year, when the firm found itself shorthanded because of Dwight Morrow's resignation and Thomas Cochran's illness.[78]

Morgan negotiated by cable the sale of Cragston, his parents' summer place, to a syndicate that proposed to turn the 733-acre property into a residential real-estate development. The sale was consummated the following year—again by cable, this time from Athens.[79]

Morgan arrived in New York on the *Majestic* on November 22 with the usual ritual of being met at the pier by Morgan bank representatives and frustrated newspaper reporters. He almost immediately went shooting at Spesutia Island over the Thanksgiving holiday and on the two following weekends. He invited his brother-in-law E. W. (Ned) Grew to Spesutia Island to shoot ducks during the second week in December and then to go by train to Climax for four days of quail shooting.[80]

Morgan reported to the secretary of the United States Steel Corporation on March 21, 1927, that he owned or controlled 2,081 shares of preferred stock and 3,833 shares of the common stock of the company. While he was in Scotland, the directors of the United States Steel Corporation met to discuss the choice of a successor to Chairman Elbert H. Gary, who had died on August 15. No action was taken, however, and it was reported that the selection would be postponed until Morgan's return.[81] A month after his return, the board met on December 27 and set up a three-man executive group among whom to divide Judge Gary's responsibilities. Morgan was named chairman to preside over board meetings and generally oversee the corporation, but he was given no executive duties and was not expected to give much—if any—more time to the company that he had as director. The other two members of the governing triumvirate were James A. Farrell, president and chief executive officer, and Myron C. Taylor, chairman of the finance committee. The naming of J. P. Morgan as chairman of the board of the United States Steel Corporation in December 1927 led to a considerable amount of misunderstanding. Morgan felt obliged to explain to his many well-wishers that he was not replacing the late Judge Gary as chief executive officer, but was merely serving as a figurehead to clarify the position of James A. Farrell, the president and real head of the company.[82]

At Christmas time, it was announced that J. P Morgan & Co. had extended credits of $25,000,000 to the Banca d'Italia of Rome, and that several London banks had joined the firm in stabilizing the Italian lira. Morgan cabled Premier Benito Mussolini congratulating him on Italy's return to the gold standard. At the end of the year, the Italian government conferred the Royal Order of the Crown of Italy on Morgan.[83]

1928

At the beginning of 1928, several new partners took their places at Morgan offices: Harold Stanley with J. P. Morgan & Co. in New York, Benjamin Joy with Morgan & Cie. in Paris, and Sir Thomas Catto with Morgan, Grenfell & Co. in London. The internal problems that had long been nagging the Paris house, Morgan, Harjes & Co., were apparently resolved with the death of Herman Harjes.[84]

On January 5, there was a ceremony at the Library at which representatives from the Japanese government decorated Morgan with the Order of the Precious Treasure, First Class, for his services in arranging the postearthquake loan.[85] Earlier that day, Morgan began a series of meetings with Daniel Guggenheim (with whom he had long been associated in Alaska ventures and Kennecott Copper).[86]

The following week there was a meeting of the Markle Foundation at 23 Wall Street—the first mention of that organization in the appointment book. In mid-January, Morgan went down to Climax; he then went on to Jekyl Island, February 11–28.[87] Upon his return, Morgan conferred with David B. Updike of the Merrymount Press of Boston about the printing of the revised Episcopal Book of Common Prayer. The revision and publication of the new prayer book dragged on through 1928.[88]

On March 15, Morgan's sister Anne came to tea at 231 Madison Avenue, and the following day Morgan sailed for France on the *Olympic*. He stopped at the Ritz in Paris for three nights and then took the train to Venice to begin the *Corsair* Mediterranean cruise. The group included Viscountess Harcourt, Boylston Beal, and the E. C. Grenfells. The cruise ended at Venice on April 23, when Morgan returned to London to catch the *Aquitania* on April 28.[89]

The month of May 1928 was broken up by service on the Nassau County Grand Jury and by attendance at the annual convention of the Episcopal Diocese of Long Island at Garden City.[90]

Early in 1928 there began a series of negotiations between Morgan and John D. Rockefeller, Jr., leading to the absorption by the New York Hospital–Cornell University Medical College of the Morgan family's favorite charity, the New York Lying-In Hospital.[91]

After Memorial Day in 1928, Morgan lunched at the United States Steel Corporation offices with George F. Baker, Jr., Myron C. Taylor, and T. W. Lamont. The next day Morgan wrote Taylor a strong vote of confidence on his part in the handling of the affairs of the company, of which Morgan was nominal chairman. The letter provides a revealing insight into the dictatorial control of the United States Steel Corporation exercised by the late E. H. Gary. He wrote: "What a pleasure and satisfaction it has been to me, ever since last January, to see how the Steel Corporation was moving along under your very careful and able guidance. The whole atmosphere is so different from what it used to be, and the Company has so completely emerged from the rut into which it had got owing to the Judge's secretive policies, that for the first time since my connection with the Company the directors have something to do and say, and have the power of getting the information to enable them both to say and to do wisely."[92]

That evening, Morgan dined with C. W. Gould and went to the Cooper Union commencement exercises, sitting on the stage in his role as trustee. The next weekend, he sailed *Phryne* to a fourth place in the Manhasset Bay races and then took *Corsair* up to New London for the rowing. This year, Morgan entertained the Harvard crew members and their fathers on *Corsair*.[93] After a busy week at the office, he sailed *Phryne* to a first at the Seawanhaka Corinthian Yacht Club and boarded *Corsair* for the trip up to Massachusetts for Harvard commencement and the class of 1889 dinner at the Union Club in Boston.[94] He got back to town in time to have lunch on the following Monday, June 25, with Col. Sosthenes Behn of International Telephone & Telegraph and to attend the meeting of the Metropolitan Opera and Real Estate Co. at the office of R. Fulton Cutting.[95]

While he was in New England, the Morgan gardeners made their usual fine showing at the Nassau County Horticultural Society flower show with six first and three second prizes, mostly with sweet peas.[96]

At the end of the week, June 30, Morgan entertained Spanish Ambassador Padilla and other guests on board *Corsair* to watch the start of the yacht race to Santander. A few days later, he sailed for the annual summer in Britain, and a month after his departure it was announced that the firm had headed a group of banks to extend a credit estimated at $25,000,000 to the Bank of Spain for the purpose of stabilizing the Spanish currency.[97] This was the latest in a series of credits from American banks under Morgan leadership to help restore order in European finances after the dislocation created by the war.

Morgan divided the summer and fall abroad between Wall Hall and Gannochy, as was his habit. The shooting season in Scotland was usually a source of great satisfaction to Morgan. The 1928 season was an exception. He returned to London disgusted.[98]

Morgan's interest in British sport stopped short of fox hunting. He had declined an invitation to hunt: "Your suggestions in regard to a day's hunting is not in the least attractive. I thank you, but I am clear off hunting since the accident to His Royal Highness— even if I had not been before."[99] The reference, of course, was to the habit of the Prince of Wales, the future Edward VIII, of falling off horses in the field.

Late in 1928, John Fleming, the manager of Wall Hall farm, won a number of prizes at agricultural shows in Britain. At Smithfield, Wall Hall entries even beat those from the royal farms. A minor project was the sending out of small quantities of wool from the farm's southdown sheep to be spun and woven into cloth for suits.[100]

Morgan's friendship with Cosmo Gordon Lang began when that prelate was Archbishop of York, "Primate of England." Morgan was, accordingly, pleased when it came out that Lang was to be promoted to Archbishop of Canterbury, "Primate of *All* England," in the summer of 1928.[101]

Morgan was kept abreast of almost everything that took place at the offices and at his several houses, even to very small details. He took a personal interest in the private lives of the staffs of the houses. He wrote to Mrs. Cameron, housekeeper of his town house at 231 Madison Avenue, to say how sorry he was that her pet bird, "Bully," had died.[102] The day after that letter was written was Election Day back in the United States. Herbert Hoover was elected president over Governor Alfred E. Smith of New York. Earlier in the year, before the Republican convention, Morgan had hoped to be able to change Coolidge's decision not to run for reelection—as expressed in his statement, "I do not choose to run."[103]

Morgan and his secretary, John Axten, sailed for New York on the *Olympic* and arrived November 21. The first meeting Morgan attended was the board meeting of the newly merged New York

Hospital. A few days later, he attended the Manville luncheon for members of the Swedish royal family and left the next day to shoot ducks at Spesutia Island. He may have caught cold sitting in a duck blind. At any rate, he was confined to 231 Madison Avenue for two days, dined with the wife of his lifelong friend James Gore King, and then went up to Boston for an overnight visit.[104]

The Dwight Morrows came to New York from Mexico City at Christmas, and Morgan went to various functions in their honor.[105]

CHAPTER X

Climax and Collapse
1929–32

1929

ON THE FIRST DAY OF 1929, THE NEWSPAPERS CARRIED THE AN-nouncement by J. P. Morgan & Co. of the promotion to partnership of three second-generation Morgan partners and two members of Drexel & Co., the Philadelphia Morgan house. Elected were Henry Sturgis Morgan, younger son of J. P. Morgan, Thomas Stilwell Lamont, son of Thomas W. Lamont, and Henry Pomeroy Davison, son of the late Henry P. Davison. The promoted Drexel partners were Thomas Newhall and Edward Hopkinson, Jr.[1]

The year started out in the usual way with meetings of the First Security Company, United States Steel Corporation and its annual directors' dinner, and the Cooper Union trustees. The first week was enlivened by the partners' luncheon at 23 Wall Street for the Italian ambassador, Signor G. de Martino, and the attaché, Signor Angelone. On January 9, Morgan had minor surgery on his leg, which kept him at home for a fortnight. On January 10, 1929, Morgan signed a contract for a new steam yacht, the fourth *Corsair*, to be built at the Bath Iron Works in Maine.[2]

J. P. Morgan & Co. did not as a rule underwrite stock issues. They were primarily a bond-issuing concern. In 1929, however, we find Morgan distributing to his grandchildren shares of United Corporation, a public-utility holding company, whose stock was underwritten by a syndicate headed by the firm.[3]

Even the conservative Morgan firm had not been able to with-
stand the pressures and temptations of the boom in the securities
market of the late 1920s. There are conflicting opinions as to who
in J. P. Morgan & Co. actually pushed for the idea, but Morgan
must take a great share of the responsibility, for his was the last
and deciding word. Frederick Lewis Allen expresses it pithily:

> Presently the Morgan firm was flirting with the brothers
> Van Sweringen; then it was backing them; by 1929 it was
> floating their giant Alleghany Corporation; and in that same
> year it entered the competition for influence over the public
> utility systems by forming another giant of the new finance,
> the United Corporation, a super-holding company for public
> utility stocks (with a little of the flavor of an investment trust
> too). Apparently the change in the atmosphere of Wall Street
> had had its effect. "It was the times."[4]

Morgan's important concern early in 1929 was his appointment
as a member with Owen D. Young of the Committee of Experts to
advise the Reparation Commission on the revision of the Dawes
Plan. Starting on February 11, the committee met throughout the
spring of 1929 in Paris.[5]

On March 30, Morgan left Paris for Venice, where he boarded
Corsair for a weekend cruise in the Adriatic.[6] He had planned a
longer Mediterranean cruise for the final extended trip of *Corsair
III*, but the cruise was cut back from twenty-four days to twelve
days by the press of work on the German reparations problem.
The truncated cruise began on April 13 and took the party to
Athens and some of the Greek islands.[7] The recently consecrated
archbishop of Canterbury was one of the yachting party. Morgan
had great affection for Cosmo Gordon Lang and presented Lam-
beth Palace, the London house of archbishops of Canterbury,
with a garden.[8]

Morgan was back in Paris on April 27. In mid-April, the conference had appeared to be on the point of collapse, but a compromise suggested by Owen D. Young was approved, and the meeting reached a successful conclusion in early June.[9]

Under the terms of the Young Plan, which had still to be
ratified by the legislatures of the signatories, German annual payments were reduced from £123,000,000 to be paid indefinitely to
£101,000,000 for thirty-seven years, followed by payments aver-

aging £85,700,000 until the fifty-ninth year, when all payments were to stop. A new Bank for International Settlements was to replace the Reparation Commission and its machinery.[10]

Morgan left the conference as soon as he could. He found the sessions frustrating, exhausting, and not very fruitful.[11] To Emile Francqui, one of his Belgian colleagues, he wrote, "I hope that our next collaboration . . . will be of an easier nature, for I found the task in Paris, as you did, exceedingly trying and difficult."[12] The amusing behind-the-scenes situation here was that Francqui had been a very stubborn obstacle to the success of the conference, but Morgan was able to win him over by a diplomatic coup of an unusual sort. Discovering that the Belgian was a dedicated pig breeder at his farm at home, Morgan sent him the greatly appreciated present of a number of prize-winning pigs from the Wall Hall piggery and by cultivating his personal goodwill secured his support for the Young Plan![13]

To a friend he wrote, "If [T. W. Lamont] says that I feel Hell has no terrors now, he is entirely wrong. What I do feel very strongly is that if Hell is anything like Paris and an International Conference combined, it has many terrors, and I shall try to avoid them."[14]

Morgan received warm congratulations on every hand for his part in the conference. Princeton gave him an honorary degree (in a group that included Sir Wilfred Grenfell and Walter Damrosch) on June 18. He wrote of the event in a revealing statement of his feelings: "I am not sufficiently used to that kind of thing to escape the slight feeling of shyness at having my obituary read aloud in my presence. . . ." The following year Belgium was to decorate him with the insigne of Grand Officier de l'Ordre de Léopold.[15]

It is impossible to assign credit or responsibility for the work of a joint enterprise like the meeting of the Committee of Experts. It was a blue-ribbon group including such notable economic figures as Sir Josiah Stamp and Dr. Hjalmar H. G. Schacht. Morgan's role at the conference was set down by Owen D. Young for T. W. Lamont to convey to the partners.

> Mr. J. P. Morgan is leaving tomorrow and I want you to get direct from me my view of the unique contribution which he has made to the success of this conference. Without him the job could not have been done. The magnet which has held the

conference together from the beginning has been the International Bank. That piece of machinery is not only essential to the plan, but if it gets off well will be the greatest contribution of the committee to the world. It would have been laughed out of existence before it could get a hearing had it not been for the prestige of Mr. Morgan and Lord Revelstoke and their wise and broadminded advice which dominated the bank plan. Then too the presence of Mr. Morgan had kept the committee together. Francqui has threatened to go home a half a dozen times on account of his marks, and when Voegler resigned Mr. Morgan saved Dr. Schacht from resigning too. These are the kind of contributions which I refer to as unique, which rest upon great reputation when backed by character, ability and fine personality. It is true that Tom [Lamont] and Nelson [Perkins] and I have had to do an enormous amount of spade work. That, although hard and essential, could have been done by others. Mr. Morgan's contribution would have been made by no one else in the world. He has shown great persistence and patience and certainly no man could have backed another with greater loyalty and strength than he has. At times he has been self-depreciating because he was not doing spade work too, but that was not his job. I want you to get the picture in clear perspective in your own minds before he comes home so that you at least will see what he in his own modesty will refuse to admit and that is, that we would have failed here had it not been for him.[16]

This statement by Young is the most informative and revealing that we have in explaining Morgan and his position in the world of finance. His strength did not lie in the originality of his thought or the power of his logic or eloquence. It lay in his own unique blend of force of character and personality, the undefinables that add up to "presence"—prestige, fairness, good sense, and experience.

June and July were an agreeable mixture of work and recreation for Morgan. He made a series of short cruises during *Corsair*'s last season as a private yacht, twice to New London for the crew races and twice to Bar Harbor. The first Bar Harbor trip included visits with his sister-in-law Rita Crosby at Manchester, Massachusetts, a stop at Bath, Maine, to look at the hull of *Corsair IV* in process of construction, and a visit with Sir Montagu Norman of the Bank of England who was visiting Mrs. John Markoe in Bar Harbor. He returned to Bar Harbor ten days later to see Norman again with a group of men including Governor Harrison of the Federal Reserve Bank and Russell Leffingwell.[17]

He attended the Cooper Union, Princeton, and Harvard graduation exercises that June. A series of five dentist appointments suggests extensive work in that department.[18] A high point of this period was Morgan's trip on June 24 to Washington in a private railroad car with Thomas W. Lamont, Owen D. Young, and Thomas Nelson Perkins to confer with President Hoover, presumably about reparations, and have lunch at the White House.[19] In between and around the edges of these activities, Morgan maintained his normal busy schedule of board and committee meetings and brief appointments with people prominent and unknown.

On July 24, Morgan sailed for Britain on the *Mauretania*. He followed a variation of his familiar schedule. Upon disembarking at Plymouth, he motored to Wall Hall, stayed there for two weeks, left for the grouse moors of Scotland on August 16, and remained until September 14, when he motored back to Wall Hall and stayed there until his departure for home on the *Olympic* on November 13.[20]

On October eighteenth, the newspapers reported that Morgan had been elected president of the Harvard Alumni Association, succeeding his 1889 classmate Allston Burr of Boston.[21]

Morgan was at the peak of his career. His recognition by fellow Harvard men and the honorary degree from Princeton came on top of his participating by invitation in the conference that seemed to settle the German reparations question, the outstanding issue left over from the war. His firm was the acknowledged leader of the banking world; they formed the syndicates that floated the loans for rehabilitating the war-stricken countries and for furnishing the credits to restore the value of their money. Then, abruptly, and immediately following the Harvard alumni honor, the collapse of the stock market in the week of October 20, 1929, began the disintegration of Morgan's world. While the drop in stock prices was sudden and dramatic, the actual decline of the business system in which Morgan flourished was a long and jerky descent. At this writing, that decline is still in progress, as emergency government expenditures designed to alleviate the economic depression that followed the fall of the securities market evolved through political expediency into a national policy of continuing deficit-spending and unbalanced budgets, with resulting inflation and a mounting national debt and interest payments to service it.

Morgan was in Britain when the crash came. In his absence, as T. W. Lamont later described it: "The Morgan firm organized a banking group to try to temper the panicky conditions and the public bewilderment by furnishing in certain key securities a temporary cushion so that urgent liquidation might be brought about in a more orderly way. This was all that was ever attempted, and that attempt was successful. Prices were bound to continue to decline if business fell off. But the banking consortium brought some order out of chaos and its modest operations served to calm a frightened public."[22]

Morgan supported his colleagues' efforts and cabled Lamont, "Very glad indeed you were able to get a strong party to work to act quickly and with judgement in the matter." Upon his return to this country a month later, he wrote Canterbury, "I . . . was made very happy by the absolutely magnificent conduct of all my partners during the 'late unpleasantness' in Wall Street. The Firm showed that it could behave just as well when I was not there, as it could have done had I been there, and I am consequently feeling very proud, and rather in the position of the successful school-master who finds his pupils doing better than he ever could himself."[23]

To those who wanted to find a scapegoat in the rich, his reply was:

"I do not believe there is any lack of a sense of responsibility on the part of men of wealth. I know that the best of these did what they could to discourage speculative excesses in the forepart of the year and to limit the panic, which developed when the bubble burst, and protect the community as far as possible from the natural consequences of the excesses of its more speculative members."[24]

Morgan continued to carry on his normal way of life. He went duck hunting at Spesutia Island. The usual round of meetings resumed: U.S. Steel, the Metropolitan Opera, the New York Trade School, the Northern-Pacific–Great Northern merger group, Discount Corporation, Metropolitan Museum, Pullman Company, New York Public Library, Century Association, Church Pension Fund, the vestry of St. John's, Lattingtown, and Cooper Union. He lunched a number of times with Owen D. Young at 23 Wall Street, attended a dinner meeting of The Creek Club governing board at Clarence Mackay's town house, dined with the Kings, went to the annual meeting of the New York Yacht Club, and entertained the Zodiac Club at dinner.[25]

He continued to make purchases, large and small. Morgan was an inveterate pipe smoker. He favored meerschaum pipes, which he ordered from F. Edwards & Co. of London. His favorite pipe tobacco was Craven mixture. He bought a painting from the dealer Thomas Agnew & Son, a portrait by the Venetian master Tintoretto, and lent it to the big exhibition of Italian paintings at Burlington House in London.[26]

He helped the American Museum of Natural History, which was in trouble, by agreeing to put up $57,167.50 to enable the museum to retain thirty-three employees likely to be let go in a drastic retrenchment move following the stock-market decline. He was strongly of the opinion, however, that the museum was operating on too ambitious a scale and should begin to economize. Earlier in the year, he had agreed to follow his usual practice and contribute $7,500 a year during 1929 and 1930 to continue the Museum's Central Asiatic expedition directed by Roy Chapman Andrews.[27]

Morgan spent Christmas at Matinicock Point, but went regularly to the office through December 31. He wrote to Grenfell with considerable satisfaction that all fifteen of his grandchildren (he was ultimately to have sixteen) sat down with him at Christmas dinner. The picture of the proud grandfather surrounded by his posterity has a slightly different perspective in the letter he wrote John Fleming congratulating him on Wall Hall's winning the fat-pig prize at Watford. (One wonders if Morgan was familiar with P. G. Wodehouse's accounts of similar victories by that peerless sow, Empress of Blandings.) To Fleming, Morgan observed: "We had a very good Christmas down on Long Island, when, for the first time we had all fifteen grandchildren seated at the same table and being fed. It really resembled nothing so much as some of the families of pigs I have seen on the farm; but it was a cheerful sight all the same."[28]

1930

On New Year's Day 1930, the papers reported that the steam yacht *Corsair* had been sold to the U.S. Department of Commerce for one dollar for use in charting navigable waters. This sale was preliminary to the launching of the new *Corsair*, fourth of that name, at Bath, Maine, on April 10. Between the relinquishing of *Corsair III* and the fitting out of the new *Corsair*, Morgan used the smaller *Navette*, Captain Greenlaw.[29]

After a week of meetings and a quick trip to Boston, Morgan took the private Pullman car Erie for Climax Lodge. He returned after a week's visit and proceeded at once to Bath, Maine, to inspect *Corsair*. After two weeks more of meetings, a dinner for Whitelaw Reid, a visit with the German ambassador, and another overnight trip to Boston including dinner with his sister-in-law Rita Crosby, he went off again by motor for three weeks at Climax and Jekyl Island.[30]

For Morgan, the major event of the spring of 1930 was the launching of the magnificent new *Corsair* at Bath on April 10. While the new yacht had been ordered during the boom period and provided employment for shipyard workers and naval architects in bad times, the commissioning of the world's most luxurious private vessel at this moment could hardly have been more regrettable for public relations.[31]

While *Corsair* was being completed, the Morgan firm was active in implementing the Young Plan resulting from the deliberations of the Committee of Experts, on which Morgan had served. The U.S. State Department approved the application of the Morgan syndicate to float in the United States about one-third of the $300,000,000 German reparations loan.[32]

June was a busy month. Following his return from *Corsair*'s maiden cruise, Morgan had meetings with such varied individuals as Stanley Baldwin's son-in-law, Gordon Munro; Cartier the jeweler; Sir Josiah Stamp, who lunched with the partners at the bank on June 6; Joseph C. Grew; Lord Ebury; and Guy Shipler of the *Churchman* magazine. On the twelfth, Morgan was present at the cornerstone-laying of the New York Hospital on Sixty-eighth Street.[33] This handsome new plant on the East River was designed by Henry R. Shepley of the Boston architectural firm Shepley, Bulfinch, Richardson & Abbott.[34]

Two days later he took *Corsair* up to New London, then continued on to Manchester for the usual visit and to Harvard commencement, at which he gave his address as president of the Harvard Alumni Association on the merits of the newly established

House Plan, which divided the undergraduate college into units like Oxford and Cambridge colleges.[35]

Two more *Corsair* cruises in July were further shakedown voyages before the big test. From July 18 to 27, Morgan crossed the Atlantic on *Corsair*. He went directly to Wall Hall. After Wall Hall came the grouse season at Gannochy beginning August 7 and lasting until September 25. There was the usual week in Paris, October 16–24. The final event of Morgan's British summer was the receiving of an honorary Oxford doctorate on November 25. The year ended with Morgan making plans for a Mediterranean cruise during the spring of 1931.[36]

1931

Nineteen thirty-one was the great *Corsair* cruise year, with three major voyages and three minor ones. In January and February, the yacht cruised in Caribbean waters,[37] in March and April in the Mediterranean,[38] in July she carried her owner across the Atlantic to begin his annual summer in Britain.[39]

Morgan remained at Wall Hall until his departure for Gannochy on August 9. He returned to London unexpectedly on September 18 because of the British financial crisis. Britain went off the gold standard on September 21. In London, Morgan was questioned about the government's move. He supported it with a public statement.[40]

He returned to New York in November in time to become involved in the receptions for Italian Foreign Secretary Dino Grandi. Grandi's visit was the occasion for a great deal of anti-Fascist activity, some of it directed against the Morgan firm, which had lent money for the rehabilitation of Italy after the war. He entertained Grandi at tea at the Morgan Library on November 23.[41]

In Washington, the Senate Finance Committee looked skeptically at the list of Morgan-managed foreign loans. This may be regarded as the very moderate opening of a series of congressional inquiries that would continue until the coming of World War II. It is axiomatic that hard times stimulate politicians to look for scapegoats in the business sector of the economy. On this occasion, Chairman Hiram Johnson gave the Morgan firm a clean bill of health.[42]

1932

The full impact of the economic downswing was not felt until two years after the stock-market collapse of October 1929. Morgan became acutely aware of it when he got back from trying to help the British and French cope with their fiscal problems in the fall of 1931. He wrote in January 1932: "Everyone has been so gloomy here since my return, that I fear I have caught some of the contagion."[43] He at once began to retrench. He suggested that the payroll at Wall Hall farm be reduced by natural attrition.[44] He wrote to Cowtan that he was compelled to let maintenance slide, "I am myself, cutting down as far as possible on all expenditure in my houses, both in England and America, and am doing nothing except that which turns out to be absolutely essential." *Corsair* remained in winter storage throughout 1932.[45]

Morgan's income was reduced by the business decline, and the demands for money were multiplied by the hard times. He wrote to Bishop Stires, "With the immediate and pressing calls for help that come from every quarter, and the business situation, it is very difficult to find any money, and I have been forced, most reluctantly as you may suppose, to cut down on my gifts, as I have in every other way. . . ."[46]

As the depression spread and unemployment increased in the spring of 1932, there was formed in New York the Block Community Organization with the objective of financing emergency work for 20,000 unemployed heads of families. Contributions were solicited from residents of some 16,000 city blocks throughout New York. Morgan had been active in unemployment relief work throughout the winter of 1931 as treasurer of the city's Emergency Work Commission under the chairmanship of Cornelius N. Bliss. He now joined the "Block-Aid" movement and helped inaugurate the drive for funds by broadcasting an appeal over radio station WJZ on the evening of Wednesday, March 23, 1932. The occasion caused considerable interest in the press with human-interest stories about his wearing a dinner jacket and Henry Physick, the butler, and others of the household staff listening to the broadcast in the servants' hall.[47] This might well have been the last stand of private philanthropy. The New Deal would shortly come into being, ushering in an era of vast and uncontrolled public welfare spending with relief becoming a way of life for millions.

The depression and its worries did not destroy Morgan's dry wit. He went to a dinner party at the house of John D. Rockefeller, Jr., one evening in April, and in the course of gathering up his hat and coat upon leaving, he inadvertently picked up an embroidered piece of linen, possibly a dressing-table cover. He wrote apologetically, "I have had it carefully done up and return it herewith. I hope you will not think that the habit of kleptomania is come on me these hard times."[48]

The Morgan firm had been leaders in railroad financing, and the railroads were particularly hard hit by the economic slump. Morgan felt keenly the unfairness of the government's favoring highway transportation at the expense of the railroads. The railroads were, in effect, taxed to subsidize their competitors, the trucks and bus lines, which used the highways without charge. He favored an evenhanded treatment by the Interstate Commerce Commission and heavy state taxes on trucks.[49]

Morgan went on his usual winter vacations in 1932, to Climax in January and to Jekyl Island in February.[50]

At the end of March, Myron C. Taylor replaced the triumvirate made up of J. P. Morgan, James A. Farrell, and himself and assumed full executive direction of the United States Steel Corporation. Morgan remained a director.[51]

In May, the Morgan tulips won the highest number of awards at the Nassau County Horticultural Society show. At the time of the flower show, Morgan was representing St. John's, Lattingtown, at the New York diocesan convention at Garden City.[52] A week later, a Leftist organization called the League for Industrial Democracy staged a minor demonstration in front of Morgan's town house, seeking to blame him for unrest in the coal mines of Harlan County, Kentucky, an alleged Morgan connection that the group did not clarify. A lawyer for the American Civil Liberties Union stood by to see that the fifteen student demonstrators' rights were preserved.[53]

The last week in May found Morgan at Camp Uncas. He motored back to New York by way of Stockbridge in the Berkshires, where he visited Dr. Riggs. June was lackluster without *Corsair* and the New London crew races, but Morgan did go up to visit his sister-in-law Rita Crosby at Manchester, and he attended Harvard commencement as usual.[54] Construction proceeded on the thirty-acre Morgan Memorial Park, the shore-front recreation area given to Glen Cove and Locust Valley in memory of his wife.

Morgan took great interest in the work and used to motor over to inspect it—riding beside the driver of a touring car, wearing a tweed cap and smoking a pipe the while. The dedication took place on July 16 with F. Trubee Davison, assistant secretary of war for aviation and son of the late Morgan partner Henry P. Davison, as speaker.[55]

Between the Fourth of July weekend and the dedication, Morgan was saddened by the death of James Gore King on July 10. King was perhaps Morgan's oldest and best friend. They had been schoolmates at St. Paul's in the 1880s, classmates at Harvard in the class of 1889, and King had served as Morgan's private lawyer for many years, setting up the Pierpont Morgan Library and Morgan Memorial Park as public institutions.[56]

An injured ankle kept Morgan housebound from July 2 to July 18, when he was allowed to go to the office for one hour. Three days later, on July 21, he sailed for Britain on the *Olympic*.[57]

Just before he left for Europe, Morgan wrote a letter to holders of Interborough Rapid Transit 7 percent notes in his capacity as chairman of the committee for Interborough ten-year secured convertible gold notes due September 1, 1932. He urged these investors to deposit their securities promptly since "the committee believes it to be in the interest of the 7 per cent note-holders to support a plan of unification on the terms which properly protect the interest of 7 per cent notes and the collateral pledged therefor."[58]

In Britain, Morgan went to Wall Hall and then up to Scotland on August 12. The Scottish shooting holiday was interrupted by the death in Switzerland at age sixty-six of Junius Spencer Morgan II—J. P. Morgan's cousin and schoolmate, a retired banker, art collector, and benefactor of Princeton University—who lived in Paris. Morgan went over to Paris for memorial services at the American Cathedral on August 23.[59]

Mention has been made of the degree to which Morgan was kept abreast of events at 23 Wall Street and elsewhere on the financial scene. On November 11, T. W. Lamont cabled from New York an account of developments at Kuhn, Loeb & Co., the friendly competitor and frequent syndicate partner of J. P. Morgan & Co. With Mortimer L. Schiff's death the previous year and Otto H. Kahn's ill health, the firm was taking in Elisha Walker as a partner and Kahn hoped (unsuccessfully) to bring in Jean Monnet. Lamont observed, "From our point of view it is important that Kuhn, Loeb & Co. should not drop to the status of a third-rate power so to speak." Morgan replied the same day, "I have, as you so well put it, a feeling of the great desirability of having Kuhn Loeb & Co. of importance in the community."[60]

A week after this exchange, Morgan sailed for New York on the North German Lloyd liner *Europa*, after a four months' absence. Interviewed in his cabin upon arriving on November 7, he was full of good humor and told newsmen that the economic outlook in England was more optimistic. F. D. Roosevelt had been elected president of the United States a fortnight before, and reporters asked if Morgan believed that things would improve in this country—using his own phrase about Britain—"now that the elections are over." He declined to prophesy. Following this interview, there was a disagreeable encounter with news photographers, who exploded flashbulbs in his face. He retreated and in the confusion drove one photographer off by brandishing his cane.[61]

CHAPTER XI

The New Deal
1933–38

THE ROOSEVELT ADMINISTRATION AND ITS DEMOCRATIC CONGRESS took office on March 4, 1933. In January and February, before the transfer of government, Morgan was away from the office the greater part of the time.[1]

Once in office, Roosevelt lost no time in asserting his leadership. He issued proclamations closing the banks and embargoing the export of gold. He sent a series of messages to Congress, together with bills that the Congress meekly passed for the purpose of reopening banks, restoring federal credit, relieving personal distress by giving out money, setting up the Civilian Conservation Corps to create employment, and stopping farm foreclosures. He pushed through measures to finance public-works construction and to regulate the securities and investment business.

Like so many conservatives, Morgan welcomed the new Roosevelt Administration. He wrote to his Harvard classmate Morris Whitridge early in 1933, "I do not rate Hoover as high as you do." He wrote Lady Buxton in March: "I think on the whole most people are feeling rather better than they were, because the new President is approaching his problems in the spirit of getting something done, instead of wrestling for a long time with a Congress of wholly uneducated people who have no courage. Of course it is quite possible that some of his cures may be the wrong ones, but, on the whole, things were so bad that almost any cure may do some good." He even wrote to Roosevelt to congratulate him on a job well handled.[2]

Morgan's enthusiasm for the new regime soon began to cool. The new administration in Washington revealed its hostility to the business community from the outset. Anti-business, anti-banking, and anti-Morgan sentiment was being whipped up by demagogic attacks. Old Morgan enemy Samuel Untermyer found a receptive audience.[3] Immediately following the inauguration of the new president, the Senate Banking and Currency Committee under Senator Duncan V. Fletcher was empowered by Senate resolution to investigate the activities of the securities business and the stock market. They engaged Ferdinand Pecora as special counsel. Morgan commented: "They have selected a little second-rate criminal lawyer, who has been Assistant District Attorney in New York, to represent the Committee and to ask the questions, and his idea appears to be to make it a criminal trial in which the accused is tried before he knows what he is accused of, and, in the meantime, must throw all his affairs open to inspection in order that the prosecutor may find something for which they can try him."[4]

Morgan was the first witness called. In the course of his testimony the articles of partnership of J. P. Morgan & Co. were read into the record, and the public learned how absolute was Morgan's authority within the firm.[5] In the testimony we have the first statement in so many words that Morgan regarded himself as semiretired at age sixty-six, although his long absences from 23 Wall Street made it increasingly apparent that almost from the end of the war the day-to-day responsibilities of the firm had been carried by the other partners. It came out in the questioning that the partners met daily, kept no minutes, but had not held regular meetings in the elder Morgan's time.

As the investigation proceeded, it soon became apparent that this was no detached search for truth conducted in accordance with the legal rules of evidence and the treatment of witnesses. Here was a politically ambitious criminal lawyer given the powers of prosecutor—and those of judge and jury as well—in a case in which the accused only learned of the crimes they were alleged to have committed when the prosecutor, without advance notice, introduced them into the "trial." The purpose of this charade was apparently to discredit those under investigation in order to satisfy popular demand for a scapegoat for the stockmarket decline and the subsequent economic depression. An integral part of the proceedings was the introduction of material that would make newspaper headlines, regardless of its relevance or accuracy. It was a virtuoso performance, because the inference of wrongdoing was present throughout, but without direct accusation of illegal actions that could be refuted by factual testimony.

At one point, Senator Carter Glass, Democrat of Virginia, author of the Federal Reserve Act and the only member of the committee with any knowledge of finance, became so outraged that he questioned the whole purpose of the investigation, saying: "I would just like to know what it is all about." Receiving no satisfactory answer, he characterized the proceedings with withering scorn: "We are having a circus, and the only things lacking now are peanuts and colored lemonade." This was greeted with laughter and applause.[6]

Much was made of the fact that Morgan and most of his partners paid almost no federal income taxes in 1930, none at all in 1931 and 1932. It was readily conceded that this was perfectly legal, but the implication in the hearings, the newspaper accounts, and the subsequent histories of the period has been that this was somehow dishonest or immoral. The fact was that while these men had received large incomes, they had sustained even greater capital losses, not paper losses, but actual losses in the given years, losses that were deductible from taxable income, just as capital gains had been included as taxable income.

In a different context, similar expressions of pious horror were registered about Morgan's real-estate taxes. Writers found it amusing and vaguely shameful that Morgan should have sued the city of Glen Cove for discriminating against him with an inequitable tax assessment on his house and surrounding grounds at East Island in 1927–33. The taxing authorities had apparently based his assessments on a presumed ability to pay rather than on a fair appraisal. On May 11, 1934, under an out-of-court settlement, Glen Cove granted a refund of $45,154. He had received a settlement of $32,800 in 1927, following a similar claim of inequality, and in 1931, a refund of $27,325.83.[7]

The old spider-web theory of interlocking corporate directorships that had lapsed into obscurity after the Pujo hearings was invoked again in an effort to prove a concentration of economic power by a small group of bankers. As at the earlier Pujo "Money

Trust" hearings, no evidence was produced by the committee or its prosecutor-counsel to show that any pressure or influence had been brought to bear by Morgan partner directors or nonpartner directors toward advancing any policy or that there was any consistent plan or purpose linking the activities of partner members within the several corporate boards on which they served. No attempt was made to show injury or loss sustained by the presence of these board members or that any illegal or even unethical action had taken place.

The impression was conveyed that the Morgan firm had sought to bribe certain allegedly preferred customers to do favors for the firm at some future date, when asked. The idea was apparently that they would want to pay off an obligation incurred when the firm invited them to buy shares of stock in Alleghany Corporation, Standard Brands, United Corporation, and Johns-Manville Asbestos at low figures, in the expectation that the market would go up.

Morgan in his June 9 statement denied the charge. He pointed out that in most instances there was no stock in existence and no market for the stock at the time the sales price was determined. The list, he said, was a compilation of those of their customers who knew the implications of speculative investment and could afford to take risks.[8] No evidence was produced to support the charges, but we can observe that for a group of sophisticated financiers, J. P. Morgan & Co. had acted with extraordinary naiveté in this sale.

One thing cannot be explained away: the firm was ill-advised to abandon its traditional policy of dealing in first-class securities and of doing business with first-class concerns. The firm's reputation was tarnished by this association with speculative common stock and with wheeler-dealers like the Van Sweringen brothers, even with the logical purpose of railroad consolidation.

It is easy, of course, to point this out with the wisdom of hindsight, but the pressures of the boom period were all toward abandoning what was regarded as a stodgy policy, and if the stock market had gone up instead of down, both the Van Sweringens and the Morgans would have been acclaimed financial geniuses!

The impression was conveyed that investment bankers as a group and J. P. Morgan & Co. specifically were acting contrary to the public interest in making postwar foreign loans and that a high pereentage of these loans had been defaulted on. The firm replied by showing that the default rate of Morgan-issued securities came to about 3 percent.

Morgan found the Pecora investigation very disagreeable.

> The experience was extraordinarily trying and fatiguing.
> To have to stand before a crowd of people and attempt, by straight answers to crooked questions, to convince the world that one is honest, is a form of insult that I do not think would be possible in any civilized country. . . . I feel very deeply the injustice caused by the misuse of the Senatorial power of investigation, in that they only want to investigate for the purpose of satisfying public curiosity, and perhaps to get some more votes for their next election.[9]

He was able to observe, however, "Mr. Pecora was not as exciting or exhausting to us as Untermyer was to Father."[10]

Throughout the entire proceedings and afterwards, the press had a field day; editorials appeared deploring the Morgans' "appearance of impropriety"; columnists expounded; constant readers wrote letters to the editor that deplored Pecora's "grandstand methods" or that attacked the rich. A lodge of the Benevolent and Protective Order of Elks gave a vote of confidence to Pecora.[11] Human interest stories abounded. The disgraceful episode of the female midget who was brought in by some publicity seeker on June 1 was exploited. "Mr. Morgan smiled feebly."[12]

After a brief holiday and an intense round of board and committee meetings, Morgan sailed on July 13 on the *Olympic* for his usual British vacation, laden with books, especially detective stories, to read on the voyage. He observed to reporters that he felt the need of a holiday—an understatement. On the day of his departure, the London *Times* published a strong vote of confidence in him, one of the very few favorable press reactions. He returned in October.[13]

Morgan's dissatisfaction with the New Deal had begun early, but, strangely, he persisted in separating in his mind the actions of Roosevelt from those of the Congress and the bureaucracy as late as November 1933.[14] By March 1934, however, this charitable point of view had disappeared. He wrote with bitterness slightly tempered by wishful thinking, "The United States will probably outlive even the attack upon it by Franklin Roosevelt, and I am particularly satisfied to see the rising tide of opposition to his fierce methods and his wholesale slaughter of reputations."[15]

1934

The first ten days of 1934 could hardly have been more varied for J. P. Morgan. He visited the Drexel office in Philadelphia on Thursday, January 4, something he almost never did. Several days later he attended a meeting of the Markle Foundation and followed it by listening to a lecture by British Oriental scholar, Lawrence Binyon, at the Library. The following few days were more normal and included meetings of First Security Co.; U.S. Steel Corporation finance committee, as well as a board meeting and annual dinner at the Pierre Hotel; Metropolitan Museum; Discount Corporation; Pullman Company; and New York Public Library Trustees.[16]

In January and February, Morgan cruised on *Corsair*. The party consisted of Morgan, the John W. Davises, Junius Morgan, Jr., and his wife, and the Louis Curtises of Boston. They sailed through the Caribbean and the Panama Canal to the Galapagos Islands and back.[17] While Morgan was away, Senator Robert M. La Follette, Jr., of Wisconsin accused the firm and Morgan personally of trying to block the proposed St. Lawrence Waterway because it planned to generate electricity at publicly owned power plants.[18]

The demagogic utterances of New Dealers from Roosevelt down, the castigation of businessmen as "economic royalists," incited the political Left to accelerate the attacks on Morgan. He rarely complained about the personal attacks, but occasionally expressed exasperation in temperate language: "I do not see any light ahead, and I am terribly bored and vexed by being eternally the target for all sorts of abuse from all over the country."[19]

The regular routine continued through the rest of the winter and spring, with several mildly noteworthy incidents. On April 2, 1934, Morgan motored out to Cold Spring Harbor to attend the funeral of Otto H. Kahn of Kuhn, Loeb & Co. Three days later, the president of Haiti dropped in at 23 Wall Street to see the partners. The ritual move from 231 Madison Avenue to Matinicock Point took place on April 13, just as it had when Jessie Morgan was alive.[20]

On Saturday, April 20, Morgan with his brother-in-law Herbert L. Satterlee and his two sons Junius and Henry reviewed the fashionable 7th Regiment, now the 107th Regiment, New York National Guard.[21] The next week he went down to Baltimore for minor eye surgery at Johns Hopkins. In May, there was the Episcopal diocesan convention at Garden City and ten days later a luncheon for visiting London partner Vivian Smith, followed by the second visit to the Philadelphia office in four months. On his return, Morgan left immediately for Camp Uncas, returning as usual by way of Stockbridge, Massachusetts, and Dr. Riggs. He returned in time to take a party of guests on *Corsair* on the day after Memorial Day to watch the naval review in New York harbor.[22]

On June 7, Morgan presented the diplomas at the Cooper Union graduation. The financier became more and more fatigued as the warm June evening progressed. His right hand became steadily more tired from shaking each graduate's hand; he mopped his head with a white linen handkerchief, and he whispered, "Nearly finished?" to the man who was handing him the diplomas. A week later he left for New England for Harvard graduation with visits on *Corsair* and New London for the races.[23] June of 1934, however, was unlike any other June in Morgan banking history. The entire character of J. P. Morgan & Co. was changed by the Banking Act of 1933, passed just prior to the Pecora hearings. This piece of legislation required banks to divorce the general banking function from the securities-underwriting function by June 16, 1934. The Morgan firm elected to remain in the banking business as a private bank.[24] This turning away from investment banking marked the end of an era. The actual transition date of June 16 found Morgan off on the *Corsair* cruising in New England waters.

Sailing on July 12, 1934, Morgan crossed the Atlantic on *Corsair* and after a visit in England went up to Gannochy for the shooting. Lord and Lady Elphinstone acted as host and hostess in Morgan's absences, since the Everard Smiths were prevented by illness from coming.[25] This is the only summer for which we have a complete list of the "guns," or hunters, and their schedule of visits. The grouse-shooting season was divided into seven periods of one week each with a complete turnover of guests each week except for the host and Lord Elphinstone.

The opening week, which began on the traditional date of August 12, there was an Elphinstone family party with the duke and duchess of York—the future King George VI and Queen Elizabeth—and her brother, the Honorable David Bowes-Lyon, and his wife. Other guests in the course of the season included the duke and duchess of Beaufort, the earl of Dalkeith, Morgan partner Harold Stanley, Sir Eric Hambro, Miss C. Mitford, the duke of Roxburghe, the future viceroy of India, the marquis of Linlithgow and his sons—the earl of Hopetoun and Lord John Hope—and Viscount Lewisham.[26]

Morgan made a number of trips to shoot ducks at Spesutia Island following his return to this country in November.[27]

The Christmas shipment of tea from China arrived in December, when an estimated six tons of "Mandarin" brand was delivered to 23 Wall Street to be distributed by J. P. Morgan, continuing his father's custom.[28]

Two days after Christmas, Morgan came down with a bad cold and was confined to his town house through New Year's Day. He was forced to miss the ball he was giving for his granddaughter, Junius's daughter Louisa, on the evening of the twenty-eighth. The sounds of dance music and revelry must have floated tantalizingly up the stairs at 231 Madison Avenue.[29]

1935

The year 1935 opened with Morgan still laid up with a cold. He soon rallied, however, and resumed his usual busy schedule.

In the middle of January, Morgan went down to Climax for a week and returned in time for the Markle Foundation meeting on January 28. He received total commissions from the Markle Estate in 1935 of $365,131.67.[30]

Recovery continued to lag at home and government expenditure to increase. Morgan felt the pinch in several ways: from the increase in taxes, from the decline in income, and from the threat to his estate from increased death duties. Morgan reacted by selling more works of art and by further cutting down on his charitable gifts.

Early in 1935, Morgan began a partial liquidation of his possessions. The first step was to offer for sale a group of paintings. The total proceeds for the year from the sale of paintings, including his collection of miniatures, came to $1,750,000.[31] Liquidation was not limited to works of art. In late February 1935, he offered for sale a tract of thirty-one acres of West Island, Glen Cove, Long Island. This was followed by the sale of Appletrees, an eighteen-acre estate in Locust Valley, and that by the sale of the commuting steam launch *Navette*.[32]

Morgan set forth his views on the economic picture in a letter to Senator Frederick Steiwer of Oregon in a reply to a telegraphic inquiry from the senator.

> It is my belief that the matters which cause the lack of confidence in the public, viz:—(a) the expenditures of such large sums of relief; (b) the unbalanced budget; (c) the excessive taxation on too narrow a base, are only symptoms of the real trouble, and would all disappear, probably fairly rapidly, if the real trouble could be remedied.
>
> This real trouble seems to be the impossibility of obtaining new money for industry by the old and well known method of the security market, and the fear on the part of industry of not being allowed to make profits, or of having those profits taken from them by excessive taxation. If, by a few comparatively simple changes in the Banking Laws and the Securities Acts, the security markets could be reopened, and industry could be convinced that it would be allowed to make and retain reasonable profits, it is my opinion that you would find the lack of confidence disappear with its causes, reemployment would take place with considerable rapidity, and tax collections be more satisfactory, which would permit a reduction in the most burdensome of them.[33]

The rest of the spring was fairly routine. Morgan spent three weeks at Jekyl Island in late February and early March. The subsequent weeks were closely scheduled: the meetings for the Metropolitan Museum, the Markle Foundation, and the New York Public Library finance committee took place on Mondays; the U.S. Steel finance committee and board and the Episcopal Church Pension Fund meetings came on Tuesdays; while the Pierpont Morgan Library trustees met on Wednesdays, as did the governors of The Creek, the Discount Corporation, and the Pullman Company.[34]

R. Fulton Cutting died in May, and Morgan attended the services on the twelfth. A week later, he went up to Hartford and made one of his rare appearances at an Aetna Insurance board meeting. The week after that, he visited Camp Uncas.

While preparations for the miniatures auction were in progress in London, Morgan decided to lay up *Corsair* for the season. Meanwhile, the tulips, roses, and sweet peas from the gardens at Matinicock Point grown under the care of head gardener James Kelly won prizes at spring flower shows around New York.[35]

With June came the Cooper Union graduation and the annual visit to New England to see his sister-in-law at Manchester, Massachusetts, and attend the Harvard graduation. On July 12 (midnight on July 11), Morgan sailed on the *Aquitania* for his annual summer visit to Britain.[36]

Morgan's standing in British official circles was a matter of interest and even of controversy. Late in July, at a royal garden party at Buckingham Palace, the king and queen were reported to have greeted Mr. Morgan with obvious affection and to have talked with him at length, to the dismay of a long line of dignitaries queued up behind him. His visit with Prime Minister Stanley Baldwin at No. 10 Downing Street even aroused questions in the House of Commons, and a sympathetic and wry editorial appeared in the *New York Times* on the absurdity of suspecting conspiracy from the encounter. Within the fortnight, Morgan entertained the duke and duchess of York, the future George VI and his wife, for the traditional August 12 opening of the grouse-shooting season at Gannochy in the Highlands.[37]

In Morgan's absence, his partners at 23 Wall Street were grappling with the reorganization problems of the bankrupt Missouri Pacific Railroad and of the other parts of the railroad empire of the Van Sweringen brothers of Cleveland controlled by an elaborate pyramid of companies with the Alleghany Corporation holding company at the top.[38]

The most important event in the Morgan story in 1935 was the formation of Morgan, Stanley & Co. to carry on the underwriting and selling of securities wholesale, which J. P. Morgan & Co. had been compelled to give up in June 1934 in accordance with the Glass-Steagall Act of 1933. Capital for the new investment banking house was put up by Morgan partners acting as individuals. The reaction of radicals to these circumstances can be readily imagined.[39]

One of the last events of the year for Morgan was the Zodiac Club dinner of December 27, held at 231 Madison Avenue. The club was a group of twelve men who met on the last Friday of each month, except during the summer. The enjoyment of food, wine, and conversation was the chief aim and activity of the society. Each club member took the name of a sign of the zodiac. New members were added to maintain the even dozen as old ones dropped out, and each assumed the zodiac sign of the member he replaced. Among the members were: Frank L. Polk of the U.S. State Department, Frank R. Appleton, Lewis Cass Ledyard, Henry Walters, Frank K. Sturgis, George Whitney, Roland Redmond (Scorpio), Princeton professor Henry Van Dyke (Leo), Vanderbilt Webb (Taurus), Dr. Austen F. Riggs, John W. Davis (Sagittarius), and Henry Fairfield Osborn. Meetings were held at Sherry's restaurant for some years, then they moved to various members' houses, but for many years, and especially during his last years, the members were guests of J. P. Morgan, Jr., at No. 231 Madison Avenue.[40]

1936

Throughout the fall of 1935, clouds were gathering for a new storm affecting J. P. Morgan and his associates. At issue was the allegation that the financial community had been instrumental in propelling the United States into World War I on the side of the Western Allies. The motive was supposed to have been to shore up the Allies in order to protect the great loans raised for them by American bankers under the leadership of J. P. Morgan & Co. A Senate investigation was launched by the Munitions Committee under the chairmanship of Senator Gerald P. Nye, Republican of South Dakota.

From January 7 to February 5, 1936, Morgan and two of his partners were interrogated by the committee. The story of the Nye hearings has been fully covered in the literature.[41] The whole episode was a public spectacle that turned out badly for Nye and the "merchants of death" theory. The committee finally admitted that there was no evidence of wrongdoing by Morgan and his partners, and the hearings fizzled out in a flurry of recriminations from senators who felt that Woodrow Wilson's endorsement of neutrality was being impugned.

While the Nye hearings were going on, King George V of England died. The death of his friend saddened Morgan. He wrote to an English friend: "the death of the King has caused a great feeling of sadness in this country as well as in yours. He was a very fine person and almost everyone knew it."[42]

In March 1936, London partners E. C. Grenfell and Vivian Smith were raised to the peerage as barons. Grenfell took the title of Lord St. Just, and Smith became Lord Bicester. Morgan sent his best wishes to the new lords by way of Charles Whigham.[43]

The spring of 1936 saw flowers from the Morgan estate once more doing well at flower shows. Morgan visited his own cyclamen exhibit at the Grand Central Palace on March 17, and his entries gathered prizes for sweet peas at the Horticultural Hall, Rockefeller Center, show in mid-June.[44]

May opened sadly, with Lewis Cass Ledyard's death and funeral at Syosset, Long Island. Two days later, Morgan was awarded the gold medal of the National Institute of Social Sciences at their annual dinner on May 6. By cheap invective, the radical press destroyed their own valid point that there was no special reason for the award.[45] But the occasion gave Morgan an opportunity to set forth his simple business creed: "Do your work; be honest; keep your word; help when you can; be fair."[46]

The liner *Queen Mary* arrived in New York on her maiden voyage on June 1, and Morgan went over to visit his old friends at the International Mercantile Marine offices to watch her steam up the harbor through a welcoming flotilla of small craft and fireboat water sprays.[47] It seemed to be the beginning of the usual June schedule. The Cooper Union graduation was held on the fourth. There were the usual meetings and lunch with George Baker at the First National Bank. On June 11, Morgan went by train to visit Rita Crosby in Manchester and attend Harvard graduation.[48] Soon after his arrival in Manchester, he suffered a coronary thrombosis. After almost three weeks at his sister-in-law's house, he was brought home to Long Island by private railway car on June 30. Word of Morgan's heart attack was withheld from the press until his return.[49]

It is clear to most observers that the strain and sense of outrage felt by the elder Morgan at the Pujo Money Trust hearings had caused his death early in 1913. It should be just as apparent that the public pillorying of the younger Morgan at the Nye "merchants of death" hearings—coming as they did on top of the Pecora hearings—contributed to the coronary thrombosis he suffered in mid-June of 1936.

Summer followed the usual routine, but at a more leisurely pace: Wall Hall, Gannochy in mid-August for the shooting, back to Wall Hall at the end of September, a brief Paris visit to keep the Paris office on its toes, another month in England, and home in mid-November—too late for the Harvard tercentenary festivities.[50]

In Britain, the year ended with the constitutional crisis over the king's involvement with an American divorcée, culminating in the forced abdication of the still-uncrowned Edward VIII and the accession of the former duke of York as George VI. Feeling ran high at the time of the abdication. Morgan belonged to the conservative group represented by the archbishop of Canterbury and Prime Minister Stanley Baldwin.[51] His judgment of Edward VIII was harsh and singularly unfeeling from an essentially humane person. He wrote to Lord Linlithgow: "What a pity that the little king had not the guts enough to do his job."[52]

1937

In mid-January 1937, Morgan began the most ambitious *Corsair* cruise ever undertaken. The route led to the West Indies with a stop at Jamaica, through the Panama Canal, then to the South Seas with visits to the Galapagos Islands, Fiji, Samoa, the Marquesas, and Tahiti. The party included Lord St. Just (E. C. Grenfell), the Everard Martin Smiths, Grenfell's sister Maud, and Lady Buxton.[53]

Upon his return, Morgan spent three weeks at the office getting caught up on accumulated business and then sailed for Europe April 21 on the *Queen Mary* for the coronation of George VI and Queen Elizabeth. Five days after his arrival in London, he had another heart attack and was compelled to miss seeing the coronation services in Westminster Abbey.[54]

He arrived back from England on the *Queen Mary* on June 7. While the *Queen Mary* was at sea, President Roosevelt and Secretary of the Treasury Morgenthau publicly denounced as tax evaders, rather than the more restrained tax avoiders, those who sought within the law to minimize their tax burdens.

Morgan lashed out at the illogicality and unfairness of the renewed appeal to popular envy. He told newspaper men who met him on arrival: "Congress should know how to levy taxes, and if it doesn't know how to collect them, then a man is a fool to pay the taxes. If stupid mistakes are made, it is up to Congress to rectify them and not for us taxpayers to do so."[55] Predictably, New Deal politicians were quick to condemn, implying piously that *they* would willingly pay more taxes than the law required rather than seek legal means of avoiding them. Secretary Morgenthau registered sanctimonious horror at Morgan's "immoral" sentiments.[56]

Morgan had only scorn for such demagoguery. He had special contempt for the statement "that the New Deal means 'subordination of the rights of property to human rights,'" observing that, "up to now the human rights in property have been among those most valued by mankind."[57]

He alternated short cruises with rest periods ashore until July 19, when he took his four oldest grandsons on a trans-Atlantic crossing on *Corsair*. The shortage of birds at Gannochy made it a disappointing season, however.[58]

Upon his return, Morgan received word that Pope Pius XI had awarded him the Grand Cross of St. Gregory the Great as an expression of appreciation for investment advice given by Morgan partners to the Holy See over a period of some ten years.[59]

The year ended with his deploring to Montagu Norman the fact that there would be no *Corsair* cruise that winter because nobody could come to keep him company.[60]

1938

The threat of a European war hung over the Western world in early 1938. The American economy, which had wallowed in continuing uncertainty and depression, began to be revived because of orders received from the European nations preparing for war. New Deal legislation designed to "prime the pump" had not worked. The use of this dubious metaphor by the administration moved Morgan to write anonymously to the *New York Herald-Tribune* a letter to the editor published on February 9:

The Well is Dry

To the New York Herald Tribune:

All this renewed talk about pump-priming overlooks the simple fact, known to every farm boy, that pump-priming accomplishes nothing when the well is dry. You don't even get back the water used for priming.

Our legislators have enacted a whole code of laws cunningly calculated to dissipate our country's income-producing capital and to discourage the initiative of enterprising men. I think we have reached the point where our well is dry and pump-priming a sheer waste.

A CITIZEN

New York, February 8, 1938

Across the newspaper clipping of this letter in the Lamont Papers is scrawled in soft lead pencil, "Partners—this from the pen of our Mr. JPM. TW."[61]

Morgan's letters continued to express his bitterness toward Roosevelt and his policies. He wrote to Montagu Norman again, "The state of affairs might be so satisfactory and helpful so easily if we did not have a crazy man in charge and my chief feeling is one of resentment at what he is putting us through."[62]

Deep as Morgan's bitterness was about the New Deal, he wrote, "All my feeling about that is over-shadowed by my feelings in the recent action of your friends, the Germans. They really are almost past believing, and I am wondering how Chamberlain manages to keep his head and temper under such provocation. It is obvious that there must come a point from which you cannot recede." The same letter mentioned Joseph Kennedy, the Roosevelt appointee as ambassador to Britain in 1938, "I share your wonder that an Irish Papist and a Wall Street punter should have been selected for the London Embassy. Of course you must expect him to have to be a New Dealer, because Franklin would not appoint anyone else."[63]

With the economic troubles of the United States and the threat of a second World War disturbing him profoundly, it is pleasant to find Morgan carrying on a correspondence also about the remarkable sighting of a blue goose with Canada geese in the pond at Beaver Dam, Long Island, and writing Robert W. Goelet about the protection of cyclamen bulbs from insect infestation by dipping them.[64]

On the first of April, Morgan set off by train for Miami, where he had chartered a houseboat for a week's cruise with his guests A. G. Millbank and John W. Davis.[65]

Morgan was wary about flying. He wrote to Charles Lindbergh, "I had the greatest pleasure from your wife's delightful book [*Listen, The Wind*]. . . . I am afraid that not even that, however, will make me really air-minded." But he finally made his first airplane flight on a small amphibian plane across Long Island Sound to New Haven on April 28 to attend a Zodiac dinner at Professor Whitridge's house. He was surprised to find how painless the experience proved to be.[66]

The following day, Henry Ford paid a fifteen-minute visit to the banker at the Wall Street office. Eyebrows were raised because part of Ford's "country boy" pose over the years had been to speak disparagingly of bankers. Following their meeting, Morgan bought a Lincoln car and gave one of his Rolls-Royces to the Ford Museum at Dearborn. Ford responded by saying publicly, "There is a constructive and a destructive Wall Street. The House of Morgan represents the constructive. I have known Mr. Morgan for many years. He backed and supported Thomas Edison, who was also my good friend."[67]

A shocking scandal in the New York financial community was the failure of the brokerage firm of Richard Whitney & Co. on March 8, 1938. Whitney had been president of the New York Stock Exchange. It was revealed that Whitney had quietly misappropriated customers' securities, employing them for his own use. This flagrant dishonesty played directly into the hands of the antibusiness elements that had long been making exaggerated accusations against the alleged villains of Wall Street. Here was an example of just such contemptible behavior. J. P. Morgan & Co. was directly involved in the Securities and Exchange Commission investigation of the Whitney affair. Thomas W. Lamont had lent money to George Whitney, a partner in the Morgan firm, to lend to his brother Richard. It came out in testimony that both George Whitney and Thomas Lamont had learned of Richard Whitney's unethical behavior as early as November 1937 and had advanced him the money to get out of his difficulties at that time. Morgan became involved because he had had to approve George Whitney's withdrawal of partnership capital from the firm to pay back to Lamont the $1,082,000 borrowed by Whitney to lend to his brother.

Put on the witness stand on May 3, 1938, by SEC counsel Gerhard Gesell, J. P. Morgan was asked to tell how much he knew of Richard Whitney's financial affairs and what he considered his public responsibility to be in light of what he knew. Strictly speaking, this information was only peripherally relevant to the investigation, but Morgan's statements could hardly have furthered public acceptance of his laissez-faire views. When asked if he had not had a responsibility to speak out when he learned something was amiss, he replied, "I had no power to go into Dick Whitney's affairs and then make a report to the Exchange that 'I did not like the look of it.'" Gesell asked, "Did you give any consideration at all to your responsibilities toward the Exchange in this particular matter?" Morgan replied, "No, none at all." Gesell then asked Morgan if he would have considered it his duty to report it to the New York Stock Exchange officials if he had known about the misuse of customers' securities. He replied in successive answers: "Well, I would not have carried the facts to the Exchange authorities if I understood the authorities knew them all and understood them." He added, "I should not anyhow." After further thought, he said, "No."[68]

Morgan's life-long interest in flowers found expression in the spring of 1938 in a new hobby, taking color photographs of botanical subjects. He wrote that his prints of drooping cherry branches in blossom had come out beautifully and he was looking forward to the rhododendrons. The following year he successfully photographed autumn foliage.[69] Morgan gardens on both sides of the Atlantic did well in flower shows in 1938, especially with chrysanthemums and begonias.[70]

The close of the academic year 1937–38 found Morgan once again participating in graduation ceremonies at Cooper Union and at Harvard.[71]

In Britain that summer, the king of England came to Gannochy as a guest for the shooting. The queen joined the party after visiting the earl of Strathmore, her father, at his seat near by. That fall, T. W. Lamont wrote to Morgan, "I attended the farewell dinner given last night for Sir Gerald and Lady Campbell. . . . Campbell spoke to me of a recent talk he had with the King in the course of which the King said to him: 'I consider Mr. Morgan the world's greatest gentleman. Whenever he comes into the room, I instinctively feel that I must arise.'"[72]

It was in other respects a very tense time. The September 1938 hurricane severely damaged the Matinicock Point area. A tidal wave did considerable tearing down of shore around West Island and Desoris Pond. Trees were broken but suffered relatively moderate damage.[73]

A week after the hurricane, there was signed on September 30, 1938, the Munich Pact between Hitler and Neville Chamberlain. Hitler's demands were granted and Czechoslovakia's defenses were destroyed. Morgan wrote that very day to congratulate Chamberlain: "What an achievement! I little thought when you were at Gannochy at tea and I said I had a hunch that there would be no war and you said hunches were the only thing to go on, and that you had the same hunch as I did, that you were going to be the one to have the imagination and courage to make that hunch come true! It never occurred to me that a single man could do so much by sheer force of courage, fairness and reasonableness."[74]

Early the following year, Morgan again supported the Chamberlain soft approach, as opposed to the more forthright demands of Winston Churchill and Lloyd George, who were out of office. He wrote of the latter, "Those two could not have behaved worse, and had they been in charge of affairs by an unfortunate accident, the world would long ago have been looking on at a War started, not because of any obligation on the part of Britain, but fought in behalf of the theory that Hitler ought to be punished."[75]

As early as January 1938, Morgan was under pressure from the Hertfordshire County Council to sell part of the Wall Hall property to be included in the Green Belt around London—with the council threatening to invoke its right of eminent domain.[76] While the final sale of the property took place after his death, Morgan had given instructions in December 1938 for winding up his tour of duty as a country squire. This was not a process that could be rushed, and the plan for liquidating the farm called for an orderly withdrawal.[77]

While he was giving up Wall Hall under duress, there is reason to believe that he welcomed the prospect of a release from responsibilities and expense, particularly with war imminent. At home he was retrenching and eliminating all along the line. He resigned from the Harvard Club of Boston, and the Metropolitan and Grolier clubs in New York at the end of the year.[78]

J. P. Morgan was a very generous man. Morgan benefactions tended to fall into several categories: education—gifts to schools, colleges, and universities, especially to Harvard University, and to students attending them; specific fields of learning often associated with specialized museums, such as natural science and archaeology; the arts—to those of the past, as with the Metropolitan Museum, and to the performing arts in the present, as with the Metropolitan Opera; health—again giving both to the supplier of medical services and to the patient; the Episcopal church; and gifts to individuals. His dismay over the shrinking of his income that resulted from the economic decline and the fiscal and regulatory legislation of the government was not because of the effect on his personal standard of living but because of its effect on his ability to give. He wrote President Butler of Columbia: "It is a great grief to me not to be able to continue to do what my Father and I did for so many years, that is, to contribute to the things we liked to help; but that time is past, and, I fear, must remain past until the New Deal is forgotten."[79]

CHAPTER XII

World War II
1939–43

1939

THE FIRST FOUR MONTHS OF 1939 WERE LARGELY SPENT AWAY FROM the office. Morgan took his usual holiday at Climax in mid-January.[1]

He called a press conference in his office on February 1 to announce the approaching admission to general partnership in J. P. Morgan & Co. on February 17 of Henry C. Alexander, J. C. Raymond Atkin, and William A. Mitchell. This was the first admission of new partners since Charles D. Dickey was admitted on January 2, 1932, and it was to be the last such admission. Changes in the firm since 1932 had included the death of Thomas Cochran, Edward T. Stotesbury, Horatio G. Lloyd, and S. Parker Gilbert. Henry S. Morgan, William Ewing, and Harold Stanley had resigned in September 1935 to create Morgan, Stanley & Co., investment bankers. Thomas Newhall had simply resigned. The full roster of partners prior to admission of the three newcomers was: J. P. Morgan, Charles Steele, Thomas W. Lamont, Junius S. Morgan, George Whitney, R. C. Leffingwell, Francis D. Bartow, Arthur M. Anderson, Thomas S. Lamont, H. P. Davison, Edward Hopkinson, Jr., and Charles D. Dickey.[2]

Three days later Morgan was off to Climax again for a week on his way to a fortnight at Jekyl Island. From there he went to Miami for a week's deep-sea fishing.[3]

The restrictions placed on private banks by New Deal legislation and the resulting problems are a recurring theme in correspondence. Morgan felt bitterly the inability of J. P. Morgan & Co. to raise capital for business concerns.[4] Morgan had gone to the aid of a number of individuals and concerns during the depression. A recurring name in the Morgan correspondence is that of Cowtan & Sons, Ltd. This London-based concern attended to the greater part of the Morgan family decorating business. When Cowtan's got into financial straits in the fall of 1925, Morgan went to their rescue with a loan of $25,000, and when the depression brought hard times to the Cowtan company, Morgan finally bought out two of the owners.[5]

Following his return from Florida, Morgan put in ten days' work at 23 Wall Street, and sailed on March 24 for England on the *Queen Mary* to join *Corsair* at Monte Carlo for what was to be her last cruise. The party was made up of the archbishop of Canterbury, Lady Buxton, Lord and Lady Elphinstone, and Miss Elphinstone. *Corsair* was under her new master, Captain G. T. Calder, who took over upon the retirement of Captain Porter. The cruise got as far as Istanbul when Morgan suddenly called the whole thing off and gave orders to cut short the voyage because of the threat of war. Morgan's decision is quite understandable: his passengers included the sister and brother-in-law of the queen of England and the archbishop of Canterbury.[6]

In spite of the threat of war, two world's fairs were in progress in the United States in the spring of 1939, one in San Francisco, the other in New York. Morgan was present at the official opening of the New York exposition's British pavilion on May 12 and of the French pavilion on May 24. The day after the opening of the French building, Morgan had some teeth extracted. The ordeal did not seriously sap his energies. He went directly from the dentist's to the Library, which had put on a special exhibition of books and manuscripts in conjunction with the exposition.[7]

A display of tulips from the Morgan gardens in the Gardens on Parade exhibit at the fair won the gold medal of the Nassau County Horticultural Society.[8]

The visit to the United States of the king and queen of England in the second week of June caused a great flurry of excitement. On Thursday, June 8, Morgan went down to Washington for the day to attend the garden party for the royal couple at the British Embassy. The following day, he boarded *Corsair* for Sandy Hook, to await the arrival there of the destroyer carrying the king and queen. Saturday morning, the tenth, *Corsair* followed the destroyer into New York harbor. That afternoon, Morgan was present at the reception at the British pavilion. When the festivities were over, he left on *Corsair* for New London for a weekend with the Harvard crews.[9] A week later, he was back in New England waters again on *Corsair* for his annual visit and the fiftieth Harvard reunion of the class of 1889. He wrote Jenny Tracy, "Wednesday, the 21st, I was at Harvard celebrating my 50th Anniversary of graduating, and 'busy' was the right word, for, like a lot of old boys, they kept it up very actively."[10]

Meanwhile, the threat of war in Europe was more immediate, but Morgan went ahead with his usual vacation plans. There was the customary grouse shooting at Gannochy in August, and again the king and queen of England were houseguests, from August 14 to 19. Along with the various aides, were Lord Eldon and the queen's brother and his wife, the David Bowes-Lyons. They had a pleasant visit despite the poor shooting.[11]

The 1939 Gannochy guest list indicates that one more shooting party took place the following week, August 21–26. There follows a hastily written notation cancelling the subsequent schedule. It reads: "The shooting at Gannochy terminated at this point because of Mr. M's return to London on account of the war crisis. Gannochy was closed up on Saturday, August 26, and Mr. Morgan returned to U.S.A. on the 'Queen Mary' sailing August 30." Within the week, the British government requested that Gannochy Lodge be turned over to the authorities as a hospital for war casualties, and Morgan agreed.[12]

The *Queen Mary* was crowded with people leaving the troubled countries of Europe. Morgan kept only a modest cabin on the ship and turned over the rest of his suite to the steamship company to help accommodate the 2,385 passengers on board. Celebrities on board included Myron C. Taylor of U.S. Steel, Dean Gildersleeve of Barnard College, the Ranee of Sarawak, the film actor Bob Hope, and Erich Maria Remarque, author of *All Quiet on the Western Front.*[13]

Morgan was as pro-Ally in World War II as he had been in World War I. He was angered by the action of the United States Congress in voting an embargo on the export of armaments to either side in the war. He conceded that nobody wanted to enter the war, but felt it was not good sense to announce to the world that no provocation would cause the United States to go to war.[14] We have noted earlier that Morgan was acquainted with Charles Lindbergh because Anne Morrow Lindbergh was the daughter of his former partner Dwight Morrow. Lindbergh's wartime pessimistic attitude toward the Allies was an exasperation to the British and a source of pain to Morgan.[15]

In December of 1939, there opened in Washington the investment banking hearings of the Temporary National Economic Committee under the chairmanship of Senator Joseph O'Mahoney, Democrat of Wyoming. The hearings were directed by the counsel for the Securities and Exchange Commission, Peter R. Nehemkis, Jr., with the help of Thurman Arnold, Assistant U.S. Attorney-General in charge of antitrust law enforcement. The SEC, in the persons of these officials, contended that a few investment banking houses, and especially Morgan, Stanley & Co., held a monopoly on security underwriting and issue in the United States. The hearings continued into the new year, with repeated attempts by the SEC to show that Morgan, Stanley & Co. was merely a front for the parent firm.[16] In a sense, the SEC was correct. In personnel and in financing, the underwriting house was indeed an extension of the firm and a continuation of the investment banking aspect of J. P. Morgan & Co. The great difference was that bank deposits were no longer at the disposal of underwriters. Since this was the chief justification for separating the two functions, the essential purpose of the law, to safeguard deposits, was achieved. It appears that Leon Henderson, head of the SEC, Arnold, and the radical press were upset because the punitive purpose of the law—to prevent Morgan partners from making money—had been legally circumvented.

On December 8, 1939, with World War II three months along, Morgan offered *Corsair* for service with the British navy in a letter to Lord Lothian, British ambassador to the United States.[17]

High point of the holiday season and one of Morgan's few relaxed and pleasant occasions since war had broken out was granddaughter Tracy Pennoyer's coming-out party at 231 Madison Avenue.[18]

1940

Morgan's whole outlook and way of life were changed by events whose full force began to be felt in early 1940. His income was rapidly shrinking from double taxation in Britain and in the United States. The war was pushing up taxes everywhere. It was almost unprecedented for Morgan to refuse a request for money from Harvard University, particularly from its library, but in January 1940 he wrote Librarian Keyes D. Metcalf that he could not help.[19] He instructed John Callahan to run Camp Uncas as cheaply as possible, with no garden and no tapping of the maple trees for sugar. He told F. A. Steward to run the Wall Hall gardens on a reduced scale and to let others win at the horticultural show—"we have swept the board for many years." At the same time, he impressed upon John Fleming the great need for economies on the farm. To Bingley, the butler, he directed that since Ambassador Kennedy, a recent tenant, would probably not be returning to Wall Hall, he should close the house and reduce the staff.[20]

In early 1940, Morgan expressed deep concern for the Finns, who had been invaded and bullied into submission by the Soviets and their fate subsequently tidied over in the United States by an adroit campaign of pro-Soviet propaganda—a campaign so skillful that Robert Sherwood's pro-Finnish play *And There Shall Be No Night* was even changed on the American stage to an indictment of Nazi tyranny instead of the Soviet tyranny of the original![21]

On February 15, a drastic change in the Morgan firm was announced. The private banking firm of J. P. Morgan & Co., a partnership (including its predecessor firms) since 1861, would become on April 1, J. P. Morgan & Co., Inc., a New York corporation. The announcement of intent was made personally by Mr. Morgan at a press conference.[22] Morgan explained the reasons to Elphinstone: "We are just at the moment in the throes of turning our business into a company, a step made necessary by the fact that so much of the capital is in a few hands, and those few hands are elderly. Death duties destroy present fortunes, and the new laws render it impossible to make any money to replace the lost money quickly. So we are turning into a company, and are going on with the same people in charge, and the stock will, I suppose, gradually get into the hands of the public. I only hope they will like it when they get it!"[23]

Morgan was not happy about the change. He wrote Grenfell that his income suffered greatly because he no longer enjoyed the tax-free income from government bonds held by the partnership. That tax advantage now accrued to the corporation. J. P. Morgan sold the seat on the New York Stock Exchange that he had held since April 25, 1895. The buyer was H. Gates Lloyd, a Morgan partner who elected to remain a member of Drexel & Co.—the Philadelphia house of the Morgan firm, which would continue as a partnership.[24]

Morgan's own position as senior partner in the old concern changed to chairman of the board of the new corporation. Thomas W. Lamont became vice-chairman of the board and chairman of the executive committee. The partners became directors, with no changes.[25]

In the early summer of 1940, Morgan wrote: "I cannot conceal from myself the fact that I am getting older rather fast of late days." His deafness increased and he got a hearing aid, but he still found it difficult to hear general conversation.[26]

Morgan wrote to Vivian Smith on June 21, 1940, that he had that day signed the papers transferring *Corsair* to the British navy. The fact was he could no longer afford to keep the ship.[27]

Another pro-British action involving very real responsibility and obvious personal inconvenience for a man of seventy-three was his taking under his protection three English children evacuated from bombarded Britain. The three were relatives of Vivian Hugh Smith, recently created Baron Bicester, a partner in Morgan, Grenfell & Co. Two-year-old George Vivian Smith and his year-old sister Ann were children of Bicester's son Hugh and his wife Lady Helen Smith, daughter of the sixth earl of Rosebery. The third was Neil Primrose (Lord Primrose), eleven-year-old half-brother of Lady Helen, and Rosebery's son by his second marriage to Eva, Lady Belper.

The children arrived with a shipload of other evacuated youngsters on the *Britannic* on July 29. Morgan met his new charges at the pier and took them out to Matinicock Point.[28] Later in the summer he wrote to Elsie Hooper, "I am getting on as well as I can and looking out for my refugees to the best of my ability. They are very pleasant small people to have around and I greatly enjoy them. I am not going off very much myself this summer, for I do not like to be too far away from the centre of my life—which is the office." The English children returned home early in 1942.[29]

In the late summer of 1940, the Western Allies were steadily losing the war to the Wehrmacht. As in the previous war, the United States was slow to recognize the dangers of an Axis victory. In the Senate, Rush D. Holt of West Virginia was particularly shrill in attacking the proposed draft. He accused "international bankers" of being behind the measure and stated on the floor of the Senate that J. P. Morgan had contributed half a million dollars to William Allen White's Committee to Defend America by Aiding the Allies. Holt subsequently "extended his remarks" in the *Congressional Record* to reduce the $500,000 to $500.[30]

It was politics as usual as the 1940 presidential election campaign warmed up. A favorite ploy was to drag the Morgan name into the campaign oratory to assure the more numerous common people that the Democrats loved them, while the Republicans were the wicked supporters of wealth and privilege.[31] The Big Lie was also flourishing in Nazi anti-American propaganda. J. P. Morgan was widely accused in the German press of helping President Roosevelt to stir up a "panic psychosis" of hostility toward the Reich.[32] Roosevelt was reelected. Morgan looked forward with dismay to four more years of abuse, but took comfort in Roosevelt's pro-British sentiments in the war.[33]

Following the incorporation of J. P. Morgan & Co., Morgan wrote that his duties and responsibilities were not as onerous as they had been before the change went into effect, so he could get away more easily and probably stay away longer.[34] In fact, however, his appointment calendar for 1940 was the most active in twenty years, because the war prevented him from taking his usual four-month sojourn in Britain. He did take a number of brief vacations throughout the year: to Climax in January, to Jekyl Island in February and March, to Florida for fishing in April, to Camp Uncas for a couple of days in late May.[35]

After *Corsair* was transferred to the British navy, Morgan chartered *Inishowen V* for the summer of 1940. So while the trip to Manchester at Harvard commencement time was by motorcar, Morgan was able to cruise in New England waters on the boat in July and August. Unfortunately, the vessel ran aground off Block Island on August 12. Nobody heard the Race Rock fog signal. Morgan was able to report to Lord Rosebery that young Neil Primrose had not been at all frightened by the accident—merely annoyed that the cruise had had to be called off.[36]

Following the return from Florida in the spring, there were very short holidays—a weekend here, four or five days there. Morgan's schedule was a long list of board and committee meetings— the familiar organizations. To all of these were now added the board of directors and the executive committee of J. P. Morgan & Co., Inc. Late in the year, there were the usual duck-hunting weekends to Canada and Spesutia Island and four days at Climax in early December.[37]

The news from Britain continued to be bleak. Sons of Morgan's friends were prisoners of war. He sent Red Cross packages to John Elphinstone and Charles Hope, Lord Linlithgow's boy, in German prison camps. Wall Hall was bombed. The Morgan, Grenfell offices in London were bombed.[38] Earlier in the year, he had received word about conditions at Morgan, Grenfell & Co. from Grenfell. His account of the office was most sad, with the whole place nearly deserted and very little work to do.[39]

His friend Lord Lothian, the British ambassador to Washington, died, having refused medical attention. Morgan wrote, "Christian Science appears to me to be worse than most diseases." He added an optimistic note: "It is most heartening to see that . . . the Italians are not any better than they were in the last war in spite of the Duce's brags."[40]

1941

Morgan had settled into a gloomy frame of mind in 1941. Between Roosevelt, Hitler, and a consciousness of aging, he saw very little cause for cheer. The American war effort was bogged down by labor demands and the post-Nye munitions investigation prejudice against military preparedness.[41] Wall Hall was windowless from bombs hastily dropped by inexperienced German fliers anxious to jettison bombs and flee from the London balloon barrage. The Morgan London offices were hit again.[42]

While feeling frustrated in business, in philanthropy, and in his desire to help the British war effort, Morgan was compelled to carry on his normal, peacetime routine. As in times past, he alternated periods of concentrated work with periods of rest and change of scene. On January 7, he met his sister Anne at Jersey City on her arrival from Europe on the *Exeter* and three weeks later went uptown to visit her. Between those two encounters, he spent a week at Climax Lodge and another week at the office and attending meetings. He was off again for most of February and half of March at Climax but was at Jekyl Island for the annual meeting of the Sans Souci Association.[43] He returned to New York in time to attend the flower show at Grand Central Palace. Morgan flowers continued to win awards in 1941. His tulips took a gold medal at the New York Horticultural Society show in May, and his chrysanthemums won most of the blue ribbons at the Nassau County Horticultural Society exhibition in the fall.[44]

Morgan was moderately social in the first half of 1941. He dined with the D. H. Morrises on January 29, attended young Paul Pennoyer's wedding on February 8, made a point of lunching at 23 Wall Street on March 28 because presidential candidate Wendell Willkie was expected. He was fairly faithful as a participant at Zodiac Club dinners and entertained the club at Matinicock Point for their May meeting. In late April, the usual group of men made a deep-sea fishing trip on *Virago* out of Miami.[45]

The spring schedule was a familiar one: the usual organization meetings, a brief visit to Camp Uncas in May, the June graduation exercises at Cooper Union and Harvard, and the annual visit to Manchester. What was not according to long-established custom was the continuous succession of board and committee meetings running straight through the summer and fall. All through the months that Morgan had formerly spent at Wall Hall or Gannochy, he now lived on Long Island, commuting to 23 Wall Street in New York almost every business day. Not since 1918 had he worked so steadily at the office. Vacation trips were limited to two or three days at Camp Uncas in August and two overnight visits to Montauk Point fishing with John Davis.[46]

Anticipating United States entry into the war, Morgan carried on a correspondence in June of 1941 with the British Museum and the National Gallery, London, on the safe storing of art works to protect them from bomb damage.[47]

The old Nye Committee merchants-of-death theory was revived in the Hearst papers and precipitated an anonymous threatening letter to Morgan.[48]

Morgan continued to fume and sputter about the prevailing short-sightedness and stupidity in the United States concerning the Nazi menace. The work stoppages by American workers in war industries infuriated him. The peace-at-any-price point of view exacerbated his fury.[49]

He sought solace in books: Fanny Burney's diary, Miller, *You Can't Do Business with Hitler*, Shirer, *Berlin Diary*, Ferrero, *The Reconstruction of Europe* (following the Congress of Vienna).[50]

Morgan made two duck-hunting trips to Long Point, Ontario, in October and a number of short trips to Spesutia during the following months.[51]

A number of Morgan's old friends died during 1941. As was his usual custom, he was frequently in attendance on these sad occasions. He was at services for Walter Frew in May, Arthur Curtiss James in early June, and George Blumenthal at the end of June, and he made a special trip to Boston for Bishop William Lawrence's funeral on November 8. His closest friend in Morgan, Grenfell—E. C. Grenfell, Baron St. Just—died on November 27.[52]

On December 7, came Pearl Harbor and American entry into the war. Morgan was gratified that the United States was finally committed to the defeat of the Axis powers.[53]

1942

The advent of American participation in World War II affected Morgan more personally than as a banker. Members of the Morgan family became involved in the war effort early. Both of his sons became naval officers. There was not a great deal that a man of seventy-four could do to help, but Morgan did what he could. He had a lifelong interest in the sea. The naval training ship *Prairie State* was one of his special interests. He participated in award ceremonies on the *Prairie State* in May and July.[54]

On August 10, he took part in a ceremony to award the Navy *E*, for excellence, to the Federal Shipbuilding & Dry Dock Company, a U.S. Steel subsidiary, Kearny, New Jersey—at which Secretary of the Navy Knox gave a "pep talk" to shipyard workers, who a year earlier had gone out on strike. Later in the month, he watched the launching at Brooklyn Navy Yard of the U.S.S. *Iowa*.[55]

Changes took place at the office. On February 3, 1942, it was announced that stock in J. P. Morgan & Co., Inc., would be sold to the general public. Smith, Barney, & Co. bought 16,500 shares of the capital stock of the bank—8.25 percent of the total outstanding—at $206 a share. Purpose of the move was to establish a market value for the shares, especially for inheritance tax purposes, and to get farther away from the family ownership among partners' descendants that had led the Securities and Exchange Commission to restrict the bank's operations.[56]

Aside from the extraordinary circumstances of war and within the firm, 1942 was very much like any other year for J. P. Morgan. Among the effects of the war, of course, was the restriction put upon his movements. As in 1941, vacations were of relatively short duration, though fairly frequent. The one exception was the four-week trip to Jekyl Island in February and March. This was to be the final season of the Jekyl Island Club. The cooperative apartment building of the Sans Souci Association closed its doors, and the proceeds of the auction of the furniture of the Morgan apartment, $875,000, was given to charity.[57]

Morgan made two trips to Climax in January. On the first, he took as guests his brother-in-law E. W. (Ned) Grew, his young associate and former partner Henry Clay Alexander, and Edwin S. S. Sunderland, the lawyer of the Davis, Polk firm. At the end of the month, he went directly from the wedding of his grand-daughter Jane Nichols and Walter Page to the train for another week at Climax.[58]

The latter half of March, all of April, and most of May saw Morgan at his regular office duties without a break. Following the annual Long Island diocesan convention at Garden City in mid-May, he spent a scant four days at Camp Uncas. The annual June visit to New England—Manchester and Harvard commencement—was very brief, only two days. A week following his return, he had minor surgery on his hand at St. Luke's Hospital.[59]

He worked through the summer, with two brief visits to Camp Uncas. On the last day of August, he went out to Conneaut, Ohio, for a voyage to Duluth, Minnesota, on board the U.S. Steel Corporation ore-carrier S.S. *Irvin*. The round trip on the Great Lakes took a week. Morgan got back in time to attend the meeting of the executive committee of J. P. Morgan & Co., Inc.[60]

He made duck-hunting trips to Long Point, Ontario, twice in October and went to Spesutia every week in November and almost as often in December. On November 11, he invited David Bowes-Lyon, brother of the queen of England, and Willis Hill Wood, and on the eighteenth, Henry Clay Alexander and Dudley Mills. Between trips, Morgan kept up his regular schedule of meetings.[61]

1943

The last year of Morgan's life began with a duck-hunting trip to Spesutia Island, Maryland, over the New Year's weekend. He returned to Spesutia within the week and upon his return to New York, following tea with his sister Louisa Satterlee, he left for Boston to attend the funeral of retired Harvard President Abbott Lawrence Lowell. His friends were dying fast. Frank L. Polk died the following month.[62] Toward the end of January, Morgan took a party of men—E. W. Grew, Dudley Mills, E. S. S. Sunderland—to Climax Lodge for a week of shooting.[63]

During January and February, Morgan conscientiously attended board and committee meetings of almost all of his concerns: U.S. Steel, Discount Corporation, the Episcopal Church Pension Fund, Cooper Union, Metropolitan Museum of Art, New York Public Library, Pullman Company, J. P. Morgan & Co., Inc.[64] He presided, as chairman of the board, at the annual stockholders' meeting of J. P. Morgan & Co., Inc., on January 20. He was disappointed that so few questions were asked from the floor.[65]

On February 21, he was present at the wedding at Locust Valley of his granddaughter Virginia "Dina" Pennoyer to Norman B. "Ike" Livermore, Jr., of San Francisco. He was reported to have been in high good humor at the reception. Next day he visited the Brooklyn Navy Yard. He then left for a Florida vacation the following day, Tuesday, February 23, after a U.S. Steel Corporation finance committee meeting.[66]

On Thursday his valet, Bernard Stewart, telephoned Morgan's secretary, John Axten, at the office, to report that they had arrived at Gasparilla Inn, Boca Grande, Florida, and that Mr. Morgan was "slightly indisposed." He had suffered a slight heart attack, following the two earlier attacks in prior years. From then on his condition rapidly deteriorated over a two-week period. The heart attack was followed by a stroke, and on March 13 he died at the age of seventy-five, the same age at which his father had died almost exactly thirty years before. Present at his bedside were his daughters Frances Pennoyer and Jane Nichols and his younger son, Harry; the elder son, Junius, was overseas with the navy.[67]

The body was taken back to New York to the Pierpont Morgan Library on March 15. The funeral was held the following day at St. George's, Stuyvesant Square. A memorial service was held in London at St. Margaret's, Westminster, on March 18. Present were representatives of the king and queen and old friends including the dowager Lady Harcourt, Lord Kindersley, and from the London office, Lord and Lady Catto and Lord and Lady Bicester.

On June 25, Morgan's two sons went up to Hartford for the day and deposited the urn containing his ashes in the family vault at Cedar Hill Cemetery.[68]

Aftermath

Morgan's death precipitated a great outpouring of writing in the press about his life and career. Most of it was laudatory—dwelling on his generosity to the causes of education, medicine, and the arts; his part in helping the Western Allies in and after World World I; his reputation for honest and fair dealing; and his position in the world of finance. The radical press, petty to the end, ignored his contributions: the Pierpont Morgan Library, the wartime loans, the postwar reconstruction loans, his role in the business community. The *New Republic* observed spitefully, "he added nothing creative or humanizing to American life, and . . . his passing subtracts nothing."[69]

Under the terms of Morgan's will, published on March 27, his two sons were named residuary legatees and major inheritors.[70]

Conclusion

WE HAVE EXAMINED A NUMBER OF ASPECTS OF THE LIFE AND CAREER of J. P. Morgan, Jr. From the welter of material consulted—inevitably incomplete and often flawed—we can make some generalizations and draw some conclusions about the man in his various roles.

Surprising as it must seem, Morgan was a shy man. He was not at ease with strangers, and this caused him at times to appear aloof and even ungracious. He dreaded public appearances and had a horror of making a speech. His few recorded speeches are on the stuffy side.

Without involving ourselves in psychological theorizing—and nothing is more tiresome or futile than amateur psychological speculation—we can certainly observe that the younger Morgan felt overshadowed by the forceful personality and great renown of his father. A recurring theme in the son's correspondence is his affection for his father, his feelings of never being able to come up to his father's level of achievement, and his wistfulness at the remoteness of the elder Morgan. Whether these feelings of inadequacy and of not quite belonging contributed to the son's diffidence can only be a matter for conjecture. It is sad that he should have felt inferior, because while his temperament was milder, he was every bit as able as his father, and at no time did he exhibit the bad judgment shown by his father in overextending his resources in buying works of art.

To people who knew him or with whom he came in frequent contact, the younger Morgan was warm, witty, and charming. This large group included people of all walks of life, from employees at the bank and hired hands on his estates to the archbishop of Canterbury and the British royal family.

Morgan had little interest in "Society" with a capital *S* (such as that found in this country at such places as Newport) and even less in the cafe society that came in after World War I. But he did observe the socially accepted rituals. He attended the approved schools, St. Paul's and Harvard, and he sent his sons to Groton and Harvard. He belonged to the right clubs—the Piping Rock, The Creek, The Links, Century, White's in London. He had the proper addresses—Murray Hill, Glen Cove, Grosvenor Square. He visited the right resorts, Jekyl Island and Bar Harbor. While not a rider to hounds, polo player, or racehorse breeder, he did race one kind of yacht and cruise in another, and he shot game birds in season, and had shooting boxes in this country and abroad. In Britain, he did not move in a fashionable set, such as the glittering coterie around Edward VII, but he was at home with a titled group of established position. The definition of a snob as one who loves a lord lacks validity unless it adds the attribute of feeling or *acting* superior because of association with titles. Morgan liked associating with the nobility, but he was not a snob. He preserved an almost boyish naiveté about his familiarity with the prominent and wellborn, as if he could hardly believe his good fortune, but he retained a Mark Twain–like sense of realism and wry American humor about the situation.

The role that suited Morgan best and that he enjoyed most was that of an English country squire. He was a conscientious landlord. He kept his property in good order, raised prizewinning farm animals, vegetables, and flowers. His gamekeepers saw to it that the birds were numerous and healthy. He maintained good relations with his neighbors and his tenants, supported the local church, and played indifferent golf with the vicar. He headed all the subscription lists for worthy causes. Mrs. Morgan played her part as a power in the local Women's Institute.

Our Morgan lacked the arrogance, ostentatiousness, and flair of his father, Pierpont Morgan. Except for *Corsair*, he did not spend money conspicuously. He was even rather dull in private life. He was a devoted husband. He had close and devoted women friends and corresponded for years with such intimates as Lady Buxton and Mrs. William Hooper. But even after the death of his wife, there is no suggestion in the record or in the recollection of people who knew him that he had inherited his father's weakness for women.

Morgan was interested in his children even after they grew up, and he enjoyed watching his grandchildren develop as they came along.

Morgan's insistence on regarding his wealth as a fund held in trust for good works resulted in very substantial achievements in the arts, health, and education and in the alleviation of misfortune.

The question naturally arises of how Morgan was able to live in rural Britain a third of the year in peacetime and still remain head of the world's major financial business. This question becomes even more pertinent when we add to this absence the other blocks of time spent away from 23 Wall Street during shooting trips to Climax Lodge, North Carolina, winter visits to Jekyl Island, Georgia, an occasional week at Camp Uncas in the Adirondacks, and *Corsair* cruises of varying lengths from Manchester, Massachusetts, and Chesapeake Bay to the eastern Mediterranean and the South Seas.

The answer, of course, lies in the nature of that senior partnership. Morgan's authority in J. P. Morgan & Co. was absolute. He was the boss. The articles of partnership gave him explicit authority to appoint and fire partners at his sole discretion. He was kept fully informed of all important matters and many lesser ones by a never-ending barrage of cablegrams and radiograms that followed him everywhere. A competent private secretary—John Axten during most of Morgan's working life—accompanied him at all times to help cope with this body of information and to frame replies.

Morgan was the undisputed head of J. P. Morgan & Co., but by his own choice he was not the chief executive officer. The man who ran the business was Thomas W. Lamont. Lamont presided at the daily partners' meetings and provided leadership where required. By the very partnership organization, however, individual partners assumed almost total responsibility for tasks informally assigned or taken on according to that partner's familiarity with or interest in a given security issue, company reorganization, or other problem.

From the effectiveness of this apparently loose partnership arrangement, it is clear that Morgan's skill at choosing partners was very great. Morgan was the man the firm turned to for advice on any and all subjects. His counsel was sought and followed on all important matters. In general, that advice was excellent, and J. P. Morgan & Co. prospered. It was not infallible, however. With the wisdom of hindsight, we see that he never should have countenanced the abandonment in early 1929 of the firm's conservative policy and have allowed it to become involved with a public-utility holding company and with the Van Sweringen brothers.

Within the firm, Morgan further dominated his associates by the affection he inspired. These realistic banking partners and the corps of supporting employees were devoted to him and were prepared to accept without rancor his occasional violent outbursts of irascibility. Outside the firm, Morgan's forceful presence—helped by his physical bulk, authoritative manner, and name—his unquestioned probity, and his reasonableness in negotiation carried enormous influence in getting people, whether businessmen or representatives of nations, to accept and to carry out the proposals he supported. Two cases in point are the $500,000,000 Anglo-French loan of 1915 and the 1929 Young Plan for German reparations settlement.

In this last connection, however, it should be noted that the ideas that he endorsed were rarely of his own inspiration. Morgan's was not an original or a creative mind. He closely scrutinized and analyzed ideas before endorsing them, but he did not dream them up.

It has already become apparent that Morgan's was a complex nature. He embodied the Puritan work ethic to a marked degree. He felt keenly his responsibility as a member of the various boards of directors of business concerns and public-service organizations on which he was invited to sit. When in town, his attendance recorded at these bodies was exemplary, even when it involved a tiring round-trip journey for a Washington meeting of the Federal Reserve Board or a monthly overnight trip to Boston for the Harvard Overseers. The secretary's diary reveals day after day with board meetings or committee meetings scheduled in exhausting succession. On the other hand, for almost half of the year, Morgan attended no meetings at all.

There is a similar relaxing of the exercise of power in the transformation of the firm brought about by the younger Morgan upon his succession to the senior partnership. Almost overnight, J. P.

Morgan & Co. abandoned its roles as a catalyst and a driving force in the creation of large business concerns in favor of the quieter function of bank and securities underwriter. In part, this shift was the result of the business trend away from mergers. In part it was a reflection of the temperament and outlook of the new senior partner. It would be a mistake to press the point too far, but influencing that temperament and outlook could have been the younger man's virtual exile, however necessary, to the quiet backwater of the firm's English house at the very time when great affairs were afoot at the home office in New York, his resulting lack of interest and of experience in those more dramatic financial adventures, and his often-stated unhappiness about and possible resentment at his isolation while they were taking place. Morgan enjoyed being busy and working hard, but he enjoyed the leisurely life of a country squire even more, and he was not forced by the need for money or an inner compulsion to put in a forty-eight week working year or to undertake bold financial enterprises.

Even though the younger Morgan created no U.S. Steel Corporation, under his quiet leadership, the firm more than any other single private agency financed and armed the Western Allies in World War I and subsequently financed the beating of swords into ploughshares. Paradoxically, the firm achieved a greater international eminence in the years 1915 to 1929 than it had enjoyed under the bolder, more active, and more imaginative Pierpont Morgan, Sr. On the other hand, the elder Morgan left behind him on his death a company of greater strength than did his son, though this was the result of the differing economic situations and government attitudes in the two periods and not of respective competences of father and son.

Morgan's relations with the political Left are a classic expression of the continuous offensive of the so-called intellectuals toward the destruction of the capitalist system, a conflict outlined by J. A. Schumpeter in his *Capitalism, Socialism and Democracy*.[1]

Morgan became a prime target of "intellectual" attack when he inherited the senior partnership on the death of his father—a casualty of like attack. He was seized upon as a symbol of all the unattractive characteristics that one could choose to attribute to the system and was made the focus of demagogic denunciation and of publicity inspired congressional investigation. To the Left, he was a godsend. The very name J. P. Morgan carried associations with the earlier "robber baron" era of American business in the uninformed popular mind. He was a banker, a calling inherently suspect to the economic illiterates uninterested in inquiring into the banker's function. He was rich, and though not as rich as was widely believed or as many other, less publicized, individuals were, he was rich enough to be pointed at as the owner of a steam yacht big enough to cross the ocean and was made the object of envy. He was a big man with big features and was easily caricatured by cartoonists, who could draw dollar signs all over his ample vest. Where he himself was at fault in contributing to his own vulnerability to public attack was his obtuseness and stubbornness in public relations. Mention has been made a number of times of his persistence in holding to the belief that he was a private person and that his views or actions were nobody's concern but his own. Not until very late in his life did he make any effort to be civil to newspaper reporters and photographers who were only carrying out their assignments in covering his arrivals and departures. The delusion that he was a private individual made Morgan regard it as nobody else's business, hence beneath his dignity, to defend himself from unfair criticism or to avoid or prevent such criticism by explaining his actions or motives either in advance or after the fact. A case in point was the decision to sell inherited works of art that people had thought were going to be given to the Metropolitan Museum of Art. The capital frozen in the art works was needed to pay cash bequests and inheritance taxes and to carry on the banking business. There was little need for a generous man to invite a reputation for parsimony by keeping quiet while the papers abused him.

We conclude that the younger Morgan was well-intentioned, unambitious, hardworking and indolent by turns, a generous man, very agreeable to those who knew him, an ardent Anglophile, a staunch churchman, and that he appeared somewhat stuffy to the world outside his own circle. His integrity was beyond question, his imagination limited, his modesty very genuine; his actual achievements were very substantial in the areas of Allied financing both during and after World War I and in German reparations settlements, as well as in corporation security underwriting, his primary job. Throughout his life, he was subjected to intermittent harassment and abuse, less on personal grounds than because he was a convenient symbol and his persecutors hoped to gain some personal or ideological advantage from being identified with the attack.

NOTES

BIBLIOGRAPHICAL NOTE

INDEX

Abbreviations Used in the Notes

BG	Belle da Costa Greene, Librarian, Pierpont Morgan Library
HSM	Henry Sturgis Morgan, younger son of J. P. Morgan, Jr.
JDF	John Douglas Forbes, author of this biography
JPM, Jr.	John Pierpont Morgan, Jr., subject of this study
JPM, Sr.	John Pierpont Morgan, father of the subject
LP	Letter press. Refers to bound volumes of letterpress copies of letters from J. P. Morgan, Jr.
Mrs. JPM, Sr.	Mrs. John Pierpont Morgan, mother of the subject
PML	Pierpont Morgan Library
SD	Secretary's diaries: bound volumes of J. P. Morgan, Jr.'s, appointment calendars

Notes

Preface

1. U.S. Congress, Senate, *Stock Exchange Practices: Hearings before the Committee on Banking and Currency on S. Res. 84 (72nd Cong.) and S. Res. 56 (73rd Cong.)*, 73rd Cong., 1st sess., 1933, Part 1, p. 4.

Introductory Note: Morgan on Morgan

1. Lamont Papers, items nos. 108–13, Baker Library, Harvard Business School.

Chapter I: "Boyhood, 1867–85"

1. Herbert L. Satterlee, *J. Pierpont Morgan, an Intimate Portrait* (New York: Macmillan, 1939), pp. 127–29. This book is a biography of the elder Morgan by his son-in-law, the husband of Louisa Morgan Satterlee. Except as noted, the information in this chapter is from Satterlee.

2. JPM, Jr., to Mrs. JPM, Sr., July 1878. Letters from J. P. Morgan, Jr., to his mother, Mrs. J. P. Morgan, Sr., during the years 1878–1924, on deposit in the Pierpont Morgan Library, New York.

3. JPM, Jr., to H. L. Satterlee, December 20, 1937, LP 45:396. Letterpress copies of letters from J. P. Morgan, Jr., bound volumes, 1905–43, vols. 1–48. J. P. Morgan, Jr., Papers.

4. Satterlee, *J. Pierpont Morgan*, p. 185.

5. JPM, Jr., to Mrs. JPM, Sr., January 20 and February 24, 1881.

6. In a letter from St. Paul's vice rector, John H. Beust, to JDF, June 23, 1975, Mr. Beust says, "I think I can confirm the [August] 1933 *Fortune* article in

its statement about the ranking and achievement of Morgan while he was a student here." The *Fortune* piece is the one already referred to in the Preface above. Characteristically, it stresses the negative and notes: "in a school of 275 to 280 he made no particular athletic mark." It lists a number of organizations (Tennis Association, Bicycle Club, Racquet Court Club) and sports (cricket, football, hockey) "for those boys who were interested—Jack Morgan rarely was." Jack Morgan's letters to his mother reveal quite a different picture, as we shall see. All subsequent statements of Jack's class standing in successive years are from the Beust letter.

7. JPM, Jr., to Mrs. JPM, Sr., October 29 and November 1, 5, 1882.

8. JPM, Jr., to Mrs. JPM, Sr., November 12 and 16, 1882.

9. JPM, Jr., to F. H. Scheffler, March 25, 1927, LP 39:380.

10. JPM, Jr., to Mrs. JPM, Sr., January 25 and 28, 1883.

11. JPM, Jr., to Mrs. JPM, Sr., February 4 and 7, 1883.

12. JPM, Jr., to Mrs. JPM, Sr., February 18 and 23, 1883.

13. JPM, Jr., to Mrs. JPM, Sr., March 11 and 18, 1883.

14. JPM, Jr., to Mrs. JPM, Sr., April 4, 1883.

15. JPM, Jr., to Mrs. JPM, Sr., April 15 and 20, 1883.

16. JPM, Jr., to Mrs. JPM, Sr., May 4, 13, 27, and June 3, 1883.

17. JPM, Jr., to Mrs. JPM, Sr., June 7, 1883.

18. JPM, Jr., to Mrs. JPM, Sr., January 24 and 27, 1884.

19. JPM, Jr., to Mrs. JPM, Sr., February 20 and 28, 1884.

20. JPM, Jr., to Mrs. JPM, Sr., March 8, 1884.

21. JPM, Jr., to Mrs. JPM, Sr., June 4, 1884.

22. JPM, Jr., to W. G. Lane, May 27, 1931, LP 42:274.

23. Satterlee, *J. Pierpont Morgan*, p. 217.

24. John K. Winkler, "Those Morgans," *World's Work*, October 1930, pp. 32–36.

25. JPM, Jr., to Mrs. JPM, Sr., February 8, 1885.

26. JPM, Jr., to Mrs. JPM, Sr., January 18 and 23, 1885.

27. JPM, Jr., to Mrs. JPM, Sr., January 8, 1885.

28. JPM, Jr., to Mrs. JPM, Sr., January 11, 1885.

29. JPM, Jr., to Mrs. JPM, Sr., January 18, 1885.

30. JPM, Jr., to Mrs. JPM, Sr., February 6, 1885.

31. JPM, Jr., to Mrs. JPM, Sr., February 15, 1885.

32. JPM, Jr., to Mrs. JPM, Sr., February 26, 1885.

33. JPM, Jr., to Mrs. JPM, Sr., March 1, 1885.

34. JPM, Jr., to Mrs. JPM, Sr., May 13 and 3, 1885.

35. JPM, Jr., to Mrs. JPM, Sr., May 10, 1885.

36. JPM, Jr., to JPM, Sr., June 25, 1885.

37. JPM, Jr., to Mrs. JPM, Sr., July 4 and 15, 1885.

Chapter II: "Harvard, *1885–89*"

1. JPM, Jr., to Mrs. JPM, Sr., October 4, 1885.
2. JPM, Jr., to Mrs. JPM, Sr., October 8, 1885.
3. JPM, Jr., to Mrs. JPM, Sr., November 6, 1885.
4. JPM, Jr., to Mrs. JPM, Sr., December 6, 1885.
5. JPM, Jr., to Mrs. JPM, Sr., December 13, 1885.
6. JPM, Jr., to Mrs. JPM, Sr., January 15, 1886.
7. JPM, Jr., to Mrs. JPM, Sr., February 14, 1886.
8. JPM, Jr., to Mrs. JPM, Sr., February 25, 1886.
9. JPM, Jr., to Mrs. JPM, Sr., February 1, 1886.
10. JPM, Jr., to Mrs. JPM, Sr., December 13, 1886.
11. JPM, Jr., to Mrs. JPM, Sr., March 10, 1886.
12. JPM, Jr., to Mrs. JPM, Sr., April 19 and June 10, 1886.
13. JPM, Jr., to Mrs. JPM, Sr., n.d. (received July 21, 1886).
14. JPM, Jr., to Mrs. JPM, Sr., September 8 [1886].
15. JPM, Jr., to Mrs. JPM, Sr., September 26, 1886.
16. JPM, Jr., to Mrs. JPM, Sr., September 19, 1886. The Reading story is outlined in *Railway World*, September 25, 1886, pp. 926 ff.
17. JPM, Jr., to Mrs. JPM, Sr., September 26, 1886.
18. JPM, Jr., to Mrs. JPM, Sr., November 14, 1886.
19. JPM, Jr., to Mrs. JPM, Sr., April 24 and 28, 1887.
20. JPM, Jr., to Mrs. JPM, Sr., April 24, 1887.
21. JPM, Jr., to Mrs. JPM, Sr., April 28, 1887.
22. JPM, Jr., to Mrs. JPM, Sr., May 14, 1887.
23. JPM, Jr., to Mrs. JPM, Sr., June 3, 1887.
24. JPM, Jr., to Mrs. JPM, Sr., June 6, 1887.
25. JPM, Jr., to Mrs. JPM, Sr., July 2, 1887.
26. JPM, Jr., to Mrs. JPM, Sr., July 10, 1887.
27. JPM, Jr., to Mrs. JPM, Sr., July 12, 1887.
28. JPM, Jr., to Mrs. JPM, Sr., July 17, 1887.
29. JPM, Jr., to Mrs. JPM, Sr., July 21, 1887.
30. JPM, Jr., to Mrs. JPM, Sr., December 4, 1887.
31. JPM, Jr., to Mrs. JPM, Sr., December 11, 1887.
32. JPM, Jr., to Mrs. JPM, Sr., January 22, 1888.
33. JPM, Jr., to Mrs. JPM, Sr., January 18, 1889.
34. Class Publications and Records, Class of 1889, Harvard University Archives, Harvard University Library, Cambridge, Mass.
35. JPM, Jr., to Mrs. JPM, Sr., June 11, 1888.
36. JPM, Jr., to Mrs. JPM, Sr., October 14, 1888.
37. JPM, Jr., to Mrs. JPM, Sr., October 18, 1888.

38. JPM, Jr., to Mrs. JPM, Sr., November 16, 1888.
39. JPM, Jr., to Mrs. JPM, Sr., October 11 and 21, 1888.
40. JPM, Jr., to Mrs. JPM, Sr., December 25, 1888.
41. JPM, Jr., to Mrs. JPM, Sr., January 13, 1889.
42. JPM, Jr., to Mrs. JPM, Sr., February 8, 1889.
43. JPM, Jr., to Mrs. JPM, Sr., March 6, 1889.
44. JPM, Jr., to Mrs. JPM, Sr., March 13, 1889.
45. JPM, Jr., to Mrs. JPM, Sr., March 21, 1889.
46. JPM, Jr., to Mrs. JPM, Sr., March 24, 1889.
47. JPM, Jr., to Mrs. JPM, Sr., May 3, 1889.
48. JPM, Jr., to Mrs. JPM, Sr., May 16, 1889.
49. Official Harvard transcript of record, J. P. Morgan, Jr., by permission of Harvard University Archives.
50. Satterlee, *J. Pierpont Morgan*, pp. 81–91.
51. JPM, Jr., to H. L. Satterlee, March 26, 1936, LP 45:159.
52. JPM, Jr., to Mrs. JPM, Sr., January 17 and July 22, 1889.
53. JPM, Jr., to Mrs. JPM, Sr., July 3 and August 4, 8, 1889.
54. JPM, Jr., to Mrs. JPM, Sr., August 18, 1889.
55. JPM, Jr., to Mrs. JPM, Sr., August 22, 1889.
56. JPM, Jr., to Mrs. JPM, Sr., August 25, 1889.
57. JPM, Jr., to Mrs. JPM, Sr., September 1 and 5, 1889.
58. JPM, Jr., to Mrs. JPM, Sr., November 21, 1889.
59. JPM, Jr., to Mrs. J. D. Prince, September 19, 1939, LP 46:307.
60. JPM, Jr., to Mrs. JPM, Sr., November 24, 1889.
61. JPM, Jr., to Mrs. JPM, Sr., December 2, 1889.

Chapter III: "Apprenticeship for Business, 1890–1905"

1. Class Publications and Records, Class of 1889, *Secretary's Report* no. 2 (1892), p. 45, Harvard University Archives.
2. Leonhard A. Keyes, *Chronological Record of Changes in J. P. Morgan & Co., New York, Drexel & Co., Philadelphia, Morgan Grenfell & Co., Limited, London, and Morgan & Cie, Paris*, undated typescript, JPM, Jr., Papers.
3. Satterlee, *J. Pierpont Morgan*, p. 275.
4. An element of confusion is introduced by the Morgans' connection with both the Sturges and the Sturgis famlies. The elder J. P. Morgan's first wife, who died shortly after their marriage, was a Sturges, and the two families maintained a friendship after her death. Jessie Grew was related to the Boston Sturgis family.
5. *New York Times*, December 12, 1890.
6. JPM, Jr., to Mrs. JPM, Sr., December 18, 1890.
7. Class Publications and Records, Class of 1889, *Secretary's Report* no. 2 (1892), p. 45, and no. 6 (1909), p. 158, Harvard University Archives.

8. Satterlee, *J. Pierpont Morgan*, p. 255.

9. Class Publications and Records, Class of 1889, *Secretary's Report*, no. 6 (1909), p. 158, Harvard University Archives.

10. JPM, Jr., to Consolidated Gas Co., April 28, 1892, LP 1892–98, p. 14.

11. JPM, Jr., to R. C. Sturgis, March 10 and August 6, 1892, LP 1892–98, pp. 4, 26.

12. JPM, Jr., to Mrs. Blake, January 5, 1893, LP 1892–98, p. 55; JPM, Jr., to S. H. Graham, April 28, 1893, LP 1892–98, p. 72; JPM, Jr., to Miss Hesse, October 23, 1893, LP 1892–98, p. 87; JPM, Jr., to W. L. Boyle, January 23, 1894, LP 1892–98, p. 112; JPM, Jr., to D. H. King, November 9, 1896, LP 1892–98, p. 203; JPM, Jr., to J. G. Agar, January 3, 1898, LP 1892–98, p. 238.

13. JPM, Jr., to Lawley & Sons, April 29, 1895, LP 1892–98, p. 176; January 5, 1897, LP 1892–98, p. 209.

14. Satterlee, *J. Pierpont Morgan*, p. 268.

15. Ibid., p. 277.

16. Class Publications and Records, Class of 1889, *Secretary's Report* no. 6 (1909), p. 158, Harvard University Archives.

17. Ibid., p. 157.

18. Satterlee, *J. Pierpont Morgan*, pp. 265–66, 273, 274, 313.

19. Ibid., pp. 277–99, 261–62, 322, 325.

20. JPM, Jr., to D. G. S. Baker, November 14, 1894, LP 1892–98, p. 158; JPM, Jr., to H. S. Brill, February 28, 1896, LP 1892–98, p. 185.

21. Class Publications and Records, Class of 1889, *Secretary's Report* no. 3 (1898), p. 57, no. 4 (1901), p. 41, and no. 6 (1909), p. 159, Harvard University Archives; HSM to JDF, in conversation, January 10, 1980.

22. JPM, Jr., to Mrs. JPM, Sr., January 17, 1898.

23. JPM, Jr., to Mrs. JPM, Sr., January 25, 1898.

24. JPM, Jr., to Mrs. JPM, Sr., January 28, 1898.

25. JPM, Jr., to Mrs. JPM, Sr., January 25, 1898; L. A. Keyes, *Chronological Record*.

26. JPM, Jr., to Mrs. JPM, Sr., January 28, 1898.

27. JPM, Jr., to Mrs. JPM, Sr., February 1, 1898.

28. JPM, Jr., to Mrs. JPM, Sr., February 2, 1898.

29. JPM, Jr., to Mrs. JPM, Sr., February 15, 1898.

30. JPM, Jr., to Mrs. JPM, Sr., February 22, 1898.

31. *London Daily Mail*, February 26, 1898.

32. JPM, Jr., to Mrs. JPM, Sr., February 25, 1898.

33. JPM, Jr., to Mrs. JPM, Sr., March 2, 1898.

34. JPM, Jr., to Mrs. JPM, Sr., March 4 and 5, 1898.

35. Ibid. L. A. Keyes, *Chronological Record*, p. 9.

36. JPM, Jr., to Mrs. JPM, Sr., March 8, 1898.

37. JPM, Jr., to Mrs. JPM, Sr., March 11, 1898.

38. JPM, Jr., to Mrs. JPM, Sr., March 16, 1898.

39. JPM, Jr., to Mrs. JPM, Sr., March 22, 1898.

40. JPM, Jr., to Mrs. JPM, Sr., March 25 and April 15, 1898.

41. JPM, Jr., to Mrs. JPM, Sr., April 20 and 29, 1898.

42. JPM, Jr., to Mrs. JPM, Sr., May 6 and 17, 1898.

43. JPM, Jr., to Mrs. JPM, Sr., March 28 and April 1, 1898.

44. JPM, Jr., to Mrs. JPM, Sr., April 11, 1898.

45. JPM, Jr., to Mrs. JPM, Sr., May 3, 6, 13, 1898.

46. JPM, Jr., to Mrs. JPM, Sr., May 3, 1898.

47. JPM, Jr., to Mrs. JPM, Sr., May 13, 1898.

48. JPM, Jr., to Mrs. JPM, Sr., May 14, 1898.

49. JPM, Jr., to Mrs. JPM, Sr., May 20, 1898.

50. JPM, Jr., to Mrs. JPM, Sr., May 27, 1898.

51. JPM, Jr., to Mrs. JPM, Sr., June 3, 1898.

52. JPM, Jr., to Mrs. JPM, Sr., June 7, 1898.

53. JPM, Jr., to Mrs. JPM, Sr., June 10, 1898. JPM, Jr., to Mrs. JPM, Sr., June 7, 1898.

54. JPM, Jr., to Mrs. JPM, Sr., June 10, 1898.

55. JPM, Jr., to Mrs. JPM, Sr., July 1, 1898.

56. JPM, Jr., to Mrs. JPM, Sr., July 6, 1898.

57. JPM, Jr., to Mrs. JPM, Sr., June 15, 1898.

58. Ibid.

59. JPM, Jr., to Mrs. JPM, Sr., June 20, 22, 1898.

60. JPM, Jr., to Mrs. JPM, Sr., June [1898].

61. JPM, Jr., to Mrs. JPM, Sr., July 8 and 13, 1898.

62. JPM, Jr., to Mrs. JPM, Sr., July 22, 1898.

63. JPM, Jr., to Mrs. JPM, Sr., July 26, 1898.

64. Ibid.

65. JPM, Jr., to Mrs. JPM, Sr., August 5, 1898.

66. JPM, Jr., to Mrs. JPM, Sr., August 9, 1898.

67. JPM, Jr., to Mrs. JPM, Sr., August 19, 1898.

68. JPM, Jr., to Mrs. JPM, Sr., August 24, 1898.

69. JPM, Jr., to Mrs. JPM, Sr., November 1 and 4, 1898.

70. JPM, Jr., to Mrs. JPM, Sr., November 11, 1898.

71. Ibid.

72. JPM, Jr., to Mrs. JPM, Sr., November 16, 1898.

73. JPM, Jr., to Mrs. JPM, Sr., November 18 and 25, 1898.

74. JPM, Jr., to Mrs. JPM, Sr., November 23, 1898. See also chapter VIII, "Morgan the Book Collector."

75. JPM, Jr., to Mrs. JPM, Sr., November 29 and December 3, 9, 14, 16, 1898.

76. JPM, Jr., to Mrs. JPM, Sr., July 6, 15, August 9, 17, November 23 and December 7, 1898.

77. JPM, Jr., to Mrs. JPM, Sr., November 4, 18 and December 8, 30, 1898.

78. JPM, Jr., to Mrs. JPM, Sr., December 23 and 28, 1898.

79. JPM, Jr., to Mrs. JPM, Sr., December 14, 1898.

80. JPM, Jr., to Mrs. JPM, Sr., December 23, 1898.

81. JPM, Jr., to Mrs. JPM, Sr., December 30, 1898.

82. JPM, Jr., to Mrs. JPM, Sr., January 7, 1899.

83. JPM, Jr., to Mrs. JPM, Sr., January 4, 1899.

84. JPM, Jr., to Mrs. JPM, Sr., January 7, 1899.

85. JPM, Jr., to Mrs. JPM, Sr., January 11, 1899.

86. JPM, Jr., to Mrs. JPM, Sr., January 20, 1899.

87. JPM, Jr., to Mrs. JPM, Sr., January 25, 1899.

88. JPM, Jr., to Mrs. JPM, Sr., January 27, 1899.

89. *London Post Office Directory*, 1900.

90. JPM, Jr., to Mrs. JPM, Sr., February 21, 1899.

91. JPM, Jr., to Mrs. JPM, Sr., March 1, 1899.

92. JPM, Jr., to Mrs. JPM, Sr., March 3, 1899.

93. JPM, Jr., to Mrs. JPM, Sr., April 28 and 24, 1899.

94. JPM, Jr., to Mrs. JPM, Sr., May 5, 1899.

95. JPM, Jr., to Mrs. JPM, Sr., April 30, 1899.

96. JPM, Jr., to Mrs. JPM, Sr., September 18, 1899.

97. JPM, Jr., to Mrs. JPM, Sr., October 3, 1899. JPM, Jr., to Mrs. JPM, Sr., October 20 and 25, 1899.

98. JPM, Jr., to Mrs. JPM, Sr., November 8, 1899.

99. JPM, Jr., to Mrs. JPM, Sr., November 24, 1899.

100. JPM, Jr., to Mrs. JPM, Sr., December 6, 1899.

101. JPM, Jr., to Mrs. JPM, Sr., December 20 and November 24, 1899.

102. JPM, Jr., to Mrs. JPM, Sr., December 9 and 13, 1899.

103. JPM, Jr., to Mrs. JPM, Sr., December 9, 20, 27, 1899.

104. JPM, Jr., to Mrs. JPM, Sr., December 27, 1899.

105. JPM, Jr., to Mrs. JPM, Sr., January 2 and 5, 1900.

106. JPM, Jr., to Mrs. JPM, Sr., February 1, 1900.

107. JPM, Jr., to Mrs. JPM, Sr., February 9, 1900.

108. JPM, Jr., to Mrs. JPM, Sr., March 2, 1900.

109. JPM, Jr., to Mrs. JPM, Sr., March 7, 1900.

110. JPM, Jr., to Mrs. JPM, Sr., March 9, 1900.

111. JPM, Jr., to Mrs. JPM, Sr., March 14, 1900.

112. Ibid.; JPM, Jr., to Mrs. JPM, Sr., March 15, 1900.

113. JPM, Jr., to Mrs. JPM, Sr., May 18, 1900.

114. JPM, Jr., to Mrs. JPM, Sr., May 23, 1900.

115. JPM, Jr., to Mrs. JPM, Sr., October 24 and 30, 1900.

116. JPM, Jr., to Mrs. JPM, Sr., November 3, 1900 and January 22, 1901.

117.   JPM, Jr., to Mrs. JPM, Sr., January 25, 1901.

118.   JPM, Jr., to Mrs. JPM, Sr., February 5 and 6, 1901.

119.   JPM, Jr.; to Mrs. JPM, Sr., February 8, 1901.

120.   JPM, Jr., to Mrs. JPM, Sr., February 15, 1901.

121.   Ibid.

122.   JPM, Jr., to Mrs. JPM, Sr., February 19, 1901.

123.   Satterlee, *J. Pierpont Morgan*, pp. 375–78.

124.   JPM, Jr., to Mrs. JPM, Sr., June 18, 1901.

125.   JPM, Jr., to Morgan, Grenfell & Co., December 6, 1910, LP 7:246.

126.   JPM, Jr., to J. W. Altham, August 27, 1920, LP 28-A:1F.

127.   JPM, Jr., to J. Anderson, August 11, 1908, LP 4:237.

128.   JPM, Jr., to Mrs. JPM, Sr., June 21, 1901. HSM to JDF, in conversation, October 1979.

129.   JPM, Jr., to Mrs. JPM, Sr., July 2, 1901.

130.   JPM, Jr., to W. H. Leslie, September 17, 1912, LP 10:235; JPM, Jr., to Sir E. Cassel, September 26, 1912, LP 10:239.

131.   JPM, Jr., to Mrs. JPM, Sr., June 20, 1901.

132.   JPM, Jr., to Mrs. JPM, Sr. [n.d. but clearly between June 20 and July 2, 1901].

133.   JPM, Jr., to Mrs. JPM, Sr., September 20, 1901.

134.   JPM, Jr., to Mrs. JPM, Sr., January 5, 1902.

135.   JPM, Jr., to Mrs. JPM, Sr., January 22, 1902.

136.   JPM, Jr., to Mrs. JPM, Sr., June 20, 1902.

137.   *Fortune*, August 1933.

138.   P. C. Knox to JPM, Jr., February 7, 1912, Philander Chase Knox File, U.S. Department of State Papers, Library of Congress.

139.   JPM, Jr., to Mrs. JPM, Sr., June 20, 1902.

140.   JPM, Jr., to Mrs. JPM, Sr., June 24, 1902.

141.   JPM, Jr., to Mrs. JPM, Sr., June 28, 1902.

142.   JPM, Jr., to Mrs. JPM, Sr., July 9, 1902.

143.   JPM, Jr., to Mrs. JPM, Sr., July 12, 1902.

144.   Ibid.

145.   Ibid.

146.   JPM, Jr., to Mrs. JPM, Sr., August 15, 1902.

147.   JPM, Jr., to Mrs. JPM, Sr., August 12, 1902.

148.   JPM, Jr., to Mrs. JPM, Sr., June 26, 1903.

149.   Ibid.

150.   JPM, Jr., to Mrs. JPM, Sr., October 16, 1903.

151.   JPM, Jr., to Mrs. JPM, Sr., October 20, 1903.

152.   JPM, Jr., to Mrs. JPM, Sr., October 23, 1903.

153.   Satterlee, *J. Pierpont Morgan*, p. 407; *New York Times*, October 15, 1904; *Social Register* (New York), 1905.

154. JPM, Jr., to J. S. Morgan & Co., February 26 and March 15, 1904, Cables 1904–6, JPM, Jr., Papers.

155. JPM, Jr., to E. C. Grenfell, March 16, 1904, and JPM, Jr., to J. S. Morgan & Co., March 24, 1904, ibid.

156. JPM, Jr., to Mrs. JPM, Sr., August 12, 1904.

157. JPM, Jr., to Mrs. JPM, Sr., November 29, 1904.

158. JPM, Jr., to Mrs. JPM, Sr., January 3, 1905.

159. Satterlee, *J. Pierpont Morgan*, p. 416.

160. JPM, Jr., to J. S. Morgan & Co., February 3 and 8, 1905, Cables 1904–6, JPM, Jr., Papers.

161. JPM, Jr., to Biles, April 11, 1905, ibid.

162. JPM, Jr., to Mrs. JPM, Sr., June 10, 1905.

163. JPM, Jr., to Mrs. JPM, Sr., June 16, 1905.

164. JPM, Jr., to Mrs. JPM, Sr., June 20, 1905.

165. Ibid.

166. J. P. Young, "Wall Street Heir Apparent," *Current Literature*, October 1910, p. 386. Satterlee, *J. Pierpont Morgan*, pp. 402–3.

167. Hugh Thompson, "The House of Morgan," *Munsey's Magazine*, June 1913, p. 357; Satterlee, *J. Pierpont Morgan*, p. 411.

168. JPM, Jr., to Mrs. JPM, Sr., October 4, 1905, Cables 1904–6, JPM, Jr., Papers.

169. JPM, Sr., to JPM, Jr., October 5 and 10, 1905, ibid.

170. JPM, Jr., to JPM, Sr., October 10 and 17, 1905, and JPM, Sr., to JPM, Jr., October 17, 1905, ibid.

171. JPM, Jr., and G. W. Perkins to JPM, Sr., October 21, 1905, and JPM, Sr., and Charles Steele to JPM, Jr., October 22, 1905, ibid.

172. JPM, Jr., and G. W. Perkins to JPM, Sr., series of cablegrams, October 23 and 24, 1905, and JPM, Sr., to JPM, Jr., and G. W. Perkins, October 23 and 24, 1905, ibid.

173. JPM, Jr., to Mrs. JPM, Sr., October 31, 1905.

174. JPM, Jr., and G. W. Perkins to JPM, Sr., October 31, 1905, Cables 1904–6, JPM, Jr., Papers.

175. JPM, Jr., to Mrs. JPM, Sr., November 6, 1905.

176. Satterlee, *J. Pierpont Morgan*, p. 426.

177. HSM to JDF, in conversation, October 1979.

Chapter IV: "The Return, 1906–13"

1. *Social Register* (New York), summer 1906.

2. JPM, Sr., to JPM, Jr., C. Steele, and G. W. Perkins, April 10, 1906, and JPM, Jr., C. Steele, and G. W. Perkins to JPM, Sr., April 11, 1906, Cables 1906–9, JPM, Jr., Papers.

3. JPM, Jr., to J. S. Morgan & Co., May 3, 1906, ibid.

4. *Encyclopaedia Britannica*, 1958, s.v. "Witte, Sergei Julievitch."

5. JPM, Jr., to Mrs. JPM, Sr., November 15, 1907.

6. George Vernadsky, *A History of Russia* (New Haven, Conn.: Yale University Press, 1929), pp. 180–84; Edward Crankshaw, *The Shadow of the Winter Palace* (New York: Viking Press, 1976), pp. 341–55.

7. *New York Times*, July 9, 1906.

8. JPM, Jr., to Mrs. JPM, Sr., October 28, 1907.

9. JPM, Jr., to Mrs. JPM, Sr., November 12, 1907.

10. JPM, Jr., to JPM, Sr., November 5, 9, 12, 13, 14 and December 2, 1907, Cables 1906–9, JPM, Jr., Papers.

11. T. W. Lamont, letter to the editor, *Harvard Alumni Bulletin*, May 1943, pp. 542–43.

12. Alexander Woollcott, "The Archer-Shee Case," *Atlantic Monthly*, February 1939, pp. 175–82.

13. JPM, Jr., to M. Archer-Shee, November 27, 1908, LP 4:413.

14. JPM, Jr., to E. C. Grenfell, January 4, 1909, Cables 1906–9, JPM, Jr., Papers.

15. JPM, Jr., to V. H. Smith, March 23, 1908, LP 4:143.

16. JPM, Jr., to E. C. Grenfell, July 3, 1908, LP 4:308.

17. JPM, Jr., to E. C. Grenfell, July 14, 1908, LP 4:289.

18. JPM, Jr., to E. C. Grenfell, January 5, 1909, LP 4:446.

19. JPM, Jr., to E. C. Grenfell, January 9, 1909, Cables 1906–9, JPM, Jr., Papers.

20. E. H. Gary to JPM, Sr., May 24, 1909, Cables 1909–11, JPM, Jr., Papers.

21. JPM, Jr., to JPM, Sr., June 26 and July 2, 1909, ibid.

22. E. C. Grenfell to JPM, Jr., December 29, 1909, ibid.

23. JPM, Jr., to V. H. Smith, September 10, 1909, LP 6:15.

24. JPM, Jr., to V. H. Smith, January 2, 1911, LP 7:279.

25. HSM to JDF, in conversation, October 1979.

26. J. Axten to S. Edwards, October 13, 1914, LP 15:321.

27. JPM, Jr., to Sir C. E. Hambro, March 24, 1926, LP 38:202.

28. JPM, Jr., to Mrs. JPM, Sr., September 13, 1919.

29. JPM, Jr., to JPM, Sr., March 18, 1911, Cables 1909–11, JPM, Jr., Papers.

30. JPM, Sr., to JPM, Jr., March 9, 1911, ibid.

31. JPM, Jr., and C. Steele to JPM, Sr., April 7, 1911, ibid.

32. Morgan, Harjes & Co. to JPM, Jr., June 2, 1911, JPM & Co. to JPM, Jr., October 18, 1911, and JPM, Jr., to JPM & Co., October 19, 1911, ibid.

33. JPM, Jr., to JPM, Sr., May 24, 1912, and JPM, Jr., to H. P. Davison, June 4, 1912, Cables 1912–13, JPM, Jr., Papers.

34. *Moody's Manual of Corporate Securities*, 4th annual number (New York: J. Moody & Co., 1903), p. 1518.

35. JPM, Jr., to E. C. Grenfell, May 29, 1908, LP 4:231. JPM, Jr., to V. H. Smith, June 30, 1908, LP 4:263. JPM, Jr., to E. C. Grenfell, July 14, 1908, LP 4:289.

36. JPM, Jr., to W. D. Guthrie, April 18, 1912, LP 9:368.

37. JPM, Jr., to H. P. Davison, April 26, 1912, LP 9:389.

38. JPM, Jr., to JPM, Sr., April 19, 1912, Cables 1912–13, JPM, Jr., Papers.

39. JPM, Jr., to E. C. Grenfell, April 30, 1912, ibid.

40. JPM, Jr., to E. C. Grenfell, September 4, 1912, LP 10:218.

41. JPM, Jr., to E. C. Grenfell, June 12, 1918, LP 23:209; *New York Times*, April 25, 1926.

42. JPM, Jr., to V. H. Smith, June 30, 1908, LP 4:263.

43. JPM, Jr., to Regatta Committees at yacht clubs of New York, Larchmont, etc., May 15, 1914, LP 14:346–51.

44. JPM, Jr., to Mrs. Meredith, July 23, 1908, LP 4:308.

45. JPM, Jr., to Rev. E. Peabody, July 19, 1909, LP 5:385.

46. JPM, Jr., to Rev. E. Peabody, March 20, 1909, LP 5:120.

47. JPM, Jr., to F. R. Swift, December 23, 1910, LP 7:264.

48. JPM, Jr., to H. P. Davison, November 5, 1909, LP 6:90.

49. JPM, Jr., to M. Worth, December 2, 1909, LP 6:108, and January 18, 1911, LP 7:322.

50. Satterlee, *J. Pierpont Morgan*, p. 522.

51. JPM, Jr., to L. Jacob, April 6, 1909, LP 5:152, and September 21, 1909, LP 6:52.

52. JPM, Jr., to Heins & LaFarge, September 13, 1909, LP 6:24; HSM to JDF, in conversation, 1977; JPM, Jr., to S. J. Stammers, July 1, 1910, LP 7:97, and May 17, 1911, LP 8:121.

53. See "Country Homes: Denham Place, Uxbridge, the Seat of Mrs. Way," *Country Life*, November 18, 1905, pp. 702–9.

54. JPM, Jr., to Mrs. JPM, Sr., June 2, 1911.

55. JPM, Jr., to JPM, Sr., January 27, 1912, Cables 1912–13, JPM, Jr., Papers. JPM, Jr. to E. C. Grenfell, February 13, 1912, LP 9:129.

56. JPM, Jr., to J. S. Ward, December 23, 1912, LP 10:322.

57. JPM, Jr., to JPM, Sr., February 1, 1912, Cables 1912–13, JPM, Jr., Papers.

58. JPM, Jr., to JPM, Sr., April 22, 1912, ibid.

59. JPM, Jr., to JPM, Sr., April 25, 1912.

60. JPM, Sr., and H. P. Davison to C. Steele and JPM, Jr., May 3, 1912, and JPM, Jr., to JPM, Sr., May 6, 1912, Cables 1912–13, JPM, Jr., Papers.

61. *New York Times*, May 31, 1911.

62. George Wheeler, *Pierpont Morgan and His Friends* (New York: Prentice-Hall, Inc., 1973) p. 290. Henry F. Pringle, *Big Frogs* (New York: Vanguard Press, 1928), p. 156.

63. P. J. Scudder, testimony, U.S. Congress, House, subcommittee of Committee on Banking and Currency, *Money Trust Investigation: Investigation of*

Financial and Monetary Conditions in the United States (under H. Res. 429 and 504), 62nd Cong., 3rd sess., 1912–13, September 18, 1912, Exhibit 134, and January 24, 1913, Exhibit 243.

64.   T. W. Lamont to H. S. Commager, March 17, 1938; Partners file, JPM, Jr., Papers.

65.   Mrs. L. M. Satterlee to JPM, Jr., February 15, 1913, Cables 1912–13, JPM, Jr., Papers.

66.   Mrs. L. M. Satterlee to JPM, Sr., February 16, 1913, ibid.

67.   Mrs. L. M. Satterlee to JPM, Jr., March 5, 1913, ibid.

68.   JPM, Jr., to C. Steele, March 4, 1913, LP 11:38.

69.   JPM, Jr., to Dr. G. A. Dixon, March 17, 1913, LP 11:89.

70.   JPM, Jr., to J. Stillman, March 12, 1913, LP 11:59.

71.   JPM, Jr., to H. L. Higginson, March 12, 1913, LP 11:66.

72.   JPM, Jr., to H. L. Satterlee, March 18, 1913, LP 11:95.

73.   T. W. Lamont to H. S. Commager, March 17, 1938, Partners file, JPM, Jr., Papers.

74.   Louis D. Brandeis, *Other People's Money and How the Bankers Use It* (New York: Frederick A. Stokes Company, 1914).

Chapter V: "The Succession, 1913–14"

1.   F. L. Allen, *The Lords of Creation* (New York: Harper & Bros., 1935), p. 200.

2.   *New York Times*, April 8, 1913.

3.   U.S. Congress, Senate, *Stock Exchange Practices: Hearings before the Committee on Banking and Currency* (on S. Res. 84, 72nd Cong., and S. Res. 56, 73rd Cong.), 73rd Cong., 1st sess., pt. II, 1933, pp. 521–26.

4.   H. P. Davison to JPM, Jr., May 4, 1913, Cables 1912–13, JPM, Jr., Papers.

5.   JPM, Jr., to W. P. Hamilton, May 5, 1913, ibid.

6.   *New York Times*, April 22, 1913; Harold Nicolson, *Dwight Morrow* (New York: Harcourt, Brace and Co., 1935), pp. 152–54.

7.   *New York Times*, September 12, 1913, and April 8, 1914.

8.   H. L. Staples and A. T. Mason, *The Fall of a Railroad Empire* (Syracuse, N.Y.: Syracuse University Press, 1947), pp. 148–50; JPM, Jr., to T. N. Vail, July 12, 1913, LP 12:105, *New York Times*, September 6, 1913.

9.   JPM, Jr. to C. A. Goodwin, February 5, 1914, LP 13:452; *New York Times*, March 9, 1914.

10.   *New York Times*, October 18, 1914.

11.   "Consolidation of Railroads," ICC *Reports*, 63 (1921):518.

12.   SD, August 30 and September 4, 6, 13, 1915.

13.   SD, August 19–September 11, 1913.

14.   SD, September 16, 1913; *Daily Telegraph* (London), quoted in the *New York Times*, January 5, 6, 1914.

15. JPM, Jr., to H. P. Davison, November 22, 1913, Cables 1913–21, JPM Jr., Papers.

16. SD, September 16–December 13, 1913.

17. *New York Times*, December 20, 1913.

18. B. C. Forbes, *Men Who Are Making America* (New York: B. C. Forbes Publishing Co., 1917), p. 257.

19. *New York Times*, January 3, 1914. JPM, Jr., to E. C. Grenfell, January 2, 1914, Cables 1913–21, JPM, Jr., Papers.

20. SD, December 30, 1913; *Commercial & Financial Chronicle* (hereafter cited as *Comm. & Fin. Chron.*), November 14, 1914.

21. *New York Times*, November 12, 1914; Allen, *The Lords of Creation*, p. 345.

22. B. C. Forbes, *Men Who Are Making America*, p. 253.

23. *New York Times*, January 27, 1914.

24. *New York Times*, February 6, 15, 16, 1914.

25. *New York Times*, February 9, 10, 12, 1915.

26. Ibid., February 10, 1915.

27. Ibid., February 21, 1915.

28. Ibid., April 16, 1915.

29. Ibid., February 3, 1916.

30. Ibid., April 14, 1916.

31. Ibid., December 18, 1917; *Comm. & Fin. Chron.*, December 22, 1917.

32. SD, 1914.

33. SD, January 26, March 27, and April 13, 1914.

34. SD, May 6, 20–23, and June 6, 13, 1914.

35. SD, June 13 and 20, 1914.

36. SD, June 15, 19, 26, 1914.

37. SD, February 11–14, October 17–31, and November 15–21, 1914.

38. SD, December 9, 2, 5, 1914.

39. JPM, Jr., to J. Stillman, July 13, 1914, LP 15:70; JPM, Jr., to J. J. Hill, December 26, 1914, LP 16:38.

40. JPM, Jr., to C. H. Howard, April 6, 1914, LP 14:195, and April 21, 1914, LP 14:260.

41. JPM, Jr., to Mrs. JPM, Sr., November 6, 1907.

42. JPM, Jr., to C. Steele, July 27, 1908, LP 4:314.

43. JPM, Jr., to H. P. Davison, June 5, 1911, LP 8:169.

44. JPM, Jr., to Mrs. JPM, Sr., June 2, 1911.

45. JPM, Jr., to Mrs. JPM, Sr., June 7, 1911.

46. U.S. Congress, House, *Report No. 726, Commission on Industrial Relations*, 62nd Cong., 2nd sess., May 16, 1912, pp. 2, 4.

47. U.S. Congress, Senate, *Industrial Relations: Final Report and Testimony* [submitted to Congress by the Commission on Industrial Relations created by the Act of August 23, 1912], 64th Cong., 1st sess., document no. 415, 1916, vol. 9, pp. 8084–8104, 8091–96.

48.   B. C. Forbes, *Men Who are Making America*, p. 254.

49.   JPM, Jr., to P. M. Warburg, December 1, 1914, LP 15:474.

50.   JPM, Jr., to Miss H. H. Brown, February 17, 1914, numerical files T, 314, JPM, Jr., Papers.

51.   JPM, Jr., to E. C. Grenfell, March 5, 1914, LP 14:61; JPM, Jr., to Henry White, June 5, 1914, LP 14:451.

52.   JPM, Jr., to Rev. R. Gillman, June 2, 1914, LP 14:434.

Chapter VI: "World War I, *1914–18*"

1.   *Comm. & Fin. Chron.*, August 1, 1914.

2.   *Comm. & Fin. Chron.*, August 8, 1914; JPM, Jr., to H. Harjes, August 3, 1914, and JPM, Jr., to Ambassador M. T. Herrick, August 3, 1914, Cables 1913–21, JPM, Jr., Papers.

3.   A. Morgan to JPM, Jr., August 11, 1914, Cables 1913–21, JPM, Jr., Papers.

4.   *New York Times*, August 16, 1914.

5.   T. W. Lamont, *Henry P. Davison: The Record of a Useful Life* (New York & London: Harper & Bros., 1933), p. 180.

6.   Ibid., pp. 218ff.

7.   J. D. Forbes, *Stettinius, Sr.: Portrait of a Morgan Partner* (Charlottesville: University Press of Virginia, 1974), pp. 44–64.

8.   Lamont, *Davison*, pp. 189ff.

9.   *New York Times*, January 19, 1915.

10.   SD, January 23–30, 1915.

11.   JPM, Jr., to Mrs. JPM, Sr., April 1, 1915.

12.   Lamont, *Davison*, p. 192.

13.   SD, vols. 1919–39.

14.   *New York Times*, March 19 and 25, 1915.

15.   *New York Times*, April 13 and 29, 1915; *Comm. & Fin. Chron.*, March 13, April 17, 24, and May 1, 1915.

16.   *New York Times*, June 23, 1915; Lamont, *Davison*, p. 192.

17.   *New York Times*, June 22, 1915.

18.   *New York Times*, June 24, 1915.

19.   SD, June 24, 25, 1915.

20.   *New York Times*, June 29, 1915.

21.   *The New Yorker*, April 4, 1931, p. 76.

22.   *New York Times*, July 6, 1915.

23.   JPM, Jr., to J. Stillman, February 4, 1916, numerical files T, 144, JPM, Jr., Papers.

24.   *Comm. & Fin. Chron.*, July 10, 1915.

25.   JPM, Jr., to J. Hamman, August 19, 1915, LP 17:96; JPM, Jr., to O. Wister, August 18, 1915, LP 17:94.

26. *New York Times*, August 17, 1915.

27. HSM to JDF, in conversation, October 1979.

28. SD, September 16–21, 1915.

29. The details of the Anglo-French loan of 1915 are covered in Lamont, *Davison*, pp. 194–200.

30. SD, October 27, 1915.

31. *New York Times*, November 27 and December 4, 28, 1915; *Comm. & Fin. Chron.*, January 1, 1916.

32. SD, November 30 and December 29, 1915.

33. SD, January 8, 9, 23, 24, 25, 1916; JPM, Jr., to E. C. Grenfell, January 24, 25, 31, 1916, Cables 1913–21, JPM, Jr., Papers; SD, February 2–29 and March 1–20, 1916.

34. Robert L. Swaine, *The Cravath Firm*, 2 vols. (New York: privately printed, 1948), 2:68.

35. *New York Times*, October 28, 1915.

36. *New York Times*, June 16, 1916.

37. *New York Times*, July 14, 1916; Nicolson, *Morrow*, p. 178.

38. Nicolson, *Morrow*, p. 178; Lamont, *Davison*, p. 202.

39. *New York Times*, November 25, 1916; *Comm. & Fin. Chron.*, December 2, 1916.

40. *New York Times*, December 18, 1916.

41. *New York Times*, January 3, 1917.

42. *New York Times*, January 5 and February 3, 13, 1917.

43. *New York Times*, January 18 and 20, 1917; Nicolson, *Morrow*, p. 178; Lamont, *Davison*, pp. 210–11.

44. *New York Times*, March 18, 1917; Nicolson, *Morrow*, p. 178; Lamont, *Davison*, p. 212; *New York Times*, March 21, 1917.

45. *New York Times*, March 10, 1917.

46. JPM, Jr., to Commandant, Third Naval District, March 6, 1917, LP 20:143.

47. *New York Times*, March 27 and 28, 1917.

48. JPM, Jr., to E. Chaplin, October 17, 1917, numerical files, 339, JPM, Jr., Papers.

49. JPM, Jr., to President Wilson, February 7, 1917, LP 20:38.

50. *New York Times*, April 10 and May 22, 1917; SD, April 8, 9, 1917.

51. SD, May 31 and June 4, 11, 19, 20, 23, 1917. See also SD, May 18, June 8, September 10, 26, and October 10, 15, 16, 22, 24, 25, 29, 1917.

52. JPM, Jr., to W. Astor, April 17, 1917, Cables 1913–21, JPM, Jr., Papers; SD, April 19, 1917.

53. JPM, Jr., to Morgan, Grenfell & Co., May 7, 1917, Morgan, Grenfell & Co. to JPM, Jr., May 8, 9, 1917, and JPM, Jr., to E. C. Grenfell, June 13, 1917, Cables 1913–21, JPM, Jr., Papers.

54. JPM, Jr., to Mrs. JPM, Sr., July 30 and August 14, 1917.

55. JPM, Jr., to Mrs. JPM, Sr., August 28, 1917.

56. JPM, Jr., to Mrs. JPM, Sr., June 9, 1917.

57. *New York Times*, June 9 and July 29, 13, 1917. See also *Comm. & Fin. Chron.*, July 14, 1917.

58. Nicolson, *Morrow*, p. 178; *New York Times*, July 29 and September 21, 26, 1917; *Comm. & Fin. Chron.*, July 28 and September 22, 28, 1917.

59. *New York Times*, January 5, 1918; *Comm. & Fin. Chron.*, January 5, 12, June 22, and July 6, 1918.

60. SD, January 13, 1918.

61. *New York Times*, March 24, 1918.

62. *New York Times*, June 5, 1918.

63. JPM, Jr., to T. D. Campbell, November 16, 1921, LP 30-A:74.

64. *New York Times*, June 18, 1918; JPM, Jr., to President F. S. Luther, April 30 and May 24, 1918, LP 23:46, 120.

65. JPM, Jr., to Mrs. JPM, Sr., January 9, 1919; HSM to JDF, in conversation, January 10, 1980.

66. JPM, Jr., to Mrs. JPM, Sr., September 3, 1918.

67. *New York Times*, October 9, 1918.

68. JPM, Jr., to George R. I., November 12, 1918, and George R. I. to JPM, Jr., November 12, 1918, Cables 1913–21, JPM, Jr., Papers.

69. SD, November 19–20 and December 4–8, 1918.

70. JPM, Jr., to Herreshoff Manufacturing Co., December 3, 1918, LP 24:258.

71. JPM, Jr. to Commdr. C. L. Arnold, December 10, 1918, LP 24:299.

72. *New York Times*, December 20, 1918.

73. JPM, Jr., to L. Sherry, December 18, 1918, LP 24:37.

Chapter VII: "The Postwar Years, *1919–23*"

1. JPM, Jr., to Mrs. JPM, Sr., January 9, 1919.

2. JPM, Jr., to Mrs. JPM, Sr., January 17, 1919.

3. JPM, Jr., to Mrs. JPM, Sr., February 1, 1919.

4. *New York Times*, January 8, 1919; JPM, Jr., to E. Shortt, January 14, 1919, LP 24-A:16.

5. *New York Times*, January 24, 1919.

6. JPM, Jr., to Rear Adm. Sir G. Gaunt, January 24, 1919, LP 24-A:16.

7. JPM, Jr., to Mrs. JPM, Sr., January 17, 1919. *Comm. & Fin. Chron.*, February 1, 1919.

8. JPM, Jr., to Mrs. JPM, Sr., January 26, 1919. JPM, Jr., to F. H. Jackson, February 10, 1919, LP 24-A:39.

9. JPM, Jr., to H. Harjes, February 10, 1919, LP 24-A:45; T. W. Lamont to JPM, Jr., May 23, 1919, Cables 1913–21, JPM, Jr., Papers.

10. See correspondence of Stettinius with Martin Egan, J. P. Morgan, and N. D. Jay in J. D. Forbes, *Stettinius*, pp. 109–11.

11. E. R. Stettinius to H. P. Davison, March 26, 1921, quoted in J. D. Forbes, *Stettinius*, p. 203.

12. *New York Times*, February 24, 1919.

13. *New York Times*, March 1, 1919.

14. JPM, Jr., to Ens. E. Nelson et al., March 7, 1919, LP 24:496.

15. *New York Times*, March 29, 1919; JPM, Jr., to G. W. Kirchwey, August 12, 1919, LP 26:33.

16. *New York Times*, January 21 and 22, 1919.

17. *New York Times*, February 8, 2, 1919.

18. JPM, Jr., to U.S. Secretary of State, May 24, 1919, LP 25:257; JPM, Jr., to Sen. H. C. Lodge, April 10, 1919, LP 25:127.

19. JPM, Jr., to Mrs. JPM, Sr., August 22, 1919.

20. *New York Times*, January 21, 25, 30, 1921.

21. *New York Times*, May 1, 1919.

22. SD, April 23, 28, 30, and May 6, 7, 8, 9, 1919.

23. *New York Times*, June 10, 12, 1919; U.S. Congress, Senate, *Investigations Relative to the Treaty of Peace with Germany: Hearings before the Committee on Foreign Relations* (Pursuant to S. Res. 64) 66th Cong., 1st sess., 1919, pt. 2, p. 52.

24. JPM, Jr., to Mrs. JPM, Sr., June 20, 1919.

25. Ibid.

26. JPM, Jr., to Mrs. JPM, Sr., August 16, 1919.

27. *New York Times*, September 23, 1919.

28. JPM, Jr., to Mrs. JPM, Sr., November 6, 1919.

29. JPM, Jr., to Mrs. JPM, Sr., October 17, 1919.

30. JPM, Jr., to Mrs. JPM, Sr., October 26, 1919.

31. Ibid.

32. JPM, Jr., to Mrs. JPM, Sr., November 6, 1919.

33. JPM, Jr., to Mrs. JPM, Sr., November 12, 1919.

34. *New York Times*, December 7, 1919.

35. JPM, Jr., to Mrs. JPM, Sr., June 20, 1919.

36. *New York Times*, November 13, 1919; J. D. Forbes, *Stettinius*, pp. 114–15, 117–26.

37. *New York Times*, January 1, 1920. See also JPM, Jr., to E. C. Grenfell, December 18, 1919, Cables 1913–21, JPM, Jr., Papers.

38. SD, August 14–December 4, 1920.

39. SD, June 1 and 10, 1920; JPM, Jr., to Sir T. Lipton, November 29, 1919, LP 26-A:137.

40. JPM, Jr., to H. P. Davison, August 12, 1920, LP 28:97. J. D. Forbes, *Stettinius*, pp. 127–36.

41. SD, August 14, 1920; JPM, Jr., to J. Fleming, December 26, 1919, LP 26:313; JPM, Jr., to Rev. E. Stogdon, February 18, 1919, LP 24-A:76; JPM, Jr., to M. Arnold, November 24, 1919, LP 26-A:122.

42. JPM, Jr., to E. C. Grenfell, March 26, 1920, LP 27:125; JPM, Jr., to

Mrs. JPM, Sr., October 18, 1921; JPM, Jr., to Mrs. JPM, Sr., November 6, 1921.

43. JPM, Jr., to Mrs. JPM, Sr., September 6, 1920. HSM to JDF, in conversation, October 1979.

44. *New York Times*, September 17, 18, 1920.

45. JPM, Jr., to Mrs. JPM, Sr., September 26, 1920.

46. JPM, Jr., to Mrs. JPM, Sr., October 10, 1920.

47. JPM, Jr., to Mrs. JPM, Sr., October 24, 1920.

48. Ibid.

49. JPM, Jr., to Mrs. JPM, Sr., n.d. (probably November 1920).

50. JPM, Jr., to H. P. Davison, August 12, 1920, LP 28:97.

51. SD, April 15, June 2, July 12, December 16, 1920, and March 10, April 20, December 14, 1921.

52. JPM, Jr., to Mrs. JPM, Sr., August 1, 1924.

53. JPM, Jr., to J. S. Morgan, Jr., October 9, 1933, Cables, England, 1933, JPM, Jr., Papers.

54. JPM, Jr., to A. L. Lowell, March 2, 1920, LP 27:41.

55. JPM, Jr., to Dr. F. Dexter, July 24, 1916, LP 17:42, April 21, 1917, LP 20:256, and April 30, 1917, LP 20:355.

56. JPM, Jr., to E. C. Grenfell, September 5, 1914, LP 15:209.

57. JPM, Jr., to M. Schiff, December 3, 1938, LP 41:439.

58. Memorandum, F. H. McKnight to D. W. Morrow, August 11, 1914, numerical files T, 383, JPM, Jr., Papers.

59. JPM, Jr., to H. F. Osborn, January 10, 1934, LP 44:211; JPM, Jr., to M. C. Norman, March 18, 1938, LP 45:489.

60. JPM, Jr., to Mrs. JPM, Sr., January 21, 1921; SD, January 18, 1921; JPM, Jr., to W. A. Gardner, January 7, 1921, LP 28:373; JPM, Jr., to Mrs. JPM, Sr., January 27 and February 7, 20, 1921.

61. JPM, Jr., to Mrs. JPM, Sr., February 2, 1921.

62. SD, March 5, 7, 12–16, 1921.

63. JPM, Jr., to Mrs. JPM, Sr., July 5, 1921; JPM, Jr., to A. Forbes, May 2, 1921, LP 29:261; JPM, Jr., to Dr. W. H. Wilmer, December 29, 1919, LP 26:311.

64. SD, March 26, 1919, June 2, 1920, March 23 and May 12, 1921.

65. JPM, Jr., to Maj. H. L. Higginson, May 17, 1915, LP 16:439; JPM, Jr., to F. L. Higginson, Jr., March 21, 1921, LP 29:75.

66. J. Axten to C. Jeeves, July 31, 1918, LP 23:343; J. Axten to H. J. Power, February 21, 1923, LP 32:345; J. Axten to Unit Construction Co., Philadelphia, February 23, 1926, LP 38:123.

67. JPM, Jr., to C. P. Brainard, December 21, 1921, LP 30:279; SD, April 13, April 21, May 20, 1921; JPM, Jr., to T. B. Wells, May 12, 1922, LP 31:277.

68. JPM, Jr., to J. Callahan, July 22, 1920, LP 28:8; J. Axten to C. G. Gunther's Sons, March 9, 1923, LP 32:378; J. Axten to Sheffield Silver Black Fox Co., January 8, 1926, LP 38:19; J. Axten to J. Callahan, July 17, 1929, LP 42:272; J. Axten to J. Callahan, April 11, 1930, LP 43:44.

69. *Comm. & Fin. Chron.*, March 26 and November 26, 1921.

70. *Comm. & Fin. Chron.*, March 26, 1921.

71. Nicolson, *Morrow*, p. 178; *New York Times*, June 14, 1921; *Comm. & Fin. Chron.*, June 18, 1921.

72. *New York Times*, August 16, 1921.

73. *New York Times*, May 19, 1922, May 3, 1923, April 28, 1924. F. V. Field, *American Participation in the China Consortiums* (Chicago: University of Chicago Press for the American Council Institute of Pacific Relations [c. 1931]), pp. 188–98.

74. SD, May 30, June 4, 11, 18, 25, and July 4, 1921; JPM, Jr., to Collector of Internal Revenue, June 29, 1921, LP 29:438.

75. JPM, Jr., to Mrs. JPM, Sr., June 29, 1921.

76. JPM, Jr., to Mrs. JPM, Sr., July 22, 1921.

77. JPM, Jr., to M. Storey, March 28, 1921, LP 29:25; JPM, Jr., to Mrs. JPM, Sr., July 12, 1921.

78. *New York Times*, July 15 and August 7, 1921.

79. J. D. Forbes, *Stettinius*, pp. 137–49.

80. *New York Times*, August 14, 1921.

81. JPM, Jr., to Mrs. JPM, Sr., July 5, 1921. SD, August 22–October 2, 1921.

82. JPM, Jr., to Mrs. JPM, Sr., October 10, 1921.

83. JPM, Jr., to Mrs. JPM, Sr., October 18, 1921.

84. SD, October 19–November 2, 1921.

85. JPM, Jr., to Mrs. JPM, Sr., October 18, 1921.

86. JPM, Jr., to Mrs. JPM, Sr., November 6, 1921.

87. JPM, Jr., to Mrs. JPM, Sr., October 31, 1921.

88. SD, December 8, 1921.

89. SD, December 15 and 16, 1921.

90. JPM, Jr., to Dr. A. F. Riggs, January 20, 1922, LP 30:395.

91. SD, January 14, 15, 16, 21, 1922.

92. JPM, Jr., to Mrs. JPM, Sr., February 12, 15, 19, 22, 28, 1922.

93. SD, March 10, 1922. JPM, Jr., to N. Tesla, January 8, 1915, LP 16:97.

94. SD, March 13, 1922.

95. .SD, March 23, April 14, 22, and May 3, 1922; J. Axten to H. P. Whitney, secretary, The Creek, June 27, 1924, LP 35:266.

96. JPM, Jr., to Rev. E. Stogdon, January 4, 1929, LP 42:38.

97. JPM, Jr., to L. M. Greer, June 11, 1935, LP 45:22; JPM, Jr., to C. Steele, April 1, 1936, LP 45:168.

98. Sir Andrew McFadyean, *Reparation Reviewed* (London: Ernest Benn, 1930), pp. 19 ff.

99. SD, May 10, 1922; *New York Times*, May 11, 1922.

100. *Comm. & Fin. Chron.*, May 27, 1922.

101. *Comm. & Fin. Chron.*, June 17, 1922; *New York Times*, June 11, 1922.

102. JPM, Jr., to J. C. Grew, November 6, 1922, LP 1922–27, p. 7.

103. *New York Times*, August 3, 1922.

104. SD, June 11, July 17–27, August 1–September 27, 1922.

105. JPM, Jr., to Mrs. JPM, Sr., September 24, 1922.

106. JPM, Jr., to Mrs. JPM, Sr., September 19, 1922.

107. JPM, Jr., to Mrs. JPM, Sr., October 15, 1922.

108. JPM, Jr., to Mrs. JPM, Sr., October 22, 1922.

109. JPM, Jr., to Dr. F. Dexter, April 30, 1923, numerical files, 154, JPM, Jr., Papers.

110. JPM, Jr., to Mrs. JPM, Sr., October 29, 1922.

111. SD, December 3; *New York Times*, December 3, 4, 1922.

112. SD, December 16, 1922.

113. *New York Times*, December 14, 20, 1922.

114. *New York Times*, January 3, 1923.

115. JPM, Jr., to E. C. Grenfell, January 3 and March 9, 1923, LP 32:164, 387.

116. *New York Times*, January 7, 1923.

117. SD, January 4, 1923; *Wall Street Journal*, January 12, 1923; *New York Times*, January 13, 14, 15, 1923.

118. JPM, Jr., to Mrs. JPM, Sr., June 20, 1919.

119. *New York Times*, June 11, 1923.

120. SD, January 10–15, 1923; SD, February 16–March 6, 1923; SD, May 3–10, 1923.

121. SD, March 31, April 7, 12, 19, 26, May 21, and June 14, 1923.

122. *New York Times*, June 22, 1923.

123. SD, June 10, 1923; *New York Times*, June 11, 1923; SD, June 21, 26, 1923; SD, June 22–25, 1923.

124. *New York Times*, June 29, 1923; SD, June 30, 1923.

125. SD, July 23, 1923; SD, July 25, 1923.

126. JPM, Jr., to J. Fleming, March 10, 1923, LP 32:406.

127. JPM, Jr., to Mrs. JPM, Sr., October 7, 1923; JPM, Jr., to Mrs. JPM, Sr., October 14, 1923.

128. *Wall Street Journal*, December 11, 1923.

Chapter VIII: "Morgan the Book Collector"

1. JPM, Jr., to Mrs. J. B. Thatcher, April 18, 1919, LP 25: 145.

2. JPM, Jr., to BG, November 12, 1919, PML file, JPM, Jr., Papers.

3. Edwin Wolf, 2d, and John F. Fleming, *Rosenbach, A Biography* (Cleveland and New York: World Publishing Company, 1960), p. 174.

4. Frederick B. Adams, Jr., *An Introduction to the Pierpont Morgan Library* (New York: Pierpont Morgan Library, 1974), p. 16.

5. [Belle da Costa Greene,] *The Pierpont Morgan Library: Review of the Activities and Major Acquisitions of the Library, 1941–1948, with a Memoir of John*

Pierpont Morgan and the Morgan Library, 1913–1943 (New York: Pierpont Morgan Library, 1949) p. 13. Hereafter cited as Greene, *Review, 1941–1948*.

6. *Illustrated Catalogue of an Exhibition Held on the Occasion of the New York World's Fair, 1940* (New York: PML, 1940), no. 20, M. 638. Hereafter cited as *World's Fair, 1940*.

7. JPM, Jr., to BG, July 28, 1922, PML file, JPM, Jr., Papers.

8. *Treasures from the Pierpont Morgan Library: Fiftieth Anniversary Exhibition, 1957* (New York: Pierpont Morgan Library, 1957), item no. 11, PML manuscript no. M. 639. Hereafter cited at *Fiftieth Anniv.*

9. *Fiftieth Anniv.*, no. 9, M. 652; Greene, *Review, 1941–1948*, p. 14.

10. M. 655 and M. 656. Archbishop Sophronios to JPM, Jr., May 26, 1922, and Morgan, Harjes & Co., Paris, to JPM, Jr., July 20, 1922, PML file, JPM, Jr., Papers.

11. M. 657. BG to JPM, Jr., July 28, 1922, and JPM, Jr., to L. Cust, August 11, 1922, ibid.

12. BG to JPM, Jr., July 28, 1922, ibid.

13. HSM to JDF, in conversation, 1974.

14. BG to JPM, Jr., August 27, 1923, PML file, JPM, Jr., Papers.

15. Archimandrite Metorphan to R. Blake, May 5 (Gregorian) or May 18 (Julian), 1922, and JPM, Jr., to R. Blake, July 26, 1922, ibid.

16. Wolf and Fleming, *Rosenbach*, p. 198.

17. JPM, Jr., to G. Upshur, December 23, 1927, LP 40:370.

18. *Mediaeval & Renaissance Manuscripts: Major Acquisitions of the Pierpont Morgan Library, 1924–1974* (New York: PML, 1974), no. 20, M. 710. Hereafter cited as *Med. & Ren., 1974*.

19. *Fiftieth Anniv.*, no. 4, M. 728; *Med. & Ren., 1974*, no. 18, M. 729.

20. *Fiftieth Anniv.*, no. 39; *Med. & Ren., 1974*, no. 402, M. 732.

21. *Med. & Ren., 1974*, no. 13, M. 736.

22. JPM, Jr., to Sir F. C. Kenyon, February 1, 1929, LP 42:123.

23. Speech of Sir John Sandys, Cambridge University, October 31, 1919, Honours and degrees file, JPM, Jr., Papers.

24. D. Veale, Registrar, Oxford University, to JPM, Jr., November 4, 1930, Honours and degrees file, JPM, Jr., Papers. *New York Times*, November 26, 1930.

25. *Fiftieth Anniv.*, no. 46; *Fiftieth Anniv.*, no. 48; JPM, Jr., to BG, November 12, 1919, PML file, JPM, Jr., Papers.

26. *Early Printed Books: Major Acquisitions of the Pierpont Morgan Library, 1924–1974* (New York: PML, 1974), no. 2. Hereafter cited as *Early Printed Books, 1974*; *Fiftieth Anniv.*, nos. 52; *Early Printed Books, 1974*, no. 49.

27. *Fiftieth Anniv.*, no. 47; *Early Printed Books, 1974*, no. 6.

28. *Early Printed Books, 1974*, nos. 24, 30.

29. *Early Printed Books, 1974*, nos. 38, 39.

30. *Early Printed Books, 1974*, no. 23.

31. JPM, Jr., to BG, November 12, 1919, PML file, JPM, Jr., Papers.

32. Howard M. Nixon, *Sixteenth-century Gold-Tooled Bookbindings in the Pierpont Morgan Library* (New York: PML, 1971), nos. 52, 59.

33. Ibid., no. 19; *Fiftieth Anniv.*, no. 61.

34. BG to JPM, Jr., February 26, 1914, PML file, JPM, Jr., Papers; JPM, Jr. to J. Seligmann, June 10, 1914, LP 14:472; JPM, Jr., to J. Seligmann, July 9, 1914, LP 15:67.

35. Rosenbach Co. bill to JPM, Jr., June 17, 1915, PML file, JPM, Jr., Papers.

36. BG to JPM, Jr., May 29, 1922, ibid.

37. BG to JPM, Jr., October 17, 1924, and JPM, Jr., to BG, October 28, 1924, ibid.

38. BG to J. Axten, September 20, 1937, ibid.

39. BG to JPM, Jr., September 26, 1924, and JPM, Jr., to BG, October 6, 1924, ibid.

40. *New York Times*, February 13, 1924.

41. *New York Times*, February 17, 1924.

42. JPM, Jr., to B. W. Morris, March 18, 1925, LP 36:379.

43. W. Winchell to R. Howson, January 31, 1933, PML file, JPM, Jr., Papers.

44. N. M. Butler to JPM, Jr., April 17, 1933, ibid.

45. JPM, Jr., to H. C. Smith, March 25, 1938, ibid.

46. BG to JPM, Jr., July 29, 1939, and JPM, Jr., to BG, August 8, 1939, ibid.

Chapter IX: "The Boom Years, *1924–28*"

1. SD, March 4, 1924.

2. *New York Times*, March 13, 1924; *Wall Street Journal*, March 19, 1924; *New York Herald-Tribune*, March 20, 1924.

3. *New York Times*, March 21, 1924.

4. JPM, Jr., to Dr. F. Dexter, May 31, 1924, LP 35:165; JPM, Jr., to Sir A. S. Shipley, May 26, 1924, LP 35:144.

5. *New York Times*, April 27, 1924.

6. *Comm. & Fin. Chron.*, July 26, 1924; SD, August 4–10, 1924.

7. JPM, Jr., to Mrs. JPM, Sr., August 24, 1924.

8. JPM, Jr., to Mrs. JPM, Sr., September 21, 1924; JPM, Jr., to H. Harjes, September 30, 1924, LP 1922–27, p. 170.

9. JPM, Jr., to Mrs. JPM, Sr., October 12, 1924.

10. SD, October 16, 17, 1924.

11. *Comm. & Fin. Chron.*, November 29, 1924.

12. *New York Times*, November 15–24, 1924.

13. JPM, Jr., to Ed. Charvet & Fils, December 15, 1924, LP 36:6.

14. Quoted in *Comm. & Fin. Chron.*, August 30, 1924.

15. *New York Times*, October 24 and November 2, 1924.

16. Ibid., January 1, 1925.

17. Ibid., January 13, 1925.

18. Ibid., March 13, 1925; SD, May 30, 1925.

19. *Comm. & Fin. Chron.*, May 2, 1925; *New York Times*, April 29 and June 3, 1925.

20. *Comm. & Fin. Chron.*, June 6, 1925, July 25, 1925, August 22, 1925.

21. *New York Times*, November 21, 1925; *Comm. & Fin. Chron.*, December 12, 1925.

22. JPM, Jr., to C. Gould, July 21, 1925, LP 37:211.

23. *Comm. & Fin. Chron.*, June 20, 27, July 4, and August 15, 1925; *New York Times*, June 18, 19, 20, 21, 22, 23, 26, 27, July 3, 4, 6, 27, and August 15, 1925.

24. *New York Times*, August 15, 1925.

25. JPM, Jr., to B. Dean, December 9, 1913, PML file, JPM, Jr., Papers.

26. BG to JPM, Jr., undated (postscript dated Paris, August 7 [1925]), PML file, JPM, Jr., Papers.

27. J. Axten to H. Poole & Co., August 31, 1925, LP 37:297.

28. JPM, Jr., to Mayor of Glen Cove, May 25, 1926, LP 38:359; JPM, Jr., to Dr. H. S. Patterson, June 19, 1926, LP 38:406.

29. JPM, Jr., to R. Thorne, March 29, 1927, LP 39:372.

30. SD, August 17–24, 1925.

31. SD, September 8–13, 1925; SD, September 19, 1925.

32. *New York Times*, August 29, 1925.

33. J. Axten to J. Fleming, June 6, 1924, LP 35:197.

34. JPM, Jr., to J. Fleming, March 19, 1925, LP 36:389, and May 21, 1925, LP 37:68.

35. SD, December 1, 1925; *New York Times*, December 2, 1925.

36. SD, December 10–12, 1925.

37. SD, January 17–March 2, March 12–21, 1926.

38. SD, March 22–May 31, 1926.

39. SD, 1926.

40. SD, January 15, March 25, April 26, May 7, 12, 28, and December 21, 1926.

41. *New York Times*, January 28, 1926.

42. *New York Times*, April 28, 1926.

43. JPM, Jr., to Joint Secretaries of the Royal Commission on Indian Currency and Finances, April 30, 1926, numerical files T, 151, JPM, Jr., Papers.

44. M. C. Norman to JPM, Jr., May 22, 1926, numerical files T, 151. JPM, Jr., Papers.

45. *New York Times*, May 18, 1926; ibid., May 22, 1926; SD, June 1–4, 1926.

46. *New York Times*, June 10 and 15, 1926.

47. JPM, Jr., to M. Whitridge, July 6, 1926, LP 38:454.

48. SD, June 11–13, 17, 1926.

49. SD, July 23–November 13, 1926.

50. *New York Times*, October 2, 1926.

51. *New York Times*, October 20, 1926.

52. *New York Times*, November 4, 16, 1926.

53. SD, November, 22, 1926; *New York Times*, quoted in *Comm. & Fin. Chron.*, November 27, 1926.

54. SD, December 13–31, 1926.

55. J. Axten to E. Franklin, December 2, 1926, LP 39:52; J. Axten to J. Fleming, December 2, 1926, LP 39:53; J. Axten to Mrs. M. Curley, December 2, 1926, LP 39:54; J. Axten to J. Callahan, December 21, 1926, LP 39:125; J. Axten to P. Wilkinson, December 21, 1926, LP 39:126; J. Axten to Benson & Hedges, December 3, 1926, LP 39:67; J. Axten to Stearn & Co., December 24, 1926, LP 39:134, and December 18, 1923, LP 34:125.

56. *New York Times*, January 1, 1927.

57. SD, January 3, 4, 5–23, February 8–March 5, 1927.

58. JPM, Jr., to Lt. Col. Sir M. Murray, May 27, 1927, LP 40:90; March 24, 1927, LP 39:380; November 7, 1929, LP 1922–27, p. 431; April 1, 1930, LP 43:20; July 5, 1934, LP 44:356; February 8, 1935, LP 44:414.

59. *New York Times*, January 19, May 20, July 6, 1927.

60. SD, April 7–12, 1927; *New York Times*, April 13, 1927.

61. *New York Times*, February 11, 1928.

62. JPM, Jr., to S. E. Morison, March 8, 1927, LP 39:335.

63. JPM, Jr., to G. W. Wheelwright, April 5, 1927, LP 39:414.

64. JPM, Jr., to M. R. James, April 25, 1927, LP 40:6.

65. JPM, Jr., to Dr. F. Dexter, August 14, 1918, LP 23:386; JPM, Jr., to Mrs. W. Hooper, September 27, 1940, LP 47:181.

66. JPM, Jr., to Lady Buxton, December 25, 1941, LP 47:359.

67. *New York Times*, April 20, 1927.

68. J. W. Suter to JPM, Jr., November 11, 1927, Prayer Book file, JPM, Jr., Papers. JPM, Jr., to J. W. Suter, December 5, 1927, LP 40:318.

69. J. Axten to H. J. Gielow, March 30, 1927, LP 39:400.

70. J. Axten to C. H. Talcott, June 18, 1927, LP 40:150; SD, May 30 and June 4, 11, 16, 18, 1927.

71. *New York Times*, June 7, 22, 1927; SD, June 20–24, 1927.

72. JPM, Jr., to L. M. Satterlee, A. Morgan, et al., July 11, 1927, LP 40:197–207.

73. SD, July 14–18, 1927.

74. *New York Times*, July 28 and August 3, 1927; JPM, Jr., to A. Steward, June 1, 1927, LP 40:115.

75. *New York Times*, August 21, 1927.

76. JPM, Jr., to BG, August 8, 1939, PML file, JPM, Jr., Papers.

77. JPM, Jr., to R. Winsor, October 21, 1927, LP 1922–27, p. 402; JPM, Jr., to P. S. du Pont, October 25, 1927, LP 1922–27, p. 414.

78. JPM, Jr., to N. D. Jay, December 27, 1927, LP 40:361.

79. *New York Times*, November 17, 1927 and April 11, 1928.

80. *New York Times*, November 23, 1927; SD, November 23–25 and December 1–2, 8–10, 1927; JPM, Jr., to E. W. Grew, November 30, 1927, LP 40:302.

81. JPM, Jr., to Secretary, U.S. Steel Corp., March 21, 1927, LP 39:367; *New York Times*, August 31, 1927.

82. *Comm. & Fin. Chron.*, December 31, 1927; JPM, Jr., to H. B. Rust, December 8, 1927, LP 40:332.

83. *Comm. & Fin. Chron.*, December 24, 1927; *New York Times*, December 26, 1927; JPM, Jr., to Italian consul general, New York, December 27, 1927, LP 40:379.

84. *New York Times*, January 4, 1928; JPM, Jr., to N. D. Jay, January 25, 1928, LP 40:456.

85. SD, January 5, 1928; *New York Times*, January 6, 1928.

86. SD, January 5 and February 8, 19, 1928.

87. SD, January 9, 15–22 and February 11–28, 1928.

88. SD, March 6, 1928; JPM, Jr., to J. Suter, December 11, 1928, LP 41:457; JPM, Jr., to S. S. Drury, December 11, 1928, LP 41:464.

89. SD, March 14, 16, 23–28, 1928; JPM, Jr., to Lady Harcourt, February 5, 1928, LP 41:10; JPM, Jr., to B. Beal, February 6, 1928, LP 41:8; JPM, Jr., to E. C. Grenfell, February 5, 1928, LP 41:10; SD, April 21–28, 1928.

90. SD, May 22, 23, 25, 29, 1928.

91. JPM, Jr., to J. D. Rockefeller, Jr., March 16 and June 6, 1928, LP 41:185, 238; JPM, Jr., to E. W. Sheldon, June 29 and July 9, 1928, LP 41:285; 323; SD, May 28, 1928.

92. SD, June 5, 1928; JPM, Jr., to M. C. Taylor, June 6, 1928, LP 41:236.

93. SD, June 6, 9, 10, 1928.

94. SD, June 15, 20–22, 1928.

95. SD, June 25, 1928.

96. *New York Times*, June 20, 1928.

97. SD, June 30 and July 12, 1928; *New York Times*, August 7, 8, 1928.

98. JPM, Jr., to J. S. Morgan, Jr., September 10, 1928, LP 1928–39, p. 16.

99. JPM, Jr., to H. D. Kirkover, March 2, 1928, LP 41:46. See also JPM, Jr., to E. Chaplin, November 6, 1922, LP 1922–27, p. 10.

100. JPM, Jr., to J. Fleming, January 4, 1929, LP 42:36; JPM, Jr., to Boyd, Jedburgh, January 17, 1930, LP 42:425.

101. JPM, Jr., to Lt. Col. Sir J. R. Chancellor, September 21, 1928, LP 1928–39, p. 36.

102. JPM, Jr., to Mrs. Cameron, November 5, 1928, LP 1929–39, p. 93.

103. JPM, Jr., to C. D. Hilles, May 28, 1928, LP 41:216.

104. SD, November 14–21, 22, November 27–December 1, November 12–15, 1928.

105. SD, December 26, 27, 1928.

Chapter X: *"Climax and Collapse, 1929–32"*

1. *New York Times*, January 1, 1929.

2. SD, January 7, 8, 9–21, 1929; JPM, Jr., to H. J. Gielow, January 11, 1929, LP 42:54.

3. JPM, Jr., to JPM & Co., January 31, 1929, LP 42:114.

4. Frederick Lewis Allen, *The Lords of Creation*, p. 346.

5. *New York Times*, February 24, 1929.

6. SD, March 30–April 3, 1929; *New York Times*, March 31, 1929.

7. JPM, Jr., to Dr. A. F. Riggs, June 11, 1929, LP 42:188; SD, April 12–22, 1929.

8. JPM, Jr., to W. A. Gardner, June 26, 1929, LP 42:209; JPM, Jr., to archbishop of Canterbury, July 16, 1929, LP 42:266; JPM, Jr., to J. Budden, March 5, 1930, LP 42:485.

9. SD, April 28–May 31, 1929; *Encyclopaedia Britannica*, 14th ed. (1929–30), *s.v.* "Young Plan."

10. *Encyclopaedia Britannica*, 14th ed. (1929–30), *s.v.* "Reparations."

11. T. W. Lamont to C. Steele and partners, June 1, 1929, Partners file, JPM, Jr., Papers.

12. JPM, Jr., to E. Francqui, July 2, 1929, LP 42:239.

13. E. Francqui to JPM, Jr., June 12, 1929, and JPM, Jr., to E. Francqui, July 2, 1929, numerical files T, 408, JPM, Jr., Papers; HSM to JDF, in conversation, October 1979.

14. JPM, Jr., to A. Woods, July 2, 1929, LP 42:244.

15. JPM, Jr., to Mrs. S. N. Warren, June 25, 1929, LP 42:202. JPM, Jr., to Vicomte de Lantsheere, May 12, 1930, LP 43:94.

16. O. D. Young to the Morgan partners, transmitted by cable by T. W. Lamont, June 1, 1929, Partners file, JPM, Jr., Papers.

17. SD, June 8–9, 15–16, July 6–11, 18–22, 1929.

18. SD, June 10, 18, 20, 12, 26, 28, July 15, 17, 1929.

19. SD, June 24, 25, 1929.

20. SD, July 24–November 13, 1929.

21. *New York Times*, October 18, 1929.

22. T. W. Lamont, letter to the editor, *Harvard Alumni Bulletin*, May 1943, pp. 542–43.

23. JPM, Jr., to T. W. Lamont, October 24, 1929, Cables, 1928–32, JPM, Jr., Papers. JPM, Jr., to archbishop of Canterbury, December 5, 1929, LP 42:341.

24. JPM, Jr., to Bishop W. Mitchell, January 31, 1930, LP 42:444.

25. SD, November 21–23, 27–30, December 19–21, November 25–27, 1929.

26. JPM, Jr., to F. Edwards & Co., December 27, 1929, LP 42:393. JPM, Jr., to B. Sherwood, December 9, 1929, LP 42:350; *New York Times*, December 19, 1929.

27. JPM, Jr., to J. H. Perkins, December 18, 1929, LP 42:377. JPM, Jr., to

director, American Museum of Natural History, June 27, 1929, LP 42:222.

28. JPM, Jr., to J. Fleming, January 6, 1930, LP 42:413. JPM, Jr., to E. C. Grenfell, December 26, 1929, LP 42:386.

29. JPM, Jr., to H. P. Thompson, December 27, 1929, LP 42:390; JPM, Jr., to M. Kerlin, December 27, 1929, LP 42:390; SD, April 10, 1930; JPM, Jr., to H. J. Greenlaw, March 4, 1930, LP 42:479.

30. SD, January 2–16, 20–22, March 2, 1930.

31. JPM, Jr., to Mrs. H. F. ("Lili") Osborn, April 9, 1930, and JPM, Jr., to Dr. A. F. Riggs, April 21, 1930, LP 43:40, 50.

32. *New York Times*, June 7, 1930.

33. SD, May 30, 31, June 3–4, 5, 6, 10, 11, 13, 27, 30, 1930.

34. J. D. Forbes, "Shepley, Bulfinch, Richardson & Abbott, an Introduction," *Journal of the Society of Architectural Historians*, fall 1958, pp. 28–29.

35. Text of address, Harvard University (and Delphic Club) file, JPM, Jr., Papers; SD, June 19, 1930.

36. SD, July 1–5, 15–16, 28–29, 31, August 7–September 25, October 15–24, 25, 1930; JPM, Jr., to the archbishop of Canterbury, December 23, 1930, LP 43: 182.

37. SD, January 16–22, February 12–14, 1931.

38. JPM, Jr., to the archbishop of Canterbury, December 23, 1930, LP 43:182; JPM, Jr. to the marquess of Linlithgow, February 19, 1931, LP 43:227; *New York Times*, March 29, April 3, 4, 12, 15, 16, 19, 28, 29, 1931.

39. JPM, Jr., to J. S. Lawrence, July 3, 1931, LP 43:294.

40. SD, July 26–September 21, 1931; *New York Times*, September 22, 1931.

41. *New York Times*, November 20, 21, 24, 1931; SD, November 23, 1931.

42. *New York Times*, February 1 and March 16, 1932.

43. JPM, Jr., to Mme. de la Bouillerie, January 8, 1932, LP 43:344.

44. JPM, Jr., to J. Fleming, January 15, 1932, LP 43:351.

45. JPM, Jr., to A. B. Cowtan, July 6, 1932, LP 43:468. JPM, Jr., to the archbishop of Canterbury, March 15, 1932, LP 43:373.

46. JPM, Jr., to Bishop E. M. Stires, March 24, 1932, LP 43:383.

47. *New York Times*, March 23, 24, 1932.

48. JPM, Jr., to J. D. Rockefeller, Jr., April 8, 1932, LP 43:398.

49. JPM, Jr., to J. A. Bolich, June 10, 1932, LP 43:455.

50. SD, January 17–23, February 9–28, 1932.

51. *New York Times*, March 30, 1932.

52. *New York Times*, May 18, 1932.

53. *New York Times*, May 26, 1932.

54. SD, May 25–31, June 18–23, 1932.

55. *New York Times*, July 8, 1932; *Comm. & Fin. Chron.*, July 23, 1932.

56. *Memorial of James Gore King* prepared by Percy D. Trafford, leaflet reprinted from *Year Book 1933* of the Association of the Bar of the City of New York, alphabetical file B, JPM, Jr., Papers.

57. SD, July 2–18, 21, 1932.

58. *New York Times*, July 19, 1932.

59. *New York Times*, August 18, 20, 24, September 3, 8; SD, August 22–23, 1932.

60. T. W. Lamont to JPM, Jr., and JPM, Jr., to T. W. Lamont, November 11, 1932, Cables, England, 1932, JPM, Jr., Papers.

61. SD, November 12, 1932; *New York Times*, November 18, 1932.

Chapter XI: "The New Deal, 1933–38"

1. SD, January 5–7, 12–14, 1933; SD, January 24, 1933; *New York Times*, January 25, 1933; SD, February 5–March 1, 1933; *New York Times*, February 9, 1933.

2. JPM, Jr., to M. Whitridge, January 9, 1933, LP 44:15; JPM, Jr., to the Countess Buxton, March 23, 1933, LP 44:63. JPM, Jr., to F. D. Roosevelt, March 16, 1933, LP 44:45.

3. *New York Times*, February 28, 1933.

4. JPM, Jr., to M. Whitridge, May 16, 1933, LP 44:100.

5. U.S. Congress, Senate, *Stock Exchange Practices: Hearings before the Committee on Banking and Currency* (on S. Res. 84, 72nd Cong., and S. Res. 56, 73rd Cong.) 73rd Cong., 1st sess., pt. II, 1933, pp. 521–26.

6. Ibid., pp. 336, 340.

7. E. P. Hoyt, Jr., *The House of Morgan* (New York: Dodd, Mead & Co., 1966), p. 372; *New York Times*, January 8, 1931.

8. *New York Times*, June 10, 1933.

9. JPM, Jr., to Bishop W. Lawrence, June 30, 1933, LP 44:135.

10. JPM, Jr., to H. Townsend, June 30, 1933, LP 44:135.

11. *New York Times*, May 28, 1933.

12. *New York Times*, June 2, 1933.

13. *New York Times*, July 14, 1933. SD, October 20, 1933.

14. JPM, Jr., to the archbishop of Canterbury, November 23, 1933, LP 44:179.

15. JPM, Jr., to G. Dunn, March 19, 1934, LP 44:231.

16. SD, January 4, 8, 9, 10, 1934.

17. JPM, Jr., to Mrs. W. Hooper, March 19, 1934, LP 44:233.

18. *New York Times*, February 13, 1934.

19. JPM, Jr., to H. F. Osborn, April 17, 1934, LP 44:271.

20. SD, April 2, 5, 13, 1934.

21. *New York Times*, April 21, 1934.

22. SD, April 25, May 15, 24, 25, 26–31, 1934.

23. *New York Times*, June 8, 1934; SD, June 14–23, 1934.

24. *New York Times*, June 8, 1934; *Business Week*, June 23, 1934, p. 34.

25. JPM, Jr., to W. R. Peabody, June 24, 1934, LP 44:340; JPM, Jr., to W. Leighton, June 25, 1934, LP 44:341.

26. List of guns, 1934, Gannochy file, JPM, Jr., Papers.

27. SD, November 28–December 1, December 6–8, 1934.

28. *New York Times*, December 2, 1934.

29. SD, December 28, 1934–January 1, 1935.

30. SD, January 14, 17–24, 28, February 19, 1935; No. 2 account of the year 1935, financial papers, JPM, Jr., Papers.

31. JPM, Jr., to G. Blumenthal, January 29, 1935, LP 44:397; *New York Times*, January 29 and March 30, 1935; No. 2 account to May 31, 1935, financial papers, JPM, Jr., Papers.

32. *New York Times*, February 22, 24, March 9, 1935.

33. JPM, Jr., to Sen. F. Steiwer, February 11, 1935, LP 44:419.

34. SD, February 12–March 9, 1935.

35. SD, May 10, 16, 23–27, 1935; *New York Times*, May 15, 26, June 12, 13, 15, 1935.

36. SD, June 6, 16–20, July 11, 1935.

37. *New York Times*, August 1, 3, 13, 1935; JPM, Jr., to Lord Elphinstone, February 8, 1935, LP 44:416.

38. *New York Times*, October 1, December 5, 20, 1935.

39. *New York Times*, September 6, 7, 1935; *New Republic*, September 25, 1935, p. 185, and October 23, 1935, p. 300.

40. SD, March 26, 1914, JPM, Jr., to F. L. Polk, January 27, 1920, LP 26:412; JPM, Jr., to F. R. Appleton, January 12, 1927, LP 39:212; SD, April 23, 1925; SD, 1914–43.

41. The story of the Nye hearings is summarized in J. D. Forbes, *Stettinius*, pp. ix–x.

42. JPM, Jr., to O. F. Morshead, January 23, 1936, LP 45:96.

43. JPM, Jr., to C. F. Whigham, March 16, 1936, LP 45:140.

44. SD, March 17, 1936; *New York Times*, March 18 and June 16, 1936.

45. SD, May 4, 6, 1936; *New Republic*, May 20, 1936, p. 44.

46. *New York Times*, May 7, 1936.

47. SD, June 1, 1936.

48. SD, June 4, 5, 9, 1936.

49. SD, June 15, 1936; *New York Times*, July 1, 1936.

50. SD, July 29–November 11, 1936.

51. JPM, Jr., to Prime Minister S. Baldwin, December 17, 1936, LP 45:299.

52. JPM, Jr., to Lord Linlithgow, January 6, 1937, LP 45:318.

53. SD, January 16–March 29, 1937; JPM, Jr., to Lord Linlithgow, January 6, 1937, LP 45:318; *New York Times*, January 5, 8, 17, 19, March 22, 28, 31, 1937.

54. SD, April 21 and 30, 1937; *New York Times*, May 13, 14, 15, 1937.

55. *New York Times*, June 8, 1937.

56. *New York Times*, June 8, 9, 1937.

57. JPM, Jr., to G. Norwood, March 12, 1936, LP 45:134.

58. SD, June 23, 1937; *New York Times*, June 6, 1937; SD, July 19, 1937; *New*

York Times, July 19, 20, 1937; JPM, Jr., to Lord Linlithgow, August 10 and September 20, 1937, numerical files T, 12, JPM, Jr., Papers.

59. JPM, Jr., to G. Fumi, December 23, 1937, LP 45:402; JPM, Jr., to A. Purves, Jr., March 10, 1938, LP 45:458.

60. JPM, Jr., to M. C. Norman, December 30, 1937, LP 45:405.

61. Lamont Papers, nos. 108–16, Baker Library, Harvard Business School.

62. JPM, Jr., to M. C. Norman, March 18, 1938, LP 45:489.

63. Ibid.

64. JPM, Jr., to Dr. J. P. Chapman, March 16, 1938, LP 45:469; JPM, Jr., to R. W. Goelet, March 21, 1938, LP 45:495.

65. JPM, Jr., to Capt. R. Busby, March 10, 1938, LP 45:461; SD, April 1–12, 1938.

66. JPM, Jr., to C. A. Lindbergh, January 27, 1938, LP 45:98. JPM, Jr., to M. Whitridge, April 19, 1938, LP 46:28; SD, April 28, 1938; *New York Times*, April 28, 1938; JPM, Jr., to W. Hunt, April 29, 1938, LP 46:42.

67. *New York Times*, June 4, 1938. SD, April 29, 1938; *New York Times*, April 30, 1938; JPM, Jr., to H. Ford, May 2, 1938, LP 46:44.

68. *New York Times*, May 4, 1938.

69. JPM, Jr., to W. R. Coe, May 2, 1938, LP 46:44; JPM, Jr., to O. N. Solbert, November 27, 1939, LP 46:362.

70. *New York Times*, March 15, 16, 1938; JPM, Jr., to S. A. Savage, March 21, 1938, LP 46:1; *New York Times*, May 21, 26, and November 11, 1938.

71. SD, June 9, 18–23, 1938; *New York Times*, June 10, 1938.

72. T. W. Lamont to JPM, Jr., October 3, 1938, Lamont Papers, nos. 108–16, Baker Library, Harvard Business School.

73. J. Kelly to JPM, Jr., September 23, 1938, Cables, England, 1938, JPM, Jr., Papers.

74. JPM, Jr., to N. Chamberlain, September 30, 1938, alphabetical file A, JPM, Jr., Papers.

75. JPM, Jr., to J. Colquhoun, January 12, 1938, LP 45:162.

76. JPM, Jr., to D. C. Tewson, January 28, 1938, LP 45:428.

77. JPM, Jr., to J. Fleming, December 19, 1938, LP 46:116.

78. JPM, Jr., to Harvard Club of Boston, to Metropolitan Club, and to Grolier Club, December 30, 1938, LP 46:37, 138; JPM, Jr., to F. T. Davison, December 19, 1938, LP 46:117.

79. JPM, Jr., to N. M. Butler, June 6, 1939, LP 46:261.

Chapter XII: "World War II, *1939–43*"

1. SD, January 12–20, 1939.

2. *New York Times*, February 2, 1939.

3. SD, February 4–March 10, 1939.

4. JPM, Jr., to Lord St. Just, February 2, 1939, LP 46:197.

5. J. Axten to Cowtan & Co., September 8, 1925, LP 37:301; JPM, Jr., to O. H. Smith, January 31 and April 27, 1939, LP 46:41, 187.

6. SD, March 24, 1939; *New York Times*, March 25, 29–30, 1939; SD, April 2, 1939; JPM, Jr., to Capt. G. T. Calder, March 17, 1939, LP 46:217; JPM, Jr., to the archbishop of Canterbury, June 5, 1939, LP 46: 257; JPM, Jr., to Lord Elphinstone, May 24, 1939, LP 46:249.

7. SD, May 12, 24, 1939; *New York Times*, May 16, 21, 1939.

8. *New York Times*, June 2, 1939.

9. JPM, Jr., to Lady Lindsay, May 10, 1939, LP 46:235; JPM, Jr., to Lord Elphinstone, June 12, 1939, LP 46:267; SD, June 8, 9, 10, 1939.

10. SD, June 17–24, 1939; JPM, Jr., to Mrs. C. E. Tracy, June 27, 1939, LP 46:276.

11. JPM, Jr., to Lord Lothian, September 8, 1939, LP 46:293.

12. Gannochy schedule, 1939, Gannochy file, JPM, Jr., Paprs; *New York Times*, August 26 and September 5, 1939.

13. JPM, Jr., to Lord St. Just, September 14, 1939, LP 46:301; *New York Times*, August 31 and September 5, 1939.

14. JPM, Jr., to Mrs. W. Hooper, November 1, 1939, LP 46:336.

15. JPM, Jr., to Lord Elphinstone, November 6, 1939, LP 46:342.

16. *New York Times*, December 15, 16, 20, 1939, and January 25, 26, 1940.

17. JPM, Jr., to Lord Lothian, December 8, 1939, LP 46:376; April 18, 1940, LP 46:488.

18. SD, December 20, 1939.

19. JPM, Jr., to K. D. Metcalf, January 3, 1940, LP 46:391.

20. JPM, Jr., to J. Callahan, February 5, 13, 1940, LP 46:420, 430; JPM, Jr., to F. A. Steward, February 6, 1940, LP 46: 422; JPM, Jr., to J. Fleming, February 6, 1940, LP 46:424; JPM, Jr., to E. Bingley, February 6, 1940, LP 46:422.

21. JPM, Jr., to Mrs. W. Hooper, February 14, 1940, LP 46:433.

22. *New York Times*, February 16, 1940; *Business Week*, February 24, 1940, pp. 16–17.

23. JPM, Jr., to Lord Elphinstone, March 30, 1940, LP 46:476.

24. JPM, Jr., to Lord St. Just, March 19, 1940, LP 46:449; *New York Times*, March 15, 1940.

25. *New York Times*, March 28, 1940.

26. JPM, Jr., to H. Kirkover, June 3, 1940, LP 47:51; JPM, Jr., to T. N. McCarler, September 18, 1940, LP 47:171.

27. JPM, Jr., to Lord Bicester, June 21, 1940, LP 47:61; JPM, Jr., to J. C. R. Peabody, May 14, 1940, LP 47:22.

28. SD, July 29, 1940; *New York Times*, July 30, 1940.

29. JPM, Jr., to Mrs. W. Hooper, July 8, 1941, LP 47:375. JPM, Jr., to Lady H. V. Smith, January 23, 1942, LP 48:14.

30. *New York Times*, August 24, 1940.

31. *New York Times*, October 25, 1940.

32. *New York Times*, February 20, 1941.

33. JPM, Jr., to Mrs. W. Hooper, December 11, 1940, LP 47:250.

34. JPM, Jr., to L. Smith, September 27, 1940, LP 47:183.

35. SD, January 13–20, February 16–March 15, April 6–17, May 30–June 2, 1940.

36. JPM, Jr., to Lord Bicester, June 21, 1940, LP 47:61; SD, June 16–20, July 10–14, 17–24, August 3–9, 12, 1940; JPM, Jr., to H. Brooks, September 24, 1940, LP 47:174; JPM, Jr., to Lord Rosebery, August 16, 1940, LP 47:122.

37. SD, September 30–October 5, November 6–9, 20–22, 27–29, December 18–19, 1–7, 1940.

38. JPM, Jr., to Mrs. W. Hooper, December 11, 1940, LP 47:250; JPM, Jr., to V. H. Smith, December 16, 1940, LP 47:255; JPM, Jr., to Lord St. Just, January 24, 1941, Partners file, JPM, Jr., Papers.

39. JPM, Jr., to Lord St. Just, March 19, 1940, LP 46:449.

40. JPM, Jr., to M. Grenfell, December 16, 1940, LP 47:253.

41. JPM, Jr., to Lord St. Just, April 25, 1940, LP 47:7.

42. JPM, Jr., to O. F. Morshead, May 14, 1941, alphabetical files B, JPM, Jr., Papers. Lord Bicester to JPM, Jr., May 23, 1941, Partners file, JPM, Jr., Papers.

43. SD, January 7–28, February 9–March 14, 1941.

44. SD, March 18, 1941; *New York Times*, May 14 and November 3, 1941.

45. SD, January 28, 29, February 8, March 27, 28, April 19–May 1, 9, 1941.

46. SD, May 15–17, June 5, 19, July 21–25, August 1–4, 10–11, 12–13, 1941.

47. JPM, Jr., to Sir K. Clark, July 29, 1941, LP 47:402; H. I. Bell to JPM, Jr., n.d., and Sir K. Clark to JPM, Jr., July 7, 1941, PML file, JPM, Jr., Papers.

48. *New York Enquirer*, June 23, 1941; T. W. Lamont to E. D. Coblentz (of the Hearst organization), July 2, 1941, Lamont Papers, no. 98-4, Baker Library, Harvard Business School. W. R. Hearst to T. W. Lamont, August 27, 1941, Lamont Papers, no. 98-4, Baker Library, Harvard Business School.

49. JPM, Jr., to Lord Bicester, June 11, 1941, LP 47:337; JPM, Jr., to Mrs. W. Hooper, July 8, 1941, LP 47:375.

50. JPM, Jr., to Mrs. W. Hooper, July 8, 1941, LP 47:375, and November 19, 1941, LP 47:487.

51. SD, October 5–10, 12–19, November 5–7, 13–15, 28–29, December 5–6, 12–13, 19–20, 26–27.

52. SD, May 27, June 7, 30, November 8, 27, 1941.

53. JPM, Jr., to Mrs. Spender-Clay, December 16, 1941, LP 48:48.

54. SD, May 8, 1942; *New York Times*, May 17 and August 1, 1942.

55. SD, August 10, 27, 1942; *New York Times*, August 11, 1942.

56. *New York Times*, February 3, 1942; *Business Week*, February 7, 1942.

57. SD, February 18–March 16, 1942; JPM, Jr., account books, 1942, financial papers, JPM, Jr., Papers.

58. SD, January 10–15, January 26–February 1, 1942.

59. SD, May 13, 21–25, June 9–11, 19, 1942.

60. SD, July 5–10; August 1–4, August 31–September 9, 1942.

61. SD, October 4–9, 11–18, 1942; SD, November 4–6, 11–13, 18–20, 25–27, December 2–5, 9–11, 30, 1942, and January 2, 1943; SD, November 11, 18, 1942.

62. SD, January 1–2, 6–7, 8–9, February 7, 1943.

63. SD, January 20–29, 1943.

64. SD, January 1–February 20, 1943.

65. *New York Times*, January 21, 1943.

66. SD, February 21, 1943; recalled in conversation by Mrs. A. J. Evers, San Francisco, summer 1975; SD, February 22, 23, 1943.

67. SD, February 25, March 3, 13, 1943; *Time*, March 23, 1943, p. 61.

68. SD, March 15, 16, 1943; *New York Times*, March 19, 1943; SD, June 25, 1943.

69. *New Republic*, March 22, 1943, p. 363.

70. *New York Times*, March 27, 1943.

Conclusion

1. Joseph A. Schumpeter, *Capitalism, Socialism, and Democracy* (New York and London: Harper & Bros., [1942]).

Bibliographical Note

The most important source for this life of the younger J. P. Morgan is the collection of his papers in the possession of his son Henry Sturgis Morgan. These include the letters from J. P. Morgan, Jr., to his mother, Mrs. J. P. Morgan, Sr., during the years 1878–1924, which are on deposit in the Pierpont Morgan Library in New York. For the period of his boyhood, young manhood, and apprenticeship for the family bank, through 1905, these letters are almost the only source and a very rich one. A running narrative for these years is provided by the biography of the elder Morgan, written by his son-in-law Herbert L. Satterlee, *J. Pierpont Morgan, an Intimate Portrait* (New York: Macmillan, 1939), but it treats of the son only incidentally to the career of the father.

For the years following 1905 and especially for the period after the elder Morgan's death in early 1913, we have in this private collection what I have called the J. P. Morgan, Jr., Papers. This is a large and uncatalogued body of letters, copies of letters, and assorted papers and documents that appear to have been thrown hastily into filing cabinets and boxes on Mr. Morgan's death and put into storage. These were made available to me by Henry Sturgis Morgan to be consulted on the premises of the Pierpont Morgan Library, although they are not formally on deposit with the library at this writing.

I have listed the contents of the J. P. Morgan, Jr., Papers below in a series of somewhat arbitrary categories, which in no way reflects their location in the filing cabinets.

1. General Correspondence

Alphabetical files

There are two separate alphabetical files, which I have called A and B, respectively. I find no system of filing to explain the separation.

Cables

Cables sent and received are filed in numerous folders with overlapping dates and titles. (The differences between "personal" cables and "private" cables eludes me.) But they do fall into two main groups: Cables (1904–43) and Cables, England (1916–38)

Office copies of letters sent—bound chronologically

Letterpress (LP) copies of letters from J. P. Morgan, Jr. Bound volumes for 1905–43 are vols. 1–48, and there are also three miscellaneous unnumbered bound volumes covering the years 1892–98, 1922–27, and 1928–29. Although the volumes of the large, continuous series are in chronological order, they are not arranged one per year.

Numerical files

There are two separate numerical files, which I have called numerical file and numerical file T, respectively. The former are in the metal filing cabinets that house the bulk of the J. P. Morgan, Jr., Papers, the latter in transfer file boxes. T is for transfer. As with the alphabetical files, no system is apparent that explains the separation.

Partners correspondence

Letters to and from the partners of J. P. Morgan & Co. are found throughout other files as well, but there is a file exclusively for partner material called Partners file.

2. Personal Material

Attempts on life
Clubs
Critics and criticism (periodical clippings)
Directorships
Final illness
Honours and [honorary] degrees
Secretary's diaries, 1913–43 (SD)
    This series of thirty-one bound volumes of appointment books, one volume per year, is a most useful source.
Thorn threat

3. Personal Finances and Property

American Gas Turbine Corporation
American Radio & Research Corporation
Appraisals of houses' contents
Camp Uncas
Corsair
Cowtan and Sons
Estate of Mrs. J. P. Morgan, Jr.
Financial papers (fragmentary):

account books, including the No. 2 Account, bank statements, cheque stubs,
   private ledgers
Gannochy
Insurance
Kuir Zinc
Securities lists
Wall Hall Properties, Ltd.
Watford Corporation

4. J. P. Morgan & Co.

Export Department
Markle Estate
New Haven Railway
Syndicate books
World War I loan negotiations

5. Public Service and Philanthropy

German reparations
   Committee of Bankers (1922)
   German Loan (1924)
   Young Plan (1929)
Harvard University (and Delphic Club)
Lying-in Hospital (including directors' minutes)
Metropolitan Museum
New York Hospital (including directors' minutes)
Philanthropy, miscellaneous files
Pierpont Morgan Library (PML)
Prayer Book (Episcopal *Book of Common Prayer*)
Nicola Tesla

6. Congressional Hearings

Nye (Munitions) Hearings

Other sources are very much less important to the study. At Harvard University, I consulted the Lamont Papers in the Manuscript Division of Baker Library, Harvard Business School, and in the Harvard University Archives, I made use of the Archibald Cary Coolidge Papers, the Abbott Lawrence Lowell Papers, and the Class of 1889 files in the Class Publications and Records. In the Library of Congress, there is some useful material in the Presidential Papers for William H. Taft and Woodrow Wilson and in the Department of State Papers, especially on Morgan's work at the coronation of Edward VII. The Merrymount Press Collection at the Huntington Library has material on the publication of the Episcopal *Book of Common Prayer* at Morgan's expense and on the Pierpont Morgan Library.
   A very useful continuing source on day-to-day happenings has been the *New*

York Times. On detailed Morgan-related matters, however, this has not always been strictly accurate. The *Commercial and Financial Chronicle* has been helpful in its own sphere.

Certain government documents have served a useful purpose. Among them are:

1. U.S. Congress, Senate, *Investigation Relative to the Treaty of Peace with Germany: Hearing before the Committee on Foreign Relations Pursuant to S. Res. 64*, 66th Cong., 1st sess., 1919.

2. U.S. Congress, Senate, *Sale of Foreign Bonds or Securities in the United States: Hearings before the Committee on Finance Pursuant to S. Res. 19*, 72nd Cong., 1st sess., 1931.

3. U.S. Congress, Senate, *Stock Exchange Practices: Hearings before the Committee on Banking and Currency on S. Res. 84 (72nd Cong.) and S. Res. 56 (73rd Cong.)*, 73rd Cong., 1st sess., 1933.

4. U.S. Congress, Senate, *Munitions Industry: Hearings before the Special Committee Investigating the Munitions Industry (pursuant to S. Res. 206 (73rd Cong.)*, 74th Cong., 2nd sess., 1937.

5. U.S. Congress, *Investigation of Concentration of Economic Power: Hearings before the Temporary National Economic Committee, Congress of the United States Pursuant to Public Resolution no. 113 (75th Cong.)*, 76th Cong., 2nd sess., 1939.

Index